Fanny Wrigley, Thomas H. Winder

The registers of the parish church of Whittington in the County of

Lancaster

Christenings, burials and weddings, 1538 to 1764

Fanny Wrigley, Thomas H. Winder

The registers of the parish church of Whittington in the County of Lancaster
Christenings, burials and weddings, 1538 to 1764

ISBN/EAN: 9783744735575

Printed in Europe, USA, Canada, Australia, Japan

Cover: Foto ©Lupo / pixelio.de

More available books at **www.hansebooks.com**

Lancashire Parish Register Society.

The Registers

OF THE

Parish Church of Whittington.

The Registers

OF THE

Parish Church of Whittington

IN THE

County of Lancaster.

Christenings, Burials, and Weddings
1538 to 1764.

TRANSCRIBED AND EDITED BY
FANNY WRIGLEY, MAB's CROSS, WIGAN,
AND
THOMAS H. WINDER, HEATON, BOLTON:
THE INDEXES BY
ALICE BRIERLEY, MAB'S CROSS, WIGAN.

*Printed by permission of the Rev. Edward Pigot, M.A.,
Rector of Whittington.*

Rochdale:

PRINTED FOR THE LANCASHIRE PARISH REGISTER SOCIETY,
BY JAMES CLEGG, AT THE ALDINE PRESS.

1899.

Preface.

W HITTINGTON—not to be confused with Withington, near Manchester, nor Whittingham, near Preston—is a pretty village situate in extreme North-East Lancashire, about one-and-a-half miles from Kirkby Lonsdale. Its Church, dedicated to S. Michael, is known to have been in existence in the fourteenth century. The Parish of Whittington comprises 4,327 acres, including the townships of Newton, Docker, and Whittington, and contains a population of 339. The adjoining parishes on the Westmoreland side are Burton and Kirkby Lonsdale, and on the Lancashire side Tunstall, Melling, and Warton. The Parish Registers share, with Whalley and Farnworth (near Widnes), the honour of commencing in 1538 — the year appointed by Vicar-General Cromwell.

The two earliest volumes have been wholly transcribed and a small part of the earliest Marriage Register kept under Lord Hardwicke's Act. The first volume comprises Christenings, Burials, and Weddings, 1538-1665, and the second volume contains Christenings and Burials 1665-1764, and Weddings up to 1753. The two earlier volumes measure twelve inches by eight inches each; the elder volume contains 148 paper leaves, very much worn at the edges, the later volume 69 parchment leaves, in good preservation: both are bound in vellum. The first "Lord Hardwicke" Marriage Register is also in excellent preservation. There are no Chapelries in the Parish.

We have to express our grateful thanks to the Rector of the Parish and his kind-hearted household for their great hospitality and for the numerous facilities they have afforded during the transcription of the Registers.

To Mrs. Henry Brierley we are wholly indebted for our excellent indexes, and to the Secretary of the Society for several useful suggestions.

We cannot trace any Episcopal transcripts.

Table of Contents.

The Registers of the Parish of Whittington.

The 13th of December in the yeare of Oū lord god 1538 and
in the yeare of the reigne of Our Souereigne lord kinge henryo
the eighth kinge of England & of france lord of Ireland de-
fendoᵖ of the fayth and in earthe immediatlye under god supreā
head of the church of the realm of England thirttie this prsent
boke pᵖpared ordeined and made witnessethe recordeth & dis-
ᶜribeth all and singuler names and syrnames of fathers and
mothers of any pson or psonns herafter to be baptised or chris-
tened at the pishe church of Whittington in Lonsdale as well
unto the yeares end as from thence and so fourth wᵗʰ the date
ɔf the moneth and yeare for ever.

CHRISTENINGS.

1538.

Richard sonne of John Patchet and Jenet his wife
    baptized vicessimo die decembris anᵒ pᵖdicto
Elizabeth daughter of Edward Ashburne ... ... 13 Januarij
Thomas Heatonn sonne of Rychard Heaton & Alice
    his wife ... ... 17 Martij
Georg sonne of James Sigswicke ... ... 19 „
Xpofer sonne of John Hewtson and Alice his wyffe 20 „

1539.

Thomas sonne of Henrie Slater and Margret his
    wyfe... ... ... 27 Aprilis
Isabell dau. of Richard Robinson and Jenet his wyfe 4 Maij
Myles son of John Baynes & Jane his wife ... ... 8 „
John son of Richard Cort and Jenet his wife ... 1 Junij·
Thomas son of Xpofer Mellinge ... ... 3 „

Jenet dau. of Thomas Whitthead and Eline his wife   4 Junij
Richard son of Hewe Myres and Isabell his wife ...   24 ,,
John son of James Dickonson   ...   .   7 Julij
J * * son of Willm Nealson & Jenet his wife ...   1 Augusti
Agnes dau. of James Heaton and Elizabeth his wife   28 Novembris

ꭓiii° die Decembris anno regni-regis henrici octavi tricessimo primo, 1539.

Ane dau. of Lawrence Cansfild and Sibell his wife   14 Decembris
Richard son of Thomas Robinson and Mabell his wife   1 Januarij
Alice dau. of Alexande Adcock and Jane his wife...   11   ,,
Elin dau. of Thomas Johnson and Maᵍret his wife   18   ,,
Richard son of Robert Couper and Madelin his wife   6 Februarij
Elizabeth dau. of Robert More and Elin his wife...   10   ,,
Xpofer son of Xpofer Borrowe and Jenet his wife...   6 Martij

1540.

Elizabeth dau. of Richard Johnson and Elizabeth
     his wyfe ...   .   17 Julie
Elizabeth dau. of Reinold Baynes and Jane his wife   18   ,,
Willm son of James Fawcet and Jenet his wife ...   20   ,,
Ane dau. of Willm Borowe and Jenet his wyfe   ...   23   ,,
Thomas son of Willm Whithead and Alice his wife   24 Augusti
Myles son of Myles Herdie and Alice his wyfe   ...   30   ,,
Barbaray dau. of Xpofer Ridell and Maᵍaret his
     wife ...   .   7 Septembris
Thomas son of James Battie and Elen his wife   ...   13   ,,
An dau. of Robert Robinson and Jenet his wyfe ...   23   ,,
Richard son of James Gibbons and Alice his wife   24   ,,
Thomas son of Bryan Robinson and Alice his wife   25   ,,
Isabell dau. of John Wilkinson and Maᵍret his wife   26   ,,
John son of William Hallanson spurria...   ...   ...   25 Octobris
Jenet dau. of the same Willm Hallanson spurria eod die
Thomas son of Robert Tydeman spurria   28   ,,
Thomas son of Reniold Borthrige ...   .   9 Novembris
Jenet dau. of Henrie Gibbons and Mᵍret his wife   10   ,,
Dorethe dau. of John Baynes and Jane his wife ...   10   ,,

ꭓiii° die Mensis Decembris ano regni regis henrici oct. ꭓꭓꭓii., 1540.

Elizabeth dau. of Thomas Bland and Jane his wife   13 Decembris
Edmund son of Thomas Whitehead and Elen his wife   20 Februarij
Isabell dau. of John Slater and Elizabeth his wife   25   ,,
Willm son of Edward Ashburne and Agnes his wife   27   ,,
Thomas son of James Gibbons and Alice his wife...   8 Martij
Gilbert son of John Robinson and Eline his wife...   20   ,,

1541.

Thomas son of Richard Hirdson and Ages his wife	26 Martij
Ane dau. of Alexander Adcock and Joane his wife	28 ,,
Reinold son of Thomas Robinson and Elizabeth his wife	20 Maij
Thomas son of Richard Makarell and Isabell his wife	23 Junij
Ane dau. of Reinold Robinson and Mabell his wife	20 Julij
Isabell dau. of Xpofer Mellinge and Elizabeth his wife	23 ,,
Elizabeth dau. of John Harison and Jane his wife	1 Augusti
Jane dau. of Giles Hardie and Alice his *	2 ,,
John son of Willm Lucas and M⁹gret his wife ...	10 ,,
Richard son of James Slater and Maud his wife ...	16 Septembris
Willm son of John Huitson and Alice his wife ...	20 ,,

ҳiii° die Decembris anno regni regis Ibenrici octavi tricessimo tertio, 1541.

Robert son of John Doddinge and Isabell his wife	14 Decembris
James son of James Battie and Elyn his wife ...	11 Januarij
Elizabeth dau. of John Pachet and Jenet his wife	15 ,,
Jenet dau. of James Heaton and M⁹gret his wife...	31 ,,
Elizabeth dau. of Robert More and Eline his wife	10 Februarij

1542.

John son of Richard Heaton and Alice his wife ...	31 Martij
Edward son of James Thornton and Alice his wife	1 Aprilis
Richard son of James Sigswick and Elizabeth his wife	20 Maij
John son of James Dickonson and Alice his wife...	26 ,,
Jane dau. of Richard Cort and Jenet his wife ...	10 Augusti
John and Thomas sonne [sic] of Alexander Adcock and Jane his wife	3 Septembris
Robert son of Xpofer Melling and Elizabeth his wife	4 ,,
Rychard son of James Gibbons and Ales his wife...	8 ,,
Isabell dau. of Lawrenc Cansfild and Sibell his wife	15 Octobris
Richard son of Robert Robinson and Jenet his wife	26 ,,
Elizabeth dau. of Olyver Dickonson and Jane his wife	26 Novembris

ҳiii° die Decembris ano regni regis Ibenrici octavi tricessimo quarto, 1542.

Alice dau. of Reynolde Banes and Jane his wife ...	6 Januarij
Agnes dau. of John Ridall and Elizabeth his wife	19 .,
Edmund son of Willm Nellson and Jenet his wife	4 Martij

1543.

Agnes dau. of Richard Johnson and Elizabeth his
wife ... ... 8 Aprilis
James son of James Walker and Jenet his wife ... 15 „
Tristram son of Robert Couper and Maude his wife 20 Septembris
John son of John Harison and Jane his wife ... 10 Novembris
Thomas son of Robert Gye and Elizabeth his wife eodem die
Jenet dau. of Edward Ashburne and Agnes his wife „
Ane dau. of James Gibbons and Alice his wife ... 20 Novembris

𝔵𝔦𝔦𝔦° 𝔡𝔦𝔢 𝔇𝔢𝔠𝔢𝔪𝔟𝔯𝔦𝔰 𝔞𝔫𝔫𝔬 𝔯𝔢𝔤𝔫𝔦 𝔯𝔢𝔤𝔦𝔰 𝔥𝔢𝔫𝔯𝔦𝔠𝔦 𝔬𝔠𝔱𝔞𝔳𝔦 𝔱𝔯𝔦𝔠𝔢𝔰𝔰𝔦𝔪𝔬 𝔮𝔲𝔦𝔫𝔱𝔬, 1543.

Mermaducke son of Briane Robinson and Alice his
wife ... ... 10 Decembris
An dau. of John Hewitson and Alice his wife ... 23 „
Mermaducke son of Thomas Robinson and Mabell
his wife ... ... 1 Januarij
Mᵍaret dau. of John Robinson and Elyn his wife 3 „
Agnes and Alice daughters of Rychard Godsalf and
Mᵍret his wife ... ... 16 Februarij
Alice dau. of Rich: Hirdson and Agnes his wife ... 18 „
Peter son of Giles Hardie and Alice his wife ... 20 „
Alice dau. of Reinalde Robinson and Mabell his wife 28 „
John son of John Slater and Elizabeth his wife ... 20 Martij

𝔵𝔦𝔦𝔦° 𝔡𝔦𝔢 𝔇𝔢𝔠𝔢𝔪𝔟𝔯𝔦𝔰 𝔞𝔫𝔫𝔬 𝔯𝔢𝔤𝔫𝔦 𝔯𝔢𝔤𝔦𝔰 𝔈𝔡𝔴𝔞𝔯𝔡𝔦 𝔰𝔢𝔵𝔱𝔦 𝔭𝔯𝔦𝔪𝔬, 1544.

Ursula dau. of Roger Banes and Jane his wife ... 26 Martij
An and Elin daughters of Rychard Johnson and
Elizabeth his wife ... ... 23 Aprilis
Thomas son of John Johnson and Agnes his wife... 10 Julie
Elin dau. of Gilbert North and Elizabeth his wife 20 „
Agnes dau. of Willm Lucas and Mᵍret his wife ... 21 Augusti
spuria Richard son of Thomas Fell, spurria, and Mᵍret
Waithman ... ... 3 Septembris
An dau. of John Ridalle and Margaret his wife ... 13 „
Elizabeth dau. of * * Holme and Christebell his
wife ... ... 20 Octobris
Mermaducke son of Mr. Bryan Hudlestou and
Mistrisse Ane his wife ... ... 13 Novembris
Joane dau. of one born spurria ... ... 12 Decembris
Ane dau. of Robert Dawnie ... ... 18 Februarij
spuria Ane dau. of the late wife of James Waller ... ... 20 „

Anno regni regis Edwardi sexti secundo, 1545.

Ane dau. of Richard Adcocke and Elizabeth his wife	13 Aprilis
Jenet dau. of Reinold Robinson and Mabell his wife	22 „
Lawrenc son of Edward Ashburne and Elizabethe his wife	10 Maij
* * son of Thomas Northe and Jenet his wife...	20 „
Reinolde son of James Johnson and M⁹gret his wife	10 Junij
Richard son of Gilbert Thornton and M⁹gret his wife	12 „
Isabell dau. of Gyles Hardie and Alice his wife ...	13 Augusti
Gilbert son of Alexander Atkinson and Mabell his wife...	20 „

Anno regni Edwardi regis sexti tertio, 1546.

John son of James Awray and Jenet his wife ...	10 Julij
Rychard son of John Robinson and Elin his wife...	12 „
M⁹gret and Jane daughters of Reinald Borthrige and Jenet his wife	14 „
Jane dau. of Richard Johnson and Elizabeth his wife	19 „
Ane dau. of Thomas Johnson and Maude his wife	10 Augusti
Richard son of Gilbert Northe and Elizabeth his wife	6 Septembris

Anno regni regis Edwardi sexto [sic] quarto, 1547.

Rowland son of Robert Burowe and Elizabeth his wife...	13 Julij
Jenet dau. of James Sigswicke and Eline his wife	23 „
Richard son of John Sigswicke and Elene his wife	3 Augusti
Gilbert son of John Warde and M⁹grete his wife...	12 „
Edmund son of Alexander Adcocke and Jane his wife...	23 „
M⁹gret dau. of Reinold Robinson and Mabell his wife	13 Septembris

Anno regni regis Edwardi sexto [sic] quinto, 1548.

Jane dau. of James Thornton and Alice his wife...	14 Decembris
Jane dau. of Thomas Johnson and Elizabeth his wife	23 Ma⁹tij
a Ethelld⁹ede dau. of Tristriam Man	13 Julij
Edward son of James Corte and Agnes his wife ...	17 „
John son of Richard Johnson and M⁹gret Borrow spuria	23 Februarij
Gilbart son of Willm Neylson and Jenet his wife	24 „
John son of Edward Hutton and Isabell his wife	25 „
Alice dau. of John Singleton and Alice his wife ...	26 M⁹tij
Isabell dau. of James Northe and Jane his wife ...	3 Maij
Tristram son of John Johnson and Agnes his wife	6 „
Eline dau. of Renold Baines and Jane his wife ...	2 Julij

spurria Anne dau. of Mr. Bryane Hudleston and Anne Atkinson...	3 Julij
Thomas son of John Huitson and Alice his wife ...	20 Augusti
John son of Renold Robinson and Mabell his wife	9 „
Ellin dau. of Xpofer Mellinge and Elizabeth his wife	10 Septembris
Edward son of Alexander Adcocke and Jane his wife	11 „
John son of Thomas Halle and Agnes his wife ...	1 Octobris
Thomas son of Gilbert Thornton and Margret his wife...	27 „
Isabell dau. of Richard Robinson and Jenet his wife	30 „
Willm son of John Sigswicke and Ellen his wife ...	2 Decembris
* * son of John Harison and Jane his wife ...	10 „
Tristriam son of Symon Sylle and Elizabeth his wife	12 „

Anno regni regis Edwardj sexto quinto [sic] 1349.

Anne dau. of Edward Ashburn and Agnes his wife	29 Decembris
Renold son of James Johnson and Mⁱgret his wife	3 Januarij
Renold son of John Slater and Elizabeth his wife	5 „
Anne dau. of Thomas North and Jenet his wife ...	23 „
Jane dau. of Edmond Newton and Isabell his wife	26 Februarij
Alice dau. Gyles Hardie and Alice his wife	2 Mⁱtij
John son of Thomas Johnson and Elizabeth his wife	10 „

1550.

Mabell dau. of James Awrey and Jenet his wife ...	18 Aprillis
spurria Willm son of John Teyler and Elizabeth Thornton	19 „
Richard son of Oliver Dickonson and Jane his wife	3 Junij
John son of Wiłłm Robinson and Mabell his wife	29 „
Peter son of Robert Burrowe and Elizabeth his wife	29 „
Richard son of Willm Ustonson and Jane his wife	4 Septembris
Richard son of Robert Robinson and Jenet his wife	7 „
Richard son of Alexander Atkinson and Mabell his wife...	13 „
Elizabeth dau. of Gilbert North and Elizabeth his wife...	15 „
Isabell and Jane daughters of Thomas Johnson and Maude his wife	26 Octob.
Renold son of Edward Whitthead and Jane his wife	18 Novembris
Willm son of Richard Heaton and Alice his wife...	26 „
Isabell dau. of James Thornton and Alice his wife	4 Decembris
Alice dau of Willm Heaton and Jane his wife ...	6 „

xiii° die Decembris ano regni regis Edwardi sexto [sic]

John son of Richard Godsalfe and Alice his wife	22 Januarij
Thomas son of James Slater and Alice his wife ...	19 Martij

[1551.]

Thomas son of John Rydall and M^{9}gret his wife...   30 Martij
Isabell dau. of Willm Borrowe and Alice his wife   13 Agusti
Jane dau. of John Dawson and Agnes his wife ...   2 Octobris
M^{9}gret dau. of James North and Jane his wife ...   13   ,,

xiii° die Decembris ano regni Marie reginae primo.

Elizabeth dau. of Richard Robinson and Jenet his
   wife...   ...   .   8 Januarij
Elen dau. of Willm Robinson and Maball his wife   18 Decembris
John son of Richard Newton and Jenet his [1] wife   6 Januarij
Richard son of John Tayler and Elizabeth his wife   22   ,,
Jane dau. of Thomas Hale and Agnes his wife ...   26   ,,

1552.

James son of Willm Heaton and Jane his wife ...   29 Apprilis
Richard and Dorothie children of Renold Baynes
   and Jane his wife   30   ,,
Alice dau. of James Awrey and Jenet his wife ...   30   ,,
Richard son of Thomas North and Jenet his wife   30   ,,
John son of Bryan Wethman and M^{9}gret Whithead   9 Mayij
Isabell [2] dau. of John Johnson and Agnes his wife   15   ,,
Robert son of John Halle and Alice his wife... ...   1 Augusti
John son of Xpofer Mellinge and Elizabeth his wife   7   ,,
Alice dau. of Edward Ashburne and Agnes his wife   15   ,,
Roland son of John Borrowe and Elizabeth his wife   8 Novembris
Eline dau. of John Harison and Jane his wife ...   11 Decembris

xiii° die Decembris ano regnoru^{9} regis et reginae Phillippi and Mariae primo et secundo.

Francis son of James Herdson and Elizabeth his
   wife...   ...   .   2 Januarij
Myles son of Tristriam Man and Isabell Willen ...   16   ,,
John son of Thomas Newton and Jennet his wife   15   ,,
Richard son of Gyles Hardie and Alice his wife ...   26   ,,
Esabell dau. of James Johnson and M^{9}gret his wife   27   ,,
Bryan son of Edmond Newton and Esabell his wife   1 Martij
Willm son of Robert Borrowe and Elizabeth his wife   3 ,,

---

[1] The words " Richard Newton and Jenet his " are struck out in
    the original.
[2] " Isabell " is written over " Elizabeth " crossed out.

1553.

Richard son of Thomas Johnson and Elizabeth his wife	16 Maij
Marmaducke son of Edward Whitthead and Jane his wife	22 Junij
Alice dau. of Gilbert North and Elizabeth his wife	6 Julij
Dorothie dau. of Renold Baynes and Jane his wife	12 ,,
Esabell dau. of Richard Corte and Alice his wife ...	12 Augusti
Añe dau. of John Claghton and Elin his wife ...	18 ,,
Esabell dau. of John Tayller and Elizabeth his wife	30 ,,
Jaue dau. of Oliver Dickonson and Jane his wife...	28 Septembris
Richard son of John Harison and Maude his wife...	2 Octobris
spurria M⁹maduke son of George Eykrigge and Alice Lucas	28 October
Thomas son of Richard Robinson and Jeuet his wife	29 Novembris

xiii° die Decembris ano regnoru⁹ regis Pbillippi et reginae Marie secdo et tertio, 1554.

M⁹gret dau. of Willm Borrowe and Alice his wife	1 Januarij
Jane dau. of Willm Heaton and Jane [1] his wife ...	23 Februarij
Elizabeth dau. of John Halle and Alice his wife ...	1 Martij
Thomas son of James North and Jane his wife ...	12 ,,
Elizabeth dau. of John Sigswicke and Elin his wife	14 ,,

1555.

Jenet dau. of Peter Hyne and Elizabeth his wife ...	15 Apprilis
spurria James son of Richard Backus and Alice Wilkinson	2 Maij
spurria Willm son of Thomas Nardsdalle and Elin Whithead	15 ,,
Jane dau. of Willm Nealson and Agnes his wife...	24 ,,
Willm sou of John Harison and Jane his wyfe ...	28 ,,
John son of Thomas Slater and Jenet his wife ...	8 Julij
Jane dau. of James Hirdson and Elizabeth his wife	6 Octobris
Elizabeth dau. of Thomas Halle and Agnes his wife	13 Novembris
Reinold son of John Johnson and Agnes his wife...	8 Decembris

xiii° die Decembris ano regnoru⁹ regis Pbilippi et reginae Marie tertio et quarto, 1555.

spurria Thomas son of Thomas Hukes and Agnes Spalton	24 Marcij

1556.

Thomas son of Richard Corte and Alice his wife ...	29 Marcij
Jaue dau. of Richard Johnson and M⁹gret his wife	3 Apprilis

[1] "Jane" written over "Alice" crossed out.

Wiħm son of Thomas Newton and Jenet his wife	28 Apprilis
Thomas son of Xpofer Ustenson and Jenet his wife	7 Maij
Jane dau. of Roland Heaton and Jenet his wife ...	28 ,,
Dorethi dau. of John Tayler and Elizabeth his wife	8 Octobris
Alice dau. of Thomas Johnson and Elizabeth his wife	12 ,,
Wiħm son of John Claghton and Elin his wif ...	22 ,,

Anno regni regis Phillippi et Marie reginae quarto et quinto, 1556.

Willm son of James Johnson and M⁹gret his wife	22 Januarij
Willm son of Robert Borrowe and Elizabeth his wife	8 Februarij
Robert son of Edmund Newton and Isabell his wife	12 ,,
Jenet dau. of Wiħm Ustenson and M⁹gret his wif	5 Martij
Robert son of James Hirdson and Dorethe his wife	20 ,,

1557.

Jenet dau. of John Halle and Alice his wife... ...	11 Maij
Richard son of Richard Cort and Alice his wife ...	24 ,,
Alice dau. of Rich. Robinson and Jenet his wife ...	28 ,,
Thomas son of Gilbert North and Elizabeth his wife	8 Junij
John son of Thomas Battie and Elizabeth his wife	13 ,,
Eline dau. of Anthonye Frereman and Sibell his wife	14 ,,
Wiħm son of John Johnson and Agnes his wife ...	8 Julij
Thomas son of Wiħm Heaton and Jane his wife ...	7 Augusti
* * son of James Northe and Jenet his wife ...	15 ,,
Ursula dau. of Renold Baynes and Jane his wife...	28 Octobris
John son of Richard Johnson and M⁹gret his wife	16 Novembris

Anno regni reginae Elizabethae primo, 1558.

Elizabeth dau. of Renold Whitthead and M⁹gret his wiffe	26 Decembris
John son of Oliver Dickonson and Jane his wife ...	1 Januarij
Edward son of John Cansfild and M⁹gret his wife	2 ,,
Richard son of Edward Northe and M⁹gerye his wife	2 ,,

1559.

Henrye son of Robert Robinson and Isabell his wife	18 Novembris
Jenet dau. of Richard Cort and Alice his wife ultimo die	,,

Anno regni reginae Elizabethae secundo, 1559.

Jenet dau. of Thomas Thornton and M⁹gret Whithead	5 Marcij

1560.

Thomas son of Thomas Smith and Jane his wife...   12 Junij
Alice dau. of Thomas Balife and Elizabeth his wife   16 Septembris
Edward son of Rich. Lucas and Agnes his wife ...   18   „
Elizabeth dau. of Bryan Dawnye and Alce his wife   21   „
Mychaell son of Rich. Johnson and M²gret his wife   29   „
Edward son of Thomas Northe and M²gret his wife   4 Octobris
Jane dau. of Bryan Bland and Agnes his wife   ...   2 November

Anno regni reginae Elizabethae tertio, 1560.

Dorethe dau. of Willm Nealson and Agnes his wife
ultimo die Januarij
Thomas son of Edward Northe and M²gerie his wife   7 Februarij

1561.

Richard son of Willm Hudleston and Cicalie his wife   16 Aprillis
Thomas son of Robert Borrowe and Elizabeth his wife   12 Maij
Myles son of John Johnson and Agnes his wife   ...   8 Septembris
Ales dau. of Robert Robinson and Isabell his wife   8 Novembris
John son of Willm Adcocke and Elizabeth his wife   8 Decembris

Anno regni reginae Elizabethae quarto, 1562.

Thomas son of John Tayler and Elizabeth his wife   8 Januarie

1562.

Agnes Smith ...   .   Ultimo die Julij
Elizabeth dau. of James Northe   ...   .   15 Augusti
Richard Balife   15   „
Ethelldred and Philippe children of Anthony Frereman
ultimo Septembris
Mathew Newton   ...   .   6 Octobris
Willm Whithead   10   „
John Robinson   ...   .   17 Novembris
Elizabeth Hudleston   ...   .   6 Decembris

Anno regni reginae Elizabethae quinto, 1562.

Thomas Bland son of Bryan Bland and Agnes his
wife ...   .   22 Decembris
Thomas Harison   ...   .   5 Januarij
Thomas Cansfild   7   „
Thomas Dickonson ...   .   10 Februarij
Stephen Johnson   23   „

1563.

Thomas Dayne	28 Martij
James Dodgtion	18 Aprilis
Alice Johnson...	8 Maij
Myles Johnson	18 Junij
ia John Werringe	3 Julij
Myles Baylye son of Thomas...	6 Augusti
John son of Xpofer Huitson	13 ,,
Alice Lupton	27 Septembris

Anno regni reginae Elizabethae sexto, 1563.

Elizabeth dau. of Mr. Edward Northe	16 Februarij
Elizabeth Corte	18 ,,

Anno regni reginae Elizabethae septimo, 1564.

Myles Borrow	3 Januarij
Alice Hvitson	10 ,,
Etheldred Harison	24 ,,
John son of John Patton	20 Februarij
Willm son of Richard Johnson	20 ,,
Jane dau. of James Northe	28 ,,
Thomas Cansfild son of John Cansfild	13 Martij
Elizabeth dau. of Willm Borrowe	14 ,,

1565.

Renond son of Richard Robinson...	ultimo die Martij
Isabell dau. of Willm Hudleston	primo die Aprilis
Mabell dau. of R * * Burrow	quinto die Aprilis

Anno regni reginae Elizabethae octavo, 1565.

Thomas son of Mr. Henrye Brabin, Gent	7 Septembris
M⁹maducke son of John Cockin	20 Octobris

Anno regni reginae Elizabethae decimo, 1567.

Willm son Mr. Henrye Brabin, gen⁹, and Alice his wife	8 Septembris
Willm son of Edmund Hardie	8 ,,
Symon son of Bryan Dañye and Alice Dawnye his wife	23 Octobris
Willm son of Henrye Pachett and Mabell his wife	25 ,,

Anno regni reginae Elizabethae undecimo, 1568.

Eline dau. of Thomas Halle and Agnes his wife ...   20 Januarij
Myles son of Richard Robinson and Alice his wife   28 Februarij
An dau. of Mr. Thomas Newton, Gent⁹ and M⁹gret
    his wife ...   .   4 Martij
James son of Thomas Sigswicke and Elin his wife   13 · „
Richard son of John Godsalfe and M⁹gret his wife   18 „

1569.

Jenet dau. of Gilbert Heaton and Alice his wife ...   3 Aprillis
Christopher son of Thomas Mellinge and Elin his wife 11   „
John son of Thomas Johnson and Alice his wife ...   21 Augusti
Mathewe son of Thomas Battie   ...   .   20 Septembris
Alexander son of Gilbert Atkinson   28   „
John son of Thomas Robinson   29   „
Edmund son of Richard Tatham and his wife   ...   18 Octobris
Thomas son of John Harison and Elin his wife ...   26   „
Myles and John children of Willm Johnson and
    Jenet his wife...   ...   .   14 Novembris
Mabell dau. of John Robinson   20   „
M⁹maducke son of Willm Mergerison   26   „
Marie dau. of one poore salter, a blynd man of
    Carnforth   14   „
Jane dau. of Willm Lupton and Agnes his wife ...   15   „
George son of John Harison and Mabell his wife...   18   „
Thomas son of Richard Whithead...   ...   .   10 Octobris

[It will be noted that several years are missing from original.]

Anno regni reginae Elizabethae decimo quinto, 1572.

Elizabeth dau. of Richard Sigswicke and Jenet his
    wif ...   .   16 Novembris

Anno regni reginae Elizabethae decimo sexto, 1573.

M⁹gret dau. of Richard Thornton and Elin his wife   14 Decembris
Robert son of Thomas Gibson and Jenet his wife...   2 Januarij
Alice dau. of John Godsalf and M⁹gret his wife   primo die   „

1574.

John son of Thomas Robinson and Elizabeth his wife 16 Aprillis
Agnes Vin dau. of John Vin and Elin his wife   ...   2 Augusti
Willm and Bryan children of Nealson and his wife   8   „
Alice dau. of John Bland and Alice his wife   ...   19 Decembris

Richard son of Bryan Dickonson ... ...   3 Januarij
Willm son of Rowland Whithead   7   ,,
M⁹gret dau. of Myles Hudleston and Catoren his wife 14 Julij
Jane dau. of Henrye Brabin and Alice his wife quarto die Augusti

Anno regni reginae Elizabethae decimo septimo, 1574.

Robert son of Edmund Burrowe ... ...   18 Decembris
Mergerie dau. of John Cansfild   ... ...   3 Januarij
Willm son of Edmund Whithead ... ...   4 Februarij

1575.

Ane dau. of Robert Pachett ... ...   26 Maij
Jane dau. of John Harries   ... ...   8 Junij
Thomas son of Edward Dickonson   ... ...   18 Julij
John son of Thomas Gibson ... ...   2 Augusti
Alice dau. of Renold Johnson   ... ...   14 Septembris
Willm son of John Vin   20   ,,
Anne dau. of Myles Hudleston   ... ...   6 Octobris
Alice dau. of Willm Slater   21   ,,
M⁹gret dau. of John Godsalf ... ...   primo die Novembris
Cateren dau. of Bryan Dawnye   14   ,,

At foot of page is written in contemporary hand,
" Richard Jackson his name
And with my pen I wrote the same."

Anno regni reginae Elizabethae decimo octavo. 1575.

Thomas son of Xpofer Hewitson and Agnes his wife   6 Februarij

1576.

Isabell dau. of M⁹maducke Hutton   ... ...   4 Aprilis
Willm son of John Heaton and Eline Boyes   ...   2 Octobris
Edward son of Thomas Gilson   10   ,,
Jenet dau. of M⁹maducke Robinson   ... ...   [sic] 16 Septembris

Anno regni reginae Elizabethae vicessimo, 1577.

Willm son of Edmund Myres   ... ...   20 Decembris
Dorothe dau. of James Awrey   ... ...   16 Januarij
Eline dau. of Thomas Mellinge   24   ,,
Eline dau. of Edward Dickonson ... ...   24 Februarij
James son of Willm Borthrigg   ... ...   16 Martij

1578.

John son of Thomas Smithe ... ...   16 Aprilis
Margerie [1] dau. of Richard Robinson ... ...   2 Maij

Anno regni reginae Elizabethae vicessimo primo, 1578.

Alice dau. of John Harries ... ...   27 Februarij

1579.

Willm son of Xpofer Hewertson ... ...   primo die Maij
Willm son of John Harison ... ...   2 Augusti
M⁹gret dau. of Willm Slater   7   „
M⁹gret dau. of Thomas Battie   19   „
Willm son of Richard Sigswicke ... ...   6 Septembris
Marye dau. of John Blande   20   „
Mabell dau. of George Toppin ... ...   3 Octobris
Renolde son of John Godsalfe   12   „
Alice dau. of Henrye Brabin   25   „
John son of Willm Sigswick ... ...   10 Novembris
Cateron dau. of John Ewean   21   „

Anno regni reginae Elizabethae vicessimo secundo, 1579.

M⁹gret dau. of M⁹maducke Hutton ... ...   20 Decembris
Eline dau. of Willm Borthrigge   26   „
Thomas son of Edmund Whitthead ... ...   17 Januarij
Willm son of Edward Warde ... ...   2 Februarij
Thomas son of Richard Northe   26   „

1580.

Anne dau. of Edward Skerret ... ...   20 Aprillis
John Kyebye ... ...   22 Maij
Renold son of John Heaton ... ...   5 Decembris
Anne dau. of John Newton, Clerke, and Dorrythie
  his wife ... ...   14 Junij
filia Xpofer Holme ... ...   14 „
Thomas Smithe ... ...   20 Julij
spuria[sic] James son of Willm Barker   26   „
spuria John son of James Robinson ... ...   14 Augusti

[1] Written over " Dorothe " crossed out.

Edmund son of Willm Jackson	14 Octobris
fillia Francisci Hirdson	16 „
Jane dau. of Gilbert Atkinson	25 Decembris

Anno regni reginae Elizabethae vicessimo tertio, 1580.

Richard son of Xpofer Metcalf	21 Februarij
George son of Edmund Myres	2 Martij
Willm son of Edmund Burrowe	7 „

1581.

Anne dau. of Richard Knight	30 Martij
John son of Richard Robinson	25 Aprilis
Elizabeth dau. of Richard Thornton	27 „
Agnes dau. of Thomas Robinson	30 Augusti
Thomas son of George Toppin	18 Novembris
Jenet dau. of John Dawnye	20 „
Jane dau. of Willm Slater	26 „

Anno regni reginae Elizabethae vicessimo quarto, 1581.

Jane dau. of John Newton and Dorothe his wif ...	28 Januarij

1582.

Jane dau. of John Harison and Eline his wife ...	25 M⁹tij
Allan son of Willm Sigswicke	20 Aprillis
Jane dau. of John Blande	20 Julie
Jane dau. of Richard Knight...	15 Septembris
Elizabeth dau. of Richard Northe...	primo die Octobris
Leonard son of John Ewean	26 „
John son of John Heaton	13 Decembris

Anno regni reginae Elizabethae vicessimo quinto 1582.

Thomas son of one Spowner of Newton	7 Aprillis
Thomas son of M⁹maducke Robinson	12 „
Elizabeth dau. of John Keysbye	27 „
Gyles son of Richard Hardie...	30 „
Jane dau. of John Godsalf	5 Septembris
Edmund son of Thomas Smithe	25 Octobris

Anno regni reginae Elizabethae vicessimo sexto, 1583.

Thomas son of John Newton, Clerke ... ...   8 M^otij

1584.

Willm son of Willm Anderson	15 Julij
Thomas son of Edmund Burrowe	9 Augusti
M⁹gret dau. of John Johnson...	29 Septembris
Catterin dau. of John Blande...	18 Octobris
Richard son of John Harison	12 ,,
Jane dau. of Richard Hirdson	7 Novembris
Isabell dau. of M⁹maduck Robinson	14 ,,
John son of Willm Slater	16 ,,

Anno regni reginae Elizabethae vicessimo septimo, 1584.

John son of Richard Thornton	16 Decembris
Thomas son of John Harries	18 Januarie
M⁹gret dau. of Rallynge Borrowe	31 ,,

1585.

Mawd dau. of John Heaton	18 Augusti
Robert son of Richard Robinson	28 Septembris

Anno regni reginae Elizabethae vicessimo octavo, 1585.

Gilbert son of Richard Thornton	28 Decembris
Henrye son of John Harries	3 Februarij
Thomas son of M⁹maducke Slater	primo die Martij
James son of Richard Johnson junior	10 ,,

1586.

Rallinge son of John Ewan	13 Maij
Bryan son of John Dawnye	27 ,,
John son of Thomas Mellinge	11 Junij
Richard son of John Newton, psonn	primo die Julij
Adam son of Willm Lansdall...	primo die Septembris
Ane dau. of Lawrence Gibson...	4 ,,
M⁹gret dau. of Willm Jackson	7 ,,
Agnes dau. of John Johnson Junior	7 Octobris

Anno regni reginae Elizabethae vicessimo nono, 1586.

Elizabeth dau. of Richard Hudleston	26 Novembris
Jane dau. of John Godsalfe	30 ,,
Ane dau. of John Bland	ultimo die ,,
Thomas son of Leonard Cansfild	21 Decembris

1587.

Willm son of Willm Sigswicke	25 Maij
John son of Robert Baynes	20 Julij
* * son of M^{o}maducke Robinson	26 ,,
M^{o}gret dau. of Thomas Whithead	20 Augusti

Anno regni reginae Elizabethae tricessimo, 1587.

Agnes dau. of Gilbert Dickonson[1]	primo die Januarij
Alexander son of Edmund Adcocke	16 ,,
Thomas son of John Heaton	3 Martij

1588.

Agnes dau. of John Bland	20 Julij
Richard son of Richard North	11 Augusti
Marmaducke son of John Newton, Clerke	16 ,,
Ane dau. of Willm Hearode	3 Novembris
John son of Leonard Carter	12 Decembris

Anno regni reginae Elizabethae tricessimo, primo, 1588.

Thomas son of Edmund Myres	9 Januarij
Alice dau. of Thomas Woodhouse	14 ,,

1589.

Elinne dau. of Robert Borrowe	13 Aprilis
Thomas son of John Ewan	30 Maij
Agnes dau. of Thomas Bland	primo die Junij
Henrye son of M^{o}maducke Robinson	4 Julij
Dorethe dau. of Richard Hudleston	6 Augusti
Anthonye son of Willm Jackson	6 Octobris
Jenet dau. of Roberte Dickonson	11 ,,
John and James children of Marmaducke Slater ...	3 Decembris

[1] In original is here written "John Gibsou de Whittington, 1652."

D

Anno regni reginae Elizabethae tricessimo secundo, 1589.

Jane dau. of James Blackburne ... ... 21 Novembris
Alice dau. of Edmund Adcoke ... ... 26 Januarij
Willm son of John Harries ... ... 9 Aprilis
Jenet dau. of Bryan Dickonson ... ... 3 Maij
spurria Elizabeth dau. of James Bland ... ... 4 „

1590. [sic]

Richard son of John Johnson ... ... 17 Maij
Agnes dau. of John Barrowe ... ... 19 „
Jane dau. of Richard Johnson Junior ... ... primo die Junij
John son of Willm Brabin ... ... 25 Junij
Thomas son of Richard Thornton ... ... 9 Augusti
Gyles son of Richard Hardie ... ... 12 „
Eline dau. of Thomas Hirdson ... ... 13 „
Elizabeth dau. of Willm Lonsdalle ... ... 19 „
Ane dau. of Thomas Heaton ... ... 24 Septembris
Jenet dau. of John Newton, psona ... ... 12 Octobris
Lawrence son of Roger Garnet of Casterton... [sic] 10 Septembris
Thomas son of Myles Beyley... ... ... 16 „
M⁹gret dau. of Thomas Godself ... ... 23 Octobris
Myles son of James Astwicke of Arkholme ... ... 6 Novembris
Richard son of John Bayley ... ... 12 „

Anno regni reginae Elizabethae tricessimo tertio, 1590.

spurria Katterin dau. of Edward Cansfild... ... ... 10 Januarij
John son of Richard Robinson ... ... 19 „
John son of Gilbert Dickonson ... ... 19 Februarij
Alice dau. of Francis Hirdson ... ... 19 „
M⁹gret and Ane daughters of John Heaton ... ... 19 „

1591.

Symon son of Renold Godself ... ... ultimo die Martij
Francis dau. of Mr. Lambert ... ... 4 Maij
Richard son of George Bachouse ... ... 16 „
Maude dau. of John Toluson... ... ... 10 „
Richard son of John Johnson ... ... 3 Augusti
Elizabeth dau. of Marmaducke Slater ... ... [sic] 9 Julij
Thomas son of Leonard Carter ... ... 17 Septembris
Willm son of Richard Hudleston ... ... 28 „
Thomas son of Xpofer Nealson ... ... 16 Octobris
John son of Robert Smithe ... ... 27 Novembris

Anno regni reginae Elizabethae tricessimo quarto, 1591.

Gilbert son of Robert Dickonson	14 Decembris
Gilbert and Richard sonnes of Thomas North ...	12 Februarij
Bryan son of Thomas Bland	16 ,,

1592.

Wiłłm son of Mᵈmaduk Slater	21 Julij
Oliver son of Richard North	9 Augusti
Wiłłm son of James Blackburn	12 Septembris
Mᵈgret dau. of John Barrowe	1 Octobris
Richard son of John Ewan	6 ,,
Mᵈgret dau. of Edmund Adcoke	10 ,,
Wiłłm son of Wiłłm Jackson	23 ,,

Anno regni reginae Elizabethae tricessimo quinto 1592.

Renold son of Thomas Whitthead	24 Novembris
Wiłłm son of Leonard Carter	17 Decembris
Thomas son of Wiłłm Borrowe de Biggins	24 ,,
Richard son of Thomas Robinson	6 Januarij
Wiłłm son of John Bland	8 ,,
John son of John Newton, psonn	24 ,,
Richard son of Mᵈmaducke Hodgeson	30 ,,
Jane dau. of John Buser	primo die Februarij
Wiłłm son of John Smith	3 ,,
Ane dau. of Richard Sigswicke	7 ,,
Alice dau. of Wiłłm Brabin	26 ,,
Jane dau. of Edward Cansfild	11 Martij
Isabell dau. of Wiłłm Margerison	16 ,,
Jane dau. of Simon Hutton	24 ,,

1593.

Dorethie dau. of Mr. Lambert	27 Aprilis
Eline dau. of John Johnson	primo die Maij
Francis dau. of Thomas Tayler	4 Maij
Elinge dau. of Thomas Hirdson	8 Septembris
John son of Richard Hardie	27 ,,
John son of Arthur Fouscrofte	30 ,,
Elinge dau. of Thomas Godsalf	13 Novembris
Richard son of John Heatonn	2 Decembris
Richard son of Xpofer Walker	3 ,,

Anno regni reginae Elizabethae tricessimo sexto, 1593.

Thomas son of Christopher Mellinge	12 Decembris
An dau. of Myles Balyfe	17 ,,
M⁹gret dau. of Willm Burton	4 Januarij
Agnes dau. of George Bachouse	27 ,,
Eling dau. of John Barrow	4 Martij
Jenet dau. of Xpofer Nealson	10 ,,

1594.

Willm son of John Toluson	21 Maij
Katerin dau. of Francis Herdson	20 ,,
An dau. of Symond Hutton	23 ,,
Elizabeth dau. of Rallinge Borrowe	24 Junij
An dau. of Willm Lansdalle	27 ,,
Jenet dau. of Richard Vstenson	2 Augusti
Elizabeth dau. of Gilbert Dickonson	11 ,,
Isabell dau. of Mr. Lambert	24 ,,

Anno regni reginae Elizabethae tricessimo septimo, 1594.

Sibell dau. of John Harries	20 Novembris
Xpofer son of Thomas Northe	20 ,,
Elizabeth dau. of John Bayley	26 ,,
Mabell dau. of Willm Patchet	13 Januarij
* * dau. of Thomas Robinson	14 ,,
Thomas son of Richard Halle	16 ,,
Elizabeth dau. of Robert Smith	26 ,,
An dau. of Richard Northe	16 Februarij
John son of John Barrow	12 Martij
M⁹gret dau. of Thomas Bland	28 ,,

1595.

Mabell dau. of John Johnson...	18 Maij
Xpofer son of John Newton, pson	20 ,,
Isabell dau. of Wilfride Brockhols...	23 ,,
John son of Richard Knight...	27 ,,
Edward son of John North	18 Julij
Willm son of James Greene	3 Augusti
Richard son of Willm Jackson	26 Septembris
Willm son of Willm Hawdwayne...	30 ,,
Isabell dau. of James Blackburne	24 Octobris
Xpofer son of Xpofer Walker...	10 Novembris

Rallynge son of James Heaton ... ... 12 Novembris
Jane dau. of Wiłłm Brabin, gentº ... ... 21 Augusti

Anno regni reginae Elizabethae tricessimo octavo, 1595.

Jane dau. of Wiłłm Whithead ... ... 4 Januarij
Richard son of George Bachouse ... ... 11 „
An dau. of Thomas Cayslie ... ... 28 „
Thomas son of Leonord Carter ... ... 15 Februarij
Robert son of Thomas Denye ... ... 21 Martij

1596.

Wiłłm son of Thomas Whithead ... ... 13 Aprilis
Ursula dau. of Symond Hutton ... ... 13 Maij
Marye dau. of Mr. Lambert ... ... 23 „
Jane dau. of Marmaducke Slater ... ... 2 Julij
Elinge dau. of Mr. John North ... ... 4 „
Jane dau. of Xpofer Mellinge... ... ... 10 „

Anno regni reginae Elizabethae tricessimo nono. 1596.

Richard son of Thomas Hirdson ... ... primo die Decembris
George son of Arthur Fowscroft ... ... 3 „
Agnes dau. of Richard Halle ... ... 26 Januarij
Wiłłm son of Thomas Heaton ... ... 9 Februarij
* * son of John Dickonson ... ... 20 „
John son of Wiłłm Patchet ... ... 6 Martij
Grace dau. of Robert Dickonson ... ... 13 „

1597.

Wiłłm son of Renold Godsalfe ... ... 8 Aprilis
* * son of Symond Battie... ... ... 12 Maij
Xpofer and Alice children of Tristriam Bowerdell 10 Julij
Thomas son of Bryan Nealson ... ... 20 Octobris

Anno regni reginae Elizabethae quadragessimo, 1597.

Elizabeth dau. of Marmaducke Cockin ... ... 8 Decembris
Robert son of John Firbancke ... ... 22 „
Jane dau. of John Johnson ... ... 22 Januarij
Wiłłm son of James Heaton ... ... 29 „
James son of John Toluson ... ... 15 Februarij
Richard son of Thomas Bland ... ... 10 Martij

1598.

An dau. of Edmund Tatham	2 Aprilis
Mergerye dau. of Mr. John North...	primo die Maij
Elizabeth dau. of James Blackburn	17 Maij
Robert son of Mr. Lambert	19 Junij
M⁹gret dau. of Mr. Thomas Blackburne	19 Julij
Katherin dau. of Willm Brabin, gent⁹	23 „
Lawrence son of Thomas Robinson	10 Augusti
Richard son of Richard Knight	13 „
M⁹gret dau. of John Barrow	24 „
James son of John Blande	3 Septembris
Willm son of Willm Whithead	8 Octobris
Willm son of Edmund Adcock	26 „
Jenet and Elizabeth daughters of Richard Halle...	2 Novembris

Anno regni reginae Elizabethae quadragessimo primo, 1598.

spuria	An dau. of Elizabeth Hudleston	10 Decembris
	An dau. of Leouard Carter	ultimo die „
	John son of Marducke Cockin	23 Februarij
	John son of Thomas Keysbie...	13 „
	Willm son of Richard Vstenson	18 Martij

1599.

Elizabeth and An daughters of Edmund Burrowe	6 Aprilis
Jane dau. of John Baylye	14 Junij
Johan dau. of Richard Robinson	10 Julij
Bryan son of James Bland	18 „
Elinge dau. of Francis Hirdson	16 „
Agnes dau. of Tristriam Bowerdell	primo die Augusti
M⁹gret dau. of James Dodgson	12 „
Jenet dau. of John Baitson	19 „
Richard son of John North, gent	19 Septembris
An dau. of William Vstenson	30 „
Xpofer son of Bryan Nealson...	3 Octobris
Willm son of Thomas Whithead	26 Novembris

Anno regni reginae Elizabethae quadragessimo secundo, 1599.

Dorothe dan. of * * Thornton	10 Decembris
Willm son of John Newton, pson	27 „
Jane dau. of Willm Patchet	20 Januarij
Agnes dau. of John Toluson	20 „

Jane dau. of Edmund Tatham	14 Februarij
Willm son of John Johnson	20 „
Elizabeth dau. of Robert Dickonson	6 Martij
Wiłłm son of Richard Johnson	7 „
Ellyn dau. of Xpofer Mellinge	8 „
John son of James Blakburne	11 „

1600.

Edmund son of Wiłłm Myres	13 Maij
Alice dau. of Richard Corte	14 „
John son of Edward Atkinson	29 „
Wiłłm son of Richard Robinson	5 Julij
Wiłłm son of Symond Hutton	20 „.
Richard son of Bryan Nealson	quinto die Augusti
Thomas son of John Robinson	„
Isabell dau. of * * * *	10 „
Wiłłm son of Renold Borthrigg	14 Septembris
Jenet dau. of Edmund Whithead	24 „
Richard son of John Knight	19 Octobris
Thomas son of Robert Cansfilde	23 „

Anno regni reginae Elizabethae quadragessimo tertio, 1600.

Francis son of Wiłłm Maddyson	19 Januarij
Jane dau. of Richard Halle	8 Februarij
Jane dau. of Bryan Gibson	8 „
Thomas son of Richard Knight	10 „
James son of Thomas North	22 „
James son of Thomas Bland	9 Martij
Agnes dau. of Marmaducke Cokin...	12 „

1601.

John son of Wiłłm Ewan	31 Martij
Jane dau. of Willm Myres	primo die Aprilis
An dau. of Thomas Dawnye	2 „
Thomas son of John Johnson younger	19 „
John son of Mr. Lambert	quinto die Maij
John son of Wiłłm Whithead	primo die Augustij
An dau. of Wiłłm Brabin, gent	„
Mꝯgret dau. of Tristriam Bowerdell	3 Octobris
John son of Wiłłm Lansdall	22 „

Anno regni reginae Elizabethae quadragessimo quarto, 1601.

Alice dau. of John Johnson	4 Decembris
James son of James Heaton	„

Elizabeth dau. of Thomas Kaysbye ... ... 10 Januarij
John son of Wiłłm Reade 30   ,,
Thomas son of James Bland ... ... quinto die Februarij

1602.

Marye dau. of Willm Myres ... ... primo die Augusti
John son of Mr. John North 11   ,,
Bryan son of Simon Dawnye ... ... 14 Septembris
Margerie dau. of Robert Cansfilde 16   ,,
Jenet dau. of Richard Godsalfe 20   ,,
Edmund son of Wiłłm Burrowe ... ... 3 Octobris
Mᵉgret dau. of Willm Patchet 24   ,,
Jane dau. of Robert Dickonson ... ... 14 Novembris
Bryan son of Francis Hirdson 15   ,,

Anno regni reginae Elizabethae quadragessimo quinto, 1602.

Elizabeth dau. of Bryan Gibson ... ... 23 Decembris
Jenet dau. of Richard Johnson 27   ,,
An dau. of Thomas Carter ... ... 2 Januarij
Bryan son of James Bland 17   ,,
Bryan son of Leonard Carter 21   ,,
John son of Thomas Tayler 28   ,,
An dau. of George Herdner, spuria ... ... 23 Februarij
Thomas son of James Blackburne ... ... 10 Martij
Alice dau. of John Toluson 18   ,,

Anno regni regis Jacobi primo, 1603.

John son of Thomas Bland ... ... 24 Aprilis
Elizabeth dau. of Xpofer Mellinge ... ... quinto die Maij
Alexander son of Bryane Nealson ... ...   ,,
Elizabeth dau. of John Robinson ... ... primo die Junij
Wiłłm son of Richard Halle ... ... 3 Julij
Ursula dau. of Wiłłm Brabin, gent ... ... 16 Octobris
George son of Richard Robinson 25   ,,
James son of Richard Knight 31   ,,
Richard son of Wiłłm Vstenson ... ... 6 Novembris
Isabell dau. of Thomas Hirdson 20   ,,
Richard son of Edmund Tatham ... ... 12 Decembris

At the top of the page is written
" Richard Jackson, his name."

spuria Elizabeth dau. of Robert Ryddinge ... ... 12 Decembris
Thomas son of Wiłłm Ewan ... ... primo die Januarij
spuria Bryan son of Oliver Dickonson 4   ,,

Anno regni don⁹j n⁹rj Jacobi regis secundo, 1604.

An dau. of Marcer * *	11 Junij
Wiłłm son of John Barrowe	12 ,,
Richard son of John Knight	22 ,,
Thomas son of John Johnson senior	9 Augusti
John son of Thomas Dawnye	28 Septembris
Xpofer son of Richard Cort	3 Octobris
An dau. of Simon Dawnye	quinto die ,,
Richard son of Renold Borthrigg	7 ,,
James son of Thomas Tayler	21 Novembris
John son of Stephen Atkinson	9 Decembris
Isabell dau. of James Halldodgeon	11 ,,
Elizabeth dau. of Tristriam Bourdell	23 ,,
John son of Richard Dawnye	3 Januarij
Alice dau. of * * Conder	19 ,,
Alice dau of Robert Cansfild	13 Februarij
M⁹gret dau. of Richard Nicholson	13 ,,
John son of Thomas Carter	24 ,,
Thomas son of Robert Cansfild	26 ,,
Elin dau. of Bryan Gibson	primo die Martij
Thomas son of Wiłłm Myres	3 ,,
John son of Thomas Bland	quinto die ,,

Anno regni dni nri Jacobi regis tertio, 1605.

John son of Thomas Northe	7 Aprilis
Agnes dau. of Thomas Whitthead	ultimo die Junij
John son of Richard Halle	17 Julij
Renold son of Richard Godsalf	11 Augusti
Thomas son of Wiłłm Brabin, Gent.	9 Septembris
Thomas son of Bryan Nealson	10 Octobris
Elin dau. of John Barrowe	22 ,,
John son of Robert Dickonson	7 Novembris
Richard son of Thomas Tayler	9 Decembris
Thomas son of Richard Dawnye	29 ,,
M⁹gret dau. of Richard Hutton	9 Januarij
Elizabeth dau. of James Bland	10 ,,
Elin dau. of John Robinson	27 ,,
James son of Xpofer Mellinge	2 Februarij
Edward son of Wiłłm Burrowe	16 Martij

Anno regni don⁹j n⁹rj Jacobi regis quarto, 1606.

Richard son of Marmaducke Cockin	8 Aprilis
Renold son of Wiłłm Whithead	14 Maij
John son of Richard Cort	18 ,,
An dau. of James Blackburne	27 Junij

E

spuria Jane dau. of George Sigswicke ... ... 23 Augusti
Edmund son of Bryan Nealson ... ... 12 Septembris
Jeffraye son of Richard Knight ... ... 17 „
Henrye son of John Johnson... ... ... 4 Decembris
John son of Willm Vstenson... ... ... 4 „
John and Jenet children of Richard Robinson ... 18 Januarij
Jenet dau. of Thomas Caysbie ... ... 19 „
Willm son of Willm Brabin, Gent. ... ... 4 Februarij
spuria M⁹gret dau. of Richard Garnet ... ... 7 Martij

Anno regni don⁹j n⁹rj Jacobi regis quinto, 1607.

Jane dau. of Thomas Hirdson ... ... 29 Martij
Agnes dau. of * * * * ... ... 26 Aprilis
Jane dau. of Edward Cockin ... ... 17 Maij
James son of Willm Gennings ... ... 14 Julij
Isabel dau. of Thomas Walker ... ... 21 „
An dau. of Willm Myres ... ... 7 Octobris
Elizabeth dau. of Willm Burrowe ... ... 8 „
James son of Edward Skayffe ... ... 9 „
Elizabeth dau. of Willm Johnson ... ... 9 „
Xpofer son of John Barrowe ... ... 12 (?) „
Elin dau. of Leonard Ewau ... ... 25 „
John son of Thomas Whormbie ... ... 18 Novembris
Thomas son of Richard Godsalfe... ... ... 18 Januarij
An dau. of James Harries ... ... 18 „
An dau. of Mr. Lambert... ... ... ultimo die „
John son of Bryan Bland ... ... 2 Martij
Elizabeth dau. of Tristriam Bowerdell ... ... 7 „
Thomas son of John Smith ... ... 13 „

Anno regni don⁹j n⁹rj Jacobi regis sexto, 1608.

Dorothe dau. of Richard Johnson, carpenter... ... 19 Aprilis
An dau. of Richard Dawnye ... ... 24 Martij
Elin dau. of Marmaducke Cockin ... ... [sic] 4 Junij
Jenet dau. of Bryan Nealson... ... ... 4 Julij
M⁹gret dau. of Thomas Ridall ... ... 17 „
John son of Richard Corte ... ... ultimo die „
John son of Edmund Burrowe ... ... quinto die Augusti
* * dau. of John Tayler ... ... 27 „
Jane dau. of Thomas Dawnye... ... ... 9 Septembris
John son of Leonard Ewan ... ... 2 Octobris
John son of Xpofer Mellinge ... ... 28 „
Agnes dau. of John Robinson ... ... 30 „
Isabell dau. of Oliver Dickonson ... ... 3 Decembris
Agnes dau. of Willm Borrowe ... ... 6 Januarij
Thomas son of Thomas Tayler ... ... 26 „
Elin dau. of George Sigswicke ... ... quinto die Martij

Anno regni don⁰j n⁰rj Jacobi regis septimo, 1609.

Alice dau. of Bryan Nealson	11 Juuij
Alice dau. of John Ewan	17 „
Marmaduke son of Edward Cockin	18 „
Alice dau. of Bryan Bland	6 Julij
Richard son of James Heaton	18 Augusti
An dau. of Richard Hutton	24 „
Richard son of John Knight	27 „
Thomas son of Richard Halle...	25 Septembris
Alice dau. of John Smithe	primo die Octobris
Willm son of Willm Vstenson	15 „
Thomas son of Robert Willson	18 „
Elin dau. of Robert Dowthwait	22 „
Henry son of Willm Brabin, gent...	3 Novembris
Nycholas son of Edwarde Dowthwait	18 „
Richard son of Robert Bethome	21 „
John son of Willm Harrison	4 Decembris
An dau. of Richard Knight	10 Martij

Anno regni don⁰j n⁰rj Jacobi regis octavo, 1610.

Katcryne dau. of Symon Dawnye...	25 Martij
M⁰gret dau. of Thomas Northe	8 Maij
Katheryne dau. of Thomas Bland	15 Julij
Robert son of Thomas Harlinge de Overhutton ...	19 Augusti
Isabell dau. of James Johnson	21 „
Thomas son of Willm Gennings	25 Septembris
Elin dau. of James Harries	Octobris
Richard son of Willm Myres...	die sexto Novembris
John son of Thomas Ridell	8 Decembris
James son of Richard Godsalfe	primo die Februarij
Richard son of Thomas Keysbie	[sic] 8 Januarij
An dau. of Richard Corte	8 „
John son of Richard Johnson, carp.	9 „
Jenet dau. of Willm Borrowe...	10 „
Elizabeth dau. of Richard Dawnye	16 „
John son of Robert Dowthwayt	23 „
Rowland son of Edmund Burrowe... [sic]	ultimo die Novembris

Anno regni don⁰j nr⁰j Jacobi regis nono, 1611.

Ellin dau. of Renold Borthrigg	29 Martij
An dau. of Richard Cansfild	primo die Aprilis
Mathew son of John Bethome	19 Aprillis
Richard son of Willm Whithead	7 Julij
Willm son of Henrie Eykrigg	18 Augusti
Richard and Marmaduke sonnes of John Robinson	3 Septembris

Bryan son of Oliver Dickonson ... ... primo die Decembris
Jane dau. of Thomas Walker, millner ... ... ultimo die Januarij
Robert son of James Blackburn ... ... 9 Februarij
Ellen dau. of Richard Dawnye ... ... 11 „
An dau. of John Browen... ... ... 26 „
Wiłłm son of Xpofer Mellinge ... ... 15 Martij

Anno regni don⁹j n⁹rj Jacobi regis decimo, 1612.

Thomas son of Henrye Robinson ... ... 7 Junij
Bryan son of John Knight ... ... 18 „
Jane dau. of James Johnson ... ... 16 Julij
Ellin dau. of Thomas Whithead ... ... 28 „
Edward and James sonnes of Robert Dowthwait... 9 Augusti
An dau. of George Sigswicke ... ... 12 „
Wiłłm son of Thomas Tayler... ... ... 23 „
Peter son of Wiłłm Burrowe... ... ... quinto die Septembris
Elizabeth dau. of Thomas Bland ... ... 27 „
Wiłłm son of John Smithe ... ... 4 Octobris
John son of John Johnson ... ... 21 „
Ellin dau. of Wiłłm Harrison ... ... 29 „
Bryan son of Thomas Dawnye ... ... primo die Januarij
Oliver son of James Heaton ... ... 3 „
Millizant dau. of Wiłłm Johnson ... ... 16 „
M⁹gret dau. of Robert Charncke ... ... 21 „
Richard son of Thomas Northe ... ... 28 „
James son of James Russell de Dallton [1] ... ...
Lydia dau. of Mr. Toppin ... ... 7 Martij
M⁹gret dau. of Robert Bethem ... ... 17 „
Ellin dau. of Xpofer Wayles ... ... 19 „

Anno regni don⁹j n⁹rj Jacobi regis undecimo, 1613.

Isabell dau. of Richard Hutton ... ... primo die Junij
Jenet dau. of Symon Dawnye ... ... 3 Augusti
Jane dau. of Richard Cansfild ... ... quinto die Septembris
John son of James Harries ... ... 27 „
Xpofer son of Thomas Tayler ... ... 12 Novembris
spuria James son of James Russell de Dalton... ... ... 23 „
Jane dau. of John Turner ... ... primo die Januarij
James son of Richard Johnson, carpenter ... ... 30 „
Thomas son of Wiłłm Sclater ... ... 8 Martij

Anno regni don⁹j n⁹rj Jacobi regis duodecimo, 1614.

John son of William Jennings ... ... 10 Aprilis
Wiłłm son of Richard Godsalfe ... ... 26 Junij
spuria Jane dau. of Henrye Eyekrigge .. .. 10 Augusti

[1] This entry has been entirely struck through.

Isabell dau. of Robert Dowthwait...   ...   .   21 Augusti
John son of Thomas Robinson   ...   .   7 Septembris
John son of Richard Dawnye...   29   „
John son of Henrie Ekrigge ...   .   30 Octobris
Rowland son of John Bethem   ...   .   17 Novembris
Isabell dau. of Thomas Bland   23   „
Ellin dau. of John Knight   ...   .   4 Decembris
Robert son of Wiłłm Burrowe   ...   .   quinto die Januarij
George son of Wiłłm Myres   6   „
Margaret dau. of Marmaducke Margerison   23   „
Anne filia Wiłłm Harrison   ...   .   secundo die Februarij
Elliñ dau. of John Slater   24   „
Jane dau. of Renold Borthrigge   28   „
John son of Bryan Widder   ...   .   quinto die Martij

Anno regni don⁹j n⁹rj Jacobi regis decimo tertio, 1615.

M⁹gret dau. of Edward Cockin   ...   .   26 Martij
Nicholas son of Edward Dowthwayt   ...   .   2 Aprilis
Thomas son of George Sigswicke   2   „
Thomas son of Wiłłm Johnson ...   .quinto die   „
Xpofer son of Robert More de puddlemyre ...   ...   14 Maij
Dorothae dau. of Richard Newton, gent.   16   „
James son of Thomas Northe...   ...   .   13 Junij
Thomas son of John Smithe   18   „
Richard son of James Johnson[1]   ...   .   1 June
An dau. of Xpofer Mellinge ...   .   6 Augusti
Wiłłm son of John Robinson   13   „
Jenet dau. of Wiłłm Whitthead ...   .   2 Septembris
Jane dau. of Thomas Northe...   25   „
John son of James Harries   ...   .   quinto die Octobris
Elizabeth dau. of Oliver Dickonson   15   „
Thomas son of Leonarde Ewan   ...   ...   quinto die Novembris
Edward son of Marmaducke Cockin   12   „
Agnes dau. of George Eakrigge   ...   .   7 Januarij
Richard son of John Hardie   25   „
Wiłłm son of Richard Dawnye   27   „
Katherin dau. of Thomas Robinson   ...   .   12 Februarij
Thomas son of Richard Hutton   18   „
James son of James Heaton ...   .   17 Martij

Anno regni d⁹nj n⁹ri Jacobi regis decimo quarto, 1616.

Anne dau. of Richard Cansfild   ...   .   12 Junij
Anne dau. of Thomas Bland ...   .
Elizabeth filia Robert Dowthwait ...   .   29 Decembris

[1] This entry is clearly a later interpolation.

Thomas son of Robert Bethem   ... ...   7 Februarij
Thomas son of Marmaduke Margerison...   8   „
Margret dau. of Wiħm Slater   18   „
Francis son of Richard Manser   ... ...   17 Martij

Anno regni ðn°i n°ri Jacobi regis ðecimo quinto, 1617.

Edward son of Thomas Tayler[1]   ... ...   Apprilis
James son of John Hardie   ... ...   24 Februarij
Lenard son of John Carter   ... ...   last day of Aprill

1618.

Jane dau. of John Carter ... ...   last day of November

Anno ðonj 1620.

James son of George Sigswicke   ... ...   2 Aprilis
Arthur son of Robert Burrowe de Lupton   18   „
Henrie son of Willm Myres ... ...   2 Maij
Alice filia Thomas North   25   „
Xpofer son of Henrie Frers ...   .   eodem die
Isabell filia John Slater ...   .   12 Augusti
Richard son of Thomas North   ... ...   quinto die Octobris
*   *   son of Richard Mansergh ...   .   „
Agnes filia Roger Lorimer   ... ...   20 Novembris
Bryan son of Thomas Barker...   26   „
Elizabeth dau. of Rowland Whitehead ... ...   15 Decembris
Elizabeth filia Wiħm Kidd   27   „
Anne filia John Dickonson   31   „
John son of Robert Bethom ...   .   18 Januarij
Jane and Alice filiae John Hardie...   26   „
Margrett filia Thomae Mellinge   ... ...   26 Februarij
Alice filia Wiħm Harries   ... ...   15 Martij
Robtt son of Thomas Whitehead of Geastwicke ...   18   „
Jane dau. of John Smith   21   „

Anno ðonj 1621.

Sonne of Gearard Whayte   ... ...   15 Julij
Jane filia Henry Brabin, gent.   ... ...   2 Septembris
Anne dau. of Wiħm Kidd[2] ...   .   20 Januarie
Bryan son of Symon Dawnie ...   .   2 Februarij

[1] Down to this entry all the entries from 1538 are made in the same hand and beautifully written. Henceforward the entries are in various hands, and the Register seems to have been kept with much less care.
[2] Here the words " sonne of John Bethom."

Richard son of Robert Robinson ... ...   7 Februarij
Willm son of a poor man at James Dodgson's   ..   4 Martij
* *   sonne of John Bethom   ... ...
* *   daughter of Thomas Bland... ... ...
* *   sonne of Duke Margison   ... ...
* *   daughter of Oljr Harrison ... ...
Elizabeth dau. of Ric⁹ Hutton   ... ...
Elizabeth dau. of Willm Burrowe ... ...   17 Martij
Katherin filia Leonard Ewan... ... ...   24 „

Anno donj 1622.

James filia Willm Harrison ... ...   22 Septembris
Thomas son of Henrie Brabin, gent. ... ...   29 Octobris
Willm son of Willm Slater ... ...   12 Januarij
Dorethie dau. of John Carter...   23   „
Bryan son of Bryan Cowper and Jane Hall   25   „
Willm son of Thomas Barker   30   „
John son of Willm Dickonson   6   „

Anno donj 1623, anno regni regis Jacobi 21.

John son of Richard Hutton ... ...   primo die Augusti
Willm son of John Smith   14   „
Xpofer son of Thomas Mellinge ... ...   ultimo die „
Agnes filia Jacobi Bordrigge ... ...   „
Henrie son of Henrie Brabin, gent.   ... ...   18 Novembris
Francis the sonne of Willm Slater   ... ...

Anno regni regis dn⁹j n⁹rj Jacobi decimo septimo, 1619.[1]

Marmeduk Slater ye sonne of Willm Slater, of
    Whittington, bapt. ye 27th of July[2]
Leonard sonne of John Johnson bapt. 2nd die Augusti[2]
Dorathy daughter of John Carter who died yonge[2] 11 June, 1620
Dorathy daughter of John Carter[3] ... ... 21 January, 1622
Agnes doughter of John Carter[3] ... ...   3 March, 1625

An don 1629.

Willm Slater son of Willm Slater   ... ...   24 June
Willm Bordrigg son of James Bordrigg   ... ...   12 September
Joseph Johnson son of Willm Johnson Webster ...   11 June

---

[1] It will have been noted that there were no entries under year 1619 in
    the proper order.
[2] Between these two entries is one deleted which is quite illegible.
[3] These three entries are made at the top of a page blank as to the re-
    mainder.

WiHm son of John Hardie ... ...primo die Novembris
James son of John Tompson de Newton ...decimo octavo „
Jane dau. of John Cockin ... ... 22 „
John son of Thomas Johnson and Jenett his wiffe 2 Februarij
* * Johnson bapti erat ... ...decimo die Junij

Here is left blank about one-third of page.

Anno don'j 1630, anno regni Caroli regis sexto.

Elizabeth dau. of Mathewe Tompson ... ... 12 Septembris
Anna spu. dau. of Arthure Dodding and Isabell
   R[ydall ?] vidua ... ... 22 Aprill
Alice dau. of Rowland Whitthead... ... ... 4 May
Thomas son of Edward S * * ourges ... ... 17 Octobris
Alice dau. of Robt Robinson ... ... 28 Novembris
Myles son of Henry Aykrigge ... ... 19 Decembris
WiHm son of Thomas Miller... ... ... 19 „
Robert son of Anthonie Dowthwait ... ... primo die Januarij
Elizabeth dau. of Robtt Bethom ... ... eodem die
Robtt son of Richard Dawnie... ... ... 20 Februarij
Jane dau. of Reinold Whitehead ... ... 16 Martij
Edward son of Thomas Dowthwait ... ... 22 „
Henrie son of Thomas Johnson ... ... 23 „

Anno regni regis Caroli septimo anno dn'j 1631.

WiHm son of John Barrowe ... ... 7 Aprilis
spuria WiHm son of Rowland Bordrigg and Elizabeth
   Lonsdale ... ... tertio die Julij
John son of WiHm Harries ... ... 17 „
Rowland son of WiHm Bordrigge ... ... 28 „
John son of Richard Manserge ... ... 12 Octobris
Margrett dau. of WiHm Slater ... ... 14 „
WiHm son of Alexander Adcocke ... ... 25 „
Thomas son of James Harries ... ... 6 Novembris
Isabell dau. of Richard Patton ... ... 20 „
John son of Rowland Whitehead ... ... 8 Decembris
Margrett dau. of Bryan Dickonson and Anne Dawnie 29 „
Anne filia Thomae Blackburne ... ... vicessimo sexto Februarij
Margrett filia Francis Brockherst and Margrett
   Patchett ... ... quinto die Martij

Anno regni regis Caroli octavo anno dn'j 1632.

Margrett filia WiHm Adcock... ... vicessimo secundo Aprilis
Jenet filia Cudbert Feyrey ... ... 17 Junij
Daniell son of WiHm Mellinge ... ... decimo septimo die Julij
Jane dau. of Edward Burrowe ... ... 12 Augusti

Katherin dau. of James Mellinge ... ... 17 Augusti
John son of Robtt Robinson 24   ,,
John son of Thomas Johnson and Margerie his wyffe 16 Septembris
Katherin filia Thomae Fawcett ... ... ultimo die ,,
Jane dau. of Anthony Whormbie ... ... 18 Octobris
James son of Richard Tatham and Dorothye his
    wyffe ... ... decimo die Novembris
Thomas son of John Eshton 17   ,,
Anne dau. of John Cockin 28   ,,
Bryan son of Thomas Johnson sen. and Jenet his
    wiffe... ... ... 19 Januarij
Symon son of Thomas Leake and Elizabeth his
    wyffe ... ... 25 Februarij
Anne dau. of Robert Bethome and Ellin his wiffe...tertio die Martij
Thomas son of Richard North and Alice his wyffe...decimo die ,,

Anno regni regis Caroli Angliae etc. nono anno donj 1633.

Wiłłm son of John Lonsdale and Ellin his wiffe ...sexto die Aprilis
Dorethie dau. of * * Wilkinson and * *
    his wiffe ... ... 5 Maij
Thomas son of Thomas Miller and Margrett his
    wiffe ... ...eodem die ,,
Wiłłm son of John Bethom ... ... 16 ,,
Wiłłm son of Wiłłm Bordrigge and Catherin his
    wiffe... ... ... penultimo die ,,
Katherin filia Wiłłm Hall and Jane his wiffe ... 29 Septembris
Richard son of Thomas Johnson Junior and Margeri
    his wyffe ... ... sexto die Octobris
Isabell dau. of John Padget and Jane his wiff bapᵈ
    the first day of May Anno pᵈd [1]
Geo. ye sonne of Richard Burrhus ... ... 3 November
Mar[grett] the daughter of Wiłłm Godsalve... ... 17   ,,
Alice ye daughter of Richard Dickonson ... eodem die ,,
Wiłłm ye sonne of Edward Burrow [?] ... ... Decembris
Dorothy dau. of Ric. Tayler 8   ,,
Henricus fillius Gullielmi Brabyn, gen,... 25   ,,
Jenet dau. of Ric. Patton ... ... 15 Februarij
Agnes dau. of Wiłłm Foster of Middleton 23   ,,
Thom son of Bryan Bland 25   ,,
Jac son of James Dodgson and Elizabeth Moore of
    Mansergh ... ... 3 Martij

Anno regni regis Caroli decimo, 1634.

Elizabeth dau. of Row: Whitehead ... ... 27 September
Ann dau. of Henry Ayckrigge ... ... 7 October

---

[1] This entry—a later interpolation—has been struck through.

F

Thom son of Alexander Adcock ... ...   9 November
Ja: son of John Harries...   15   „
Myles son of Richard North ... ...   7 December
Ric: son of Wiłłm Bordrick ... ...   7 Januarij
Edmunde son of Wiłłm Adcock   15   „
Ann dau. of Ja: Melling...   20   „
Wiłłm son of Geo. Ward, gent. ... ...   10 February

1636 [?]¹

Wiłłm son of Richard Dickonson ... ...   23 December
Robt. son of Wiłłm Brabbyn, gent ... ...   1 Januarij
Eliza: dau. of John Pagett ... ...   eodem die
Ann dau. of Ric. Sharpe the piper ... ...   22 Januarij
John son of Wiłłm Melling ... ...   24 February

Anno regni regis Caroli decimo tertio, 1637.

John son of John Dawny ... ...   9 Aprill
Alice dau. of Wiłłm Godsalf   16   „
Judith dau. of John Bland   25   „
Christofer son of Richard Tayler ... .,. ... ...   16 May
John son of Thom Robinson ... ...   20 August
Marmaduke son of Ric. Cocking ... ...   17 Sept.
Jenet dau. of Ja: Melling   17   „
Margrett dau. of Bryan Dickonson   24   „
Jane dau. of John Harries ... ...   18 Octobris
Alice dau. of Willm Adcock ... ...   16 Novem⁹
Ellen dau. of Wiłłm Johnson of Durham ... ...   30 Decemb
Bryan son of Bryan Bland ... ...   21 January
Richarde son of James Godsalfe   30   „
Isabell dau. of Wiłłm Bordrick ... ...   8 Febr.
Francis son of Wiłł Stithe   14   „

14° Anno regis Caroli 1638.

Mary dau. of Wm. Burrwo ... ...   16 May
Isabell dau. of Cuthbert Feray ... ...   22 Aprill
John son of Sander Adcock... ... ...   14 June
Alice dau. of Ric Patton   19   „
spur. Jenet dau. of Ric Chamelhouse and Ellen Halstead
      servant at Docker Hall... ... ...   9 July
Xpofer son of Edward Burrow   28   „
Margaret dau. of Ric. North of Docker ... ...   5 August
Ellen dau. of John Cockin   16   „

¹ Apparently a leaf has been lost here containing entries for remainder of
   1634, whole of 1635, and part of 1636.

Ellen ye daughter of one John Towers dwelling in
London, * supposed to be base begotten of ye
boddy of *[1] Ann Harries of Newton   ...   ...   9 September
Jane dau. of James Melling ...   .   17 October
Richard son of Wm. Hall   ...   .   3 February
Isabell ye dau. [2]   ...   .
Margaret dau. of Bryan Dickonson   16   ,,
Isabell dau. of Robt. Robinson   21   ,,

Anno regni regis Caroli decimo quinto anno dn'i 1639.

Chr Tayler ye sonne of Chr Tayler   ...   ...   18 May
Edward Tayler ye sonne of Thoma⁹ Tayler ...   ...   11 July
Isabell ye daughter of John Bland the younger ...   6 September
Jane ye daughter of John Harries...   15   ,,
Richard ye sonne of James Godsalfe   29   ,,
Andrewe ye sonne of Randall Kew   ...   ...   first December
Hellin ye daughter of Nicholas Dowthwaite...   ...   22   ,,
Thomas Bland and Jane Bland both ye children of
John Bland of Newton ...   .   10 Januarie
Ellen ye daughter of Thom⁹ Milner   26   ,,
Tho: ye sonne of Willm Stythe   ...   .   2 Februarie
Jane ye daughter of Wm. Adcocke   2   ,,
Henry ye sonne of Thom⁹ Johnson ye younger ...   17 March

Ano regni regis Caroli decimo sexto and anno dn⁹i 1640.

Richard ye sonne of Mr. Robinson of ye Parke, gent   24 Maij
James ye sonne of Thomas Newby of Docker   ...   7 June
Oliver ye sonne of Ric. North of Docker   ...   ...   8 July
Edwarde ye sonne of Edwarde Burrow...   25   ,,
Isabell ye daughter of Ric Patton...   ...   ...   11 August
John ye sonne of Ric. Cocking of Newton   30   ,,
Isabell ye daughter of Robt. Jackson of Newton ...   12 Sept.

Christenings from ye death of Mr. Daniell, M.A.

Ellen ye daughter of Jo: Cort   ...   .   4 October
Edward ye sonne of Rich. Dickonson of Docker ...   15 November
Dorothye dau. of Wiłłm Godsalfe ...   .   7 December
Marmaduke son of Thomas Robinson   22   ,,
Richard son of Thomas Hutton   27   ,,

[1] The words between the asterisks are struck through in the original.
[2] Struck through in the original.

Anno regni regis dn'j n'rj Caroli Angliae decimo septimo, 1641.

Jane dau. of Thomas Tayler	...undecimo die Aprilis
Alice dau. of Wi{{m Harling	26 Septembris
Jane fillia Robertt Eskrigg	12 Decembris
James son of Nicholas Bramell	20 Januarie
Agnes dau. of Nicholas Dowthwaite ...	decimo tertio Februarij

Anno regni don'j n'rj Caroli Angliae etc. decimo octavo anno dn'i 1642.

Bryan son of John Bland de Hill in Newton...	tertio die Aprilis
Jenett filia Willm Slater de Newton	eodem die ,,
Margrett dau. of James Godsalfe	,, ,,
Ellen filia Johan Whitehead	primo die Maij
Henrie son of John Harries	12 Junij
Isabell filla Bryan Dickonson...	29 ,,
Anne dau. of Randall Keene	25 Augusti
Elizabeth dau. of Richard North	4 Septembris
Eline dau. of Wi{{m Styth	20 ,,
Thomas son of Thomas Johnson Junior	22 Novembris
Thomas and John the sonnes of Wi{{m Hall ...	24 ,,
spuria Margrett the daughter of Thomas Sclater and Alice Dawnie	27 ,,
Marie dau. of Mr. Richard Jackson parson of Whittington	2 Decembris
Ellin dau. of Bryan Bland son of Thomas * * *	14 Januarij
Symon son of Wi{{m Adcocke	29 ,,
Jane dau. of Edward Burrowe	2 Februarij
John son of Richard * *	22 ,,

Anno regni regis dn'j n'rj Caroli Angliae etc. decimo nono, 1643.

John son of Wi{{m Harlinge...	2 May
Richard son of John Cort	2 Junij
Alce dau. of Thomas Robinson	4 ,,
Thomas son of Richard Cockin	28 ,,
Elizabeth dau. of Thomas Taylor	8 July
Symond son of Bryane Dawnie	21 Octobris
Janne dau. of Richard North...	9 Novembris
John son of Wi{{m Slater	19 Januarij
Janne dau. of Wi{{m Godsalff Junior	eodem die

Anno regni regis don'j n'rj Caroli Anglia etc. vicessimo, 1644.

Edward son of Nicholas Dowthwayt ...	vicessimo tertio die Junij
Elizabeth dau. of Robert Eskrigg	6 October
Bryan son of Thomas Johnson	first day of January
Edward son of Edward Cockin and Janne his wife	6 October
Daniell son of Mr. Richard Jackson pson of Whittington	19 Februarie
Elizabeth dau. of John Ewan...	decimo sexto Decembris
Dorethy dau. of John Taylor and Anne Harison ...	25 May
John son òf Thomas Taylor	4 June

Anno regni regis don'j n'rj Caroli Angliae etc. vicessimo primo, 1645.

Margret dau. of James Godsalff	19 October
Margret dau. of Robertt Willson and Jenett Ewan	vicessimo sexto ,,
Thomas son of John Wyldman	2 November
John son of Robertt Jackson de Newton	11 ,,
* * dau. of Willm Slater de W⁹tn ...	decimo octavo Decembris
Janet dau. of John Bland Junr.	quarto die Januarij
Anne dau. of John Johnson	primo die Februari
Margrett dau. of Willm Godsalff	9 ,,
Robertt son of Edward Burrow	16 ,,
Thomas son of Christopher Foster [1]	3 Aprilis
* * dau. of James Aaura [? Awrey] .	vicessimo secundo Februarij
Jane dau. of Richard Cockin	primo die Martij
Elliu dau. of Richard Whittehead	...nono die ,,
Rodger son of Mr. Richard Jackson pson of Whittington	15 ,,
Thomas son of John Harries	...vicessimo nono Decembris

Anno regni regis don'j n'ri Caroli Angliae etc. vicessimo secundo, 1646.

Alice dau. of Thomas Slater	...decimo die Maij
Elizabeth dau. of Nicholas Dowthwayt...	28 June
Richard son of Richard Backhousse	sexto die Augusti
John son of Thomas Hutton	13 ,,
James son of Willm Styth [2]	20 September

[1] Evidently interlined but in contemporary hand.
[2] In margin is here written " the one and 20 of August."

Anno regni Caroli Angliae vicessimo tertio, 1647.

Jenett son of Thomas Smith	7 Februarij
Rowland son of Tho. Johnson junior	14 ,,
Janne dau. of Robtt Batersbie	21 ,,
Oliver son of Bryan Dicconson	first March
Tho. son of Simon Dawney	25 Julij

Anno regni regis dn°j n°rj Angliae etc. vicessimo quarto, 1648.

John son of Richard Hardy	first March
Wiłłm son of Wiłłm Styth	ultimo die Aprilis
Ann dau. of Bryan Dickonson	3 Septembris
Ellin dau. of Robtt Jackson and Anne his wiff ...	17 ,,

[Here follow in original the grants of pews printed at the end of this volume. Next in order in original follow Burials from 1651-1665 (inclusive), printed under Burials in their proper chronological order.] Then comes the following:—
"Thomas Thistlethwaite came to be ye clerk and scoolmaster upon ye 28th day of July (1692)
" Henry Eckridge clerk at ye parish church of Whittington 1700
"Thomas Brabin sonn of Mr. Thomas Brabin was bapt. ye 2 day of December 1649 "[1]

Jane dau. of Richard Cockin	September
Thomas son of Bryan Canstfeild	27 ,,
Mary dau. of James North	8 October
Wiłłm son of Richard Betham	22 ,,
Dorothy[2] dau. of John Willdman	29 ,,
Alice dau. of Barian Dawny	decimo nono die Novembris
John son of John Johnson	eodem ,,
Thomas son of John Bland	last day of December

1649.

Thomas Brabin son of Mr. Thomas Brabin	2 December
Margret dau. of Thomas Johnson	18 March

1650.

Wiłłm son of Wiłłm Slater de Newton	7 Aprill
Lenard son of Mr. Richard Jackson	21 ,,
Richard son of Thomas Tayler	eodem die ,,

[1] This entry is struck out but appears entered in its proper chronological order as printed herein.
[2] Written over "Jane."

Richard son of Richard Hardy	... ...	28 Aprill
John son of Wiłłm Margison...	... ...	29 December
John son of Wiłłm Stith	... ...	20 January
Wiłłm son of Robert Batersbie	... ...	2 March
Wiłłm Slater son of Mard Slater ...	... ...	23 ,,

1651.

Elin dau. of John Hares...	... ...	5 Aprill
Jane dau. of Thomas Hutton...	... ...	16 ,,
An dau. of Nicholas Douthwhet	... ...	29 ,,
Jane dau. of Richard Whithead	... ...	9 June
John son of Thomas Smith	... ...	14 September
Henry son of Mr. Thomas Brabin ...	... ...	21 ,,
Mary dau. of George Preston...	... ...	eodem die ,,
George son of Thomas Carus Esʳ...	... ...	6 October
Jenet dau. of Wiłłm Smith ...	... ...	12 ,,

1652.

Henry son of Thomas Roˡ * *	... ...	7 February
Elizabeth Godsalfe dau. of Wiłłm Godsalfe ...	...	13 ,,

𝕬nno 1653.

Jane West dau. of George West de Kirkby	... ...	16 Aprill
Margret dau. of Thomas Johnson ...	... ...	1 ,,
Isabel Stith dau. of Wiłłm Stith ...	... ...	14 May
Jenet dau. of Nicholas Dawthwhet	... ...	12 June
Allis dau. of Richard Johnson	... ...	25 September
Thomas son of James Vapor ...	... ...	9 October
Mayry dau. of Mr. Richard Jackson, pson	... ...	19 ,,
Dorothy dau. of John Johnson	... .	23 ,,
Cristapher Tayler son of Thomas Tayler	... ...	25 Desember
Wiłłm Smith son of Thomas Smith	...	ye first day of January

1654.

* * ˢHaris fillia Thomas Haris...	... ...	26 March
Jane dau. of Josias Eamason de Kirkby	... ...	9 Aprill
Isabell Cokin fillia Marmaduke Cockin...	... ...	23 ,,
Jane Dawny fillia Bryan Dawny	... ...	21 May
John Bland fillius John Bland	... ...	28 ,,
John son of Danjel Cuningam	... ...	28 ,,
Jane Hardy fillia James Hardy	... ...	27 June

[1] Top of leaf worn off.
[2] Edge of leaf torn off.

Anna Turner dau. of Wiłłm Turner ... ...   16 July
James Godsalfe ... ...   23 ,,
Ellin Swenson de Kirby ... ...   23 ,,
Jane Robinson fillia Thomas Robinson ... ...   29 October
Jane dau. of Richard Hardy ... ...   5 November
James Bordrigge fillius Wiłłm Bordrigge ... ...   26 ,,
Richard Betham son of Richard Betham ... ...   19 Desember
Margret Tounson fillia Wiłłm Townson ... ...   26 ,,
Isabell Backhouse fillia George Ba[ckhouse]...ye fourt day of March
Grace Eameson fillia John Eamarson de Kirby ...   eleventh ,,

1655.

James Johnson fillius Richard Johnson ... ...   18 March
Thomas fillius John Johnson, natus erat septimo die Aprillis and
    bapt. erat octo die Aprillis
Anas elligittima filia Thomas Dickconson and Dorothy Adison natus
    erat 13 Maij
Wiłłm fillius Richard Cockin natus erat 11 day of June and bap.
    erat 17 day
John fillius Robert Willson natus erat 22 day of Juune and bap.
    erat 24 day of June
Thomas fillius Bryan Manser natus erat quinte die July and bap.
    erat the 8 day of July
Bryan sonne of Bryan Dawny natus 27 day and bap. erat 29 of July
Jane daughter of John Dawny natus [sic] erat 23 day of July and
    bap. erat 29 day
An Cort daughter of John Cort was borne ye 4 day of August and
    bat. ye 5 day
John samson sonne of Edward Samson natus erat 30 day of August
    and bap. erat the second day of September
Abigal Jackson daughter of Mr. Richard Jackson, pson, natus [sic]
    erat 15 day of September and bap. erat ye 16 day of September
Elizabeth daughter of George Willson natus [sic] erat 25 day of
    October and baptizatus [sic] erat 28 day of October
William sonne of Christapher Laurence natus erat 31 day of October
    and bap. erat quarta dies [sic] Novembris
Jane daughter of John Hardy natus [sic] erat 26 day of November
    and bap. erat 2 day of Desember
Allice daughter of John Bland natus [sic] erat ye first day of Desem-
    ber and bap. erat 2 day of Desember
Francis Stith sonn of Wiłłm Stith natus erat 5 day of Decembe et
    natus [sic] erat 9 day of December
Sarah daughter of Wiłłm Margison natus [sic] erat 6 day et bap.
    erat 9 December
Allice Haris daughter of Thomas Haris natus [sic] erat 11 day et
    bap. erat 16 day of December
Willm son of Robert Burrow... ... ...bapp   23 March

1656.

Mary dau. of Thomas Douthwaite Junior	28 March
John son of Thomas Tayler	27 Aprill
Alice dau. of James Godshalfe	4 May
Elling dau. of Willm Adcocke	17 ,,
John son of Nicholas Dowthaite	8 June
Alice dau. of Thom¹	6 July
Willm son of Joseph Johnson	9 November
John son of Thomas Hutton	23 ,,
Thomas son of Robert Wilson	14 December
James son of James Melling	21 ,,
Richard son of George Backhouse...	15 February
John son of Willm Johnson	8 March
An dau. of Thomas Robinson...	22 ,,

1657.

John son of John Johnson	3 May
Isaac son of Brian Dawny	28 June
Mary dau. of Edward Douthwait	19 July
Vigessima Jackson...	6 September
Brian son of Thomas Smith	20 ,,
* * ² dau. of Willm S [ti]th showmaker	30 ,,
Elizabeth dau. of Henry Mires	10 October
Alice dau. of Willm Slater	18 ,,
Richard son of Marmaducke Cocking	6 December
Willm son of Willm Bordridge Junior	27 ,,
Edward son of James North	same day
Richard and Thomas two sones of John Dawny of Newton at one birth	13 January
Willm son of Thomas Tayler, waller	14 February

1658.

Richard son of Brian Barker of Broome feilds of the Parish of Melling	11 Aprill
Agnes dau. of Richard Cort son of Arthur Cort of Arram	18 ,,
John son of William Barker of the Parish of Melling	6 May
Margret dau. of Brian Nealson of Newton shoomaker	15 August
Agnes dau. of Richard Cockin of Newton carpinter	22 ,,
Dorothy dau. of Brian Dawny and Dorothy Carter his wife	19 September
Alice dau. of Willm Johnson...	3 October
Alexander son of Willm Adcocke...	31 ,,

¹ Top of leaf torn off.
² Christian name of child and middle of surname torn out.

James son of Lieuetenant John Bland... ... ...   31 October
Isabell dau. of Willm Margison of Docker ... ...   12 December
* * ¹ dau. of Joseph Johnson   21   ,,
Thomas son of Thomas Smith of Newton   29   ,,
Alice dau. of Thomas Whitbead, schoolmaster at
    Arram, came from the Parish of Orton in West-
    merland ... ...   9 January
Alice dau. of Willm Slater of Whittington ... ...   20 February
Elling dau. of John Butterfield of Docker Hill miller   27   ,,

1659.

Henry son of Robert Burrow... ... ...   17 Aprill
Elizabeth dau. of Richard Johnson and Jane dau.
    of Robert Wilson dwelling in Chapel Lane in
    Newton both baptized ... ...   20 [?] ,,
Dorothy dau. of John² ... ...   16 December

1660.

Agnes dau. of Willm Adcocke   ... ...   13 January
Thomas son of Edward Douthwait   ... ...   7 June
Jane dau. of John Dawny of Newton ... ...   20 January
Grace dau. of Henry Myres ... ...   11 November
Willm son of Thomas Stith and Agnes dau. of
    Thomas Tayler   ... ...bapt. both   10 March
Elling dau. of Willm Slater of Whittington... ...   24   ,,
Ruth Jackson and Mary Jackson   25   ,,

1661.³

* *   sone of Robert Burrow of Whitt: ... ...   21 Aprill
Jane dau. of Thomas Harris of Newton   ... ...   5 May
Mary⁴ dau of John Miller Taylor...   12   ,,
Willm son of Willm Margison and Mary daughter
    of Brian Dawny baptized both   19   ,,
John son of George Garnet of Kirby Lonsdale and
    Elizabeth daughter of John Richardson of the
    said Kirby Lonsdale also both baptized... ...   1 September
Willm son of Francis Da[wny ?]   15   ,,
Edmond son of Richard Tatham of Newton ... ...   13 October
Jane dau. of Marmaducke Cocking   27   ,,

¹ Edge of leaf torn off.
² Top of leaf torn off.
³ The entries commencing here and ending 2 July, 1665, are repeated in
    vol. ii. of original Registers, but as there are some interesting varia-
    tions between the entries in the two volumes it was thought well to
    print both sets of entries.
⁴ Written over " Agnes " struck out.

John son of Richard Johnson the Leaser of a part
   of Sellett to present ... ... 19 January
Mary daughter of John Johnson bapt. the second day of February
   in the New funt the first child the said funt erected in the 14th
   year of the Reigne of our Soverign Lord Charles the second
Wiłłm son of James Hardy ... ... 9 February
* * ¹ dau. of Henry Pattison 16   ,,

Anno ōn²j 1662.

Elizabeth dau. of Thomas Hutton... ... ... 18 May
Elizabeth dau. of Wiłłm Tolson and An² Booth
               both baptized 1 June
Jane dau. of Mr. John Foxcroft ... ... 30 September
Thomas son of Thomas Stith ... ... 8 January
Jenet dau. of Thomas Smyth of Kirby 11   ,,
An dau. of Henry³ ... ... 1 February
Elling dau. of Henry Smyth of Arram 22   ,,
Richard son of John Jackson... ... ... 22 March

1663.

Elizabeth dau. of Wiłłm Margison ... ... 5 Aprill
John son of Brian Manser ... ... 21 ,,
Margret dau. of Wiłłm Slater ... ... 10 May
John son of Nicholas Croft sometime Laborer in
   Coolemines ... ... 17 ,,
John son of John Miller and Christopher sone of
   Wiłłm Barker... ... ... 14 June
* * ⁴ sone of John Troughton [web]ster ... ... 21 ,,
Jane dau. of Richard Nort⁵ North ... ... 16 August
John son of John Smyth of Aram 30   ,,
Elizabeth dau. of Bryan Nealson shoomaker... ... 4 October
Richard son of Joseph Johnson webster 11   ,,
Margret dau. of Nicholas Atkinsō and Alice dau. of
   Thomas Harling both of Kirby Lonsdale bap-
   tized both 4   ,,
Richard son of Tho⁶ ... ... 15 November
Thomas son of Richard Tatham junior de Newton 13 December
John son of John Bland on the High Greene in
   Newton 27   ,,

¹ Top corner of leaf torn off.
² Over "An" are the letters D : W : B : probably meaning daughter of
    W * * Booth.
³ Corner of leaf torn off.
⁴ Top corner of leaf torn off.
⁵ This is as it is written, but probably it appears in this form because there
    was not room to finish the word "Nort" at end of the line and it was
    repeated at beginning of next.
⁶ Top of leaf torn off.

Richard son of Richard Johnson ... ...   24 January
John and Jenet both at one birth children of Thomas
    Doughwaite of Newton   31   „
*   *   ¹ dau. of James Melling   ... ...   14 March

1664.

Richard son of John Dawny of Newton the North
    end therof   ... ...   27 March
Jenet dau. of Thomas Robinson of Churchland ...   24 Aprill
Elizabeth dau. of Willm Adcocke ... ...   1 May
Jane dau. of Edward Moore Kirb sadler   ... ...   24 July
An dau. of Thomas Dicconson miller the thirty one being last of July
Jane dau. of Edward Douthwaite ... ...   28 August
Richard son of Thomas [Hutton] postlehwitt   ...   2 October
Edward son of Willm Burrow   30   „
Mary dau. of Thomas Whithead Reader and School-
    maister inhabiting at Arram ... ...   6 November
John son of Christopher Lawrence and Katheraine
    daughter of John Johnson both bapt. ... ...   18 December
John son of Richard Tatham elder   ... ...   22 January
Elling dau. of Willm Margison of Docker ... ...   19 March

1665.

Alice dau. of Thomas Hodgon   ... ...   2 Aprill
*   *   ² of John Troughton   10   „
Elizabeth dau. of Thomas Styth shoomaker... ...   23   „
Thomas son of Robert Blackburne taylor   ... ...   14 May
An dau. of Mr. John Foxcroft   29   „
Annas dau. of Willm Toluson   ... ...   2 July

[Here follow the Entries relating to Collections printed at end of
    this volume.]

¹ Top corner of leaf torn off.
² Top of leaf cut off.

[Here commences Volume II. of Original Register.]

A Register of all Christnings Marriages and Burialls in Whittington parrish from the yeare D⁰ni 1661.

[From here to 2 July, 1665, is a repetition with variations of the contents of Volume I. of Register for same period already printed.]

1661.

Robert sone of Robert Burrow bapt the one & twentith day of April Anno pʳ dᵗ

Jane daughter of Thomas Harris of Newton bapt the fift day of May Anno pʳ dᵗ

Mary daughter of John Miller Taylor bapt 12th day of May Anno pʳ dᵗ

Willm sone of Willm Margison & Mary daughter of Bryan Dawny both bapt 19 May

John sone of George Garnet & Elizabeth daughter of John Richardson both born in Kirby Lonsdale and baptised the 1 Sep.

Willm sone of Francis Doleman [1]	15 September
Edmund sone of Richard Tatham	13 October
Jane daughter of Marmaduke Cocking	27 „
John sone of Richard Johnson	29 January
Mary daughter of John Johnson	2 February
Willm sone of James Hardy	9 „
An daughter of Henry Pattison	16 „

1662.

Elizabeth daughter of Thomas Hutton	18 March
Elizabeth daughter of Willm Johnson & An daughter of Willm Booth ... ... both	1 June
Jane daughter of Mr. John Foxcroft	30 September
Thomas sone of Thomas Stith schomaker	8 January
Jenet daughter of Thomas Smyth of Kirby Lonsdale	11 „
An daughter of Henry Mires	1 February
Elling daughter of Henry Smyth of Arram	22 „
Richard sone of John Jackson	22 March

1663.

Elizabeth daughter of Willm Margison	5 Aprill
John sone of Bryan Manser	21 „

---

[1] Henceforward the word "bapt." which always occurs in the original is omitted.

John son of John Miller [1]	14 June
Margret daughter of Willm Slater of Whittington	10 May
John sone of Nicholas Cross	17 ,,
Christopher sone of Willm Barker of the High ...	14 June
Leonard sone of John Troughton	21 ,,
Jane daughter of Richard North of Newton... ...	16 August
John sone of John Smyth of Arram	30 ,,
Elizabeth daughter of Bryan Nealson shomaker ...	4 Octob
Richard sone of Joseph Johnson	11 ,,
Margret daughter of Nicholas Attkinson & Alice daughter of Thomas Harling both of Kirby ...	18 ,,
Richard sone of Thomas Taylor, waller	15 Novem
Thomas sone of Richard Tatham Junior	13 Decem
John sone of John Bland of the Fir Greene in Newton	27 ,,
Richard sone of Richard Johnson	24 January
John & Jenet children at one birth of Thomas Dawthaite of Newton, webster	31 ,,
Jane daughter of James Melling	13 March

1664.

Richard sone of John Dawny of the Yeat	27 March
Jenet daughter of Thomas Robinson of Churchl:...	24 Aprill
Elizabeth daughter of Willm Adcocke	1 May
Jane daughter of Edward Moore of Kirby sadler...	24 July
An daughter of Thomas Dicconson miler	31 ,,
Jane daughter of Edward Douthwaite	28 August
Richard son of Thomas Hutton	2 Octob
Edward sone of Willm Burrow	30 ,,
Mary daughter of Thomas Whithead of Arram ...	6 Novemb
John sone of Christopher Laurence carpinter & Katherine daughter of John Johnson both	18 December
John sone of Richard Tatham thelder	22 January
Elling daughter of Willm Margison	19 March

1665.

Alice daughter of Thomas Hogon	2 Aprill
Hanna daughter of John Troughton web:	15 ,,
Elizabeth daughter of Thomas Styth	23 ,,
Thomas sone of Robert Blackburne	14 May
An daughter of Mr. John Foxcroft	29 ,,
Agnes daughter of Willm Johnson	2 July
James sone of James Harris	9 October
Thomas sone of Thomas North	27 November
Willm sone of Willm Slater	6 Decem
Thomas sone of John Miller	10 ,,
Robert sone of Willm Burrow	18 February

[1] Interpolation.

1666.

Nathan sone of Thomas Douthwaite web:	15 July
John sone of Brian Bland	22 ,,
Jenet daughter of John Wildman Younger	9 Sep
Brian and Mathew sones of Brian Nealson	23 ,,
Alice daughter of James Curteous	4 Novē
John sone of Willm Adcock	23 Jañu
Henry sone of Oliuer Birch	15 February

1667.

Christopher sone of Thomas Hodgon	25 March
Thomas sone of Richard North of Newton	31 ,,
Richard sone of Robert Skirrow	14 Aprill
Richard sone of Richard Cort	10 May
Thomas sone of John Dawny of Newton north yeat	23 June
Thomas sone of Henry Johnson opposit Parsonage	8 Sept:
Dorothy daughter of Richard Tatham Sen:	15 ,,
Richard sone of Thomas Taylor west end of the step	20 Octo:
Elizabeth daughter of Thomas Towerson	3 Nov:
Abigaile daughter of James Curteous	24 ,,
Willm sone of Willm Margison	1 Decem
Elizabeth daughter of John Johnson	15 ,,
Isabell daughter of John Shaw ... ... the last day of February

1668.

James sone of John Miller	26 Aprill
James sone of Edward Douthwaite	7 June
John sone of Robert Topping	21 ,,
Edward sone of Marmaducke Cocking	26 July
John sone of Henry Mealis	2 August
Margret daughter of Robert Kellet spur:	29 ,,
Margret daughter of Richard Robinson	11 September
Willm sone of Myles Eykridge	13 ,,
Dorothy daughter of Symond Dawny	18 October
Mayry daughter of Richard Lancaster	22 Novem
Elizabeth daughter of Willm Burrow	29 ,,
Thomas sone of Willm Miller	6 December
John sone of Robert Blackburne & Agnes daughter of Rowland Braythait ... ... both	3 January
Marmaducke sone of Thomas Hutton	28 February
John sone of Thomas Shaw	14 March

1669.

Katheraine doughter of James Harris	4 Aprill
Katheraine doughter of Thomas Harris	18 ,,

Willm sone of Henry Myres ... ...   30 May
Sibilla daughter of Thomas Peandreth of Dalton...   30 ,,
James sone of Thomas Towerson ... ...   1 August
John sone of Edmond Burrow   ... ...   14 Decem
Alice doughter of James Curteous... ... ...   19 ,,
Robert sone of Henry Johnson   ... ...   25 ,,
Jane daughter of Richard North of Whitt: ... ...   26 ,,
Isabell daughter of Brian Bland ... ...   2 Jan:
Elizabeth daughter of Mr. Thomas Walker & Jane
    daughter of Thomas Stith   ... ...both   30 ,,
Robert sone of Robert Topping ... ...   6 February

1670.

Margret daughter of Richard Cort   ... ...   3 Aprill
Jane daughter of John Johnson   ... ... ,...   24 ,,
Katherine daughter of Thomas Taylor ... ...   3 July
Margret daughter of Willm Margison ... ...   25 ,,
John sone of Richard Robinson of the Corner   ...   21 August
Richard sone of Edward Dicconson of Docker   ...   9 October
Willm sone of Thomas Wattson ... ...   30 ,,
Margret daughter of Oliuer Birch... ... ...   15 November
John sone of Edmond Burrow   ... ...   18 December
An daughter of Richard Proctor ... ...   22 January
Elizabeth daughter of John Miller   ... ...   19 February

1671.

Jenet daughter of Robert Toppin ... ...   9 Aprill
Agnes daughter of John Cort Ju: sp: ... ...   24 ,,
Esther dau. of Andrew Cue ... ...   30 ,,
Lidea dau. of Richard Lancaster & Johanna dau.
    of Mark Bentham spu: ... ...both   2 July
Thomas sone of Robert Greensworth spur: ... ...   7 ,,
Jenet daughter of James Harris ... ...   20 August
John sone of Willm Miller   ... ...   17 Septemb:
An dau. of Willm Gibson   ... ...   1 Octr.
Willm son of Willm Cumerlond   ... ...   4 ,,
Elizabeth dau. of John Towerson ... ...   22 ,,
Roger sone of Willm Dodshon   ... ...   1 January
Thomas sone of James Curteous ... ...   14 ,,

1672.

Robert sone of Richard Robinson ... ...   14 Aprill
John sone of Rowland Braithait ... ...   26 May
Agnes dau. of Willm Burrow   ... ...   16 June
John sone of Henry Johnson & Thomas son of
    Thomas Watson   ... ...both   25 August

Ann dau. of Miles Eykridge	29 Sep
Willm sone of Robert Toppin	6 Octob
Richard sone of Oliuer North	3 November
Alice dau. of Thomas Bland	17 ,,
Agnes dau. of Marmaduk Cocking & Mary dau. of	
Andrew Cue ... ...both	24 ,,
Jane dau. of John Wildman Juñ	5 January

Anno Domini 1673.

Elling and Alice daughters of Willm Lonsdale ...	20 April
Thomas filius Gulielmi Thistlethwaite Ludi	
Magister [1]	1 May [?]
John son of Edward Dauthaite	4 ,,
Elizabeth dau. of Mr. Tho Brabin natus [1]	31 ,,
Thomas sone of Thomas Shaw	18 ,,
Richard sone of Richard North	1 June
John sone of Richard Cort wēb :	8 ,,
Willm son of Edmund Burrow	15 ,,
Richard sone of Mr. Willm Jackson borne 4th day	
being Munday and bapt the 21st day being	
Thursday of the month August	
John sone of Christopher Taylor	7 September
Elizabeth dau. of John Shaw...	
Isabell dau. of Richard Robinson	12 Octr
Margret dau. of Willm Miller	26 ,,
Alice dau. of Willm Gibson	2 Novr
Isaack sone of Richard Lancaster & George sone of	
John Miller ... ...both	14 December

1674.

George sone of Thomas Wattson & Isable dau. of	
Willm Slater of Newton... ... ...both	26 Apr
Jane dau. of John Cort Ju:	31 May
Elizabeth dau. of John Robinson & John sone of	
Robert Toppin ... ...both	5 July
Katherine dau. of Edmond Adcocke	2 August
John sone of John Wildman Jun:...	20 Septr
Margret dau. of Arthur Willson of old towne of the	
Parish of Kirby Lonsdale	27 ,,
Rowland sone of Henry Johnson	18 Octr
Richard sone of Robert Cornthait	6 Decem
Isabell dau. of Marmaducke Cocking	10 January
Tho: son of Mr. Tho: Bribin natus [1]	6 February
Elling dau. of Willm Lancet of Lupton	7 ,,

[1] Interpolations.

H

1675.

Jane dau. of Mr. Willm Slater	28 March
Edward soue of Robert Blackburne	20 June
Thomas sone of Thomas Bland	27 „
Isabell dau. of Willm Burrow	4 July
Charles sone of Mr. John Buckley	6 „
Elizabeth dau. of Willm Whithead	18 „
Willm sone of Willm Slater of Newton	5 Septem
Robert sone of Oliuer North	12 „
Willm sone of John Shaw	21 Nove
Henry sone of Miles Eykridge	30 Januari
Alice dau. of Richard North	27 February
Mary dau. of Mark Bentham spuria	19 March

1676.

Richard sone of James Corner	2 Aprill
George sone of Edmund Burrow	9 „
Elling dau. of Mr. Olliuer Dicconson	23 „
Henry sone of Robert Cornthwaite	23 „
John sone of James Curteous	30 „
Agnes dau. of Christopher Taylor	20 August
Isabell dau. of John Robinson	8 October
Robert sone of William Millers	29 „
Thomas sone of Thomas Bland	5 November
Thomas sone of Andrew Cue	17 December

1677.

George sonne of Mr. John Buckley	27 March
Mary dau. of Richard Cort	1 Aprill
William son of Edmond Adcock	8 „
Ellin dau. of Edward Douthwaite...	13 May
John sonne of Rowland Burrow & Margret dau. of Robert Topping ... ...both	20 „
Mary dau. of Edmond Burrow	27 „
Dorothy dau. of Thomas Read	3 June
Bryan son of John Wildman	5 August
John sone of Thomas Watson	12 „
Agnes dau. of Richard Robinson	14 October
Allis dau. of Willm Whitehead	28 „
John son of William Slater	25 Novemb
Agnes dau. of Thomas Bland	10 February

1678.

Henry son of Thomas Hutton and Agnes dau. of John Robinson ... ...both	14 Aprill

Isabell dau. of Marmaduke Cocking of Newton ... 28 Aprill
Rebecca dau. of George Hackforth ... ... 2 May
Job son of James Corney ... ... 9 June
Thomas son of Christopher Taylor ... ... 16 ,,
Margret dau. of William Bateson of the parish of
    Melling ... ... 18 Aug
Richard son of Rowland Burrow ... ... 20 Octr
Richard sone of Richard Godsall and Judith Harris 28 ,,
Thomas sone of Robert Toppin ... ... 1 Dec
James sone of Edward Dowthwaite ... ... 15 ,,
Thomas sone of Richard North ... ... 19 Jany
Jane dau. of Edmond Adcocke ... ... 26 ,,
Michael sone of Tho Brabing gentl natus [1] ... ... 7 August

Anno Domini 1679.

Elizabeth dau. of Edmond Burrow ... ... 29 June
Edward sone of Thomas Newby ... ... 26 Oct
Jane dau. of Richard Corte ... ... 7 Dec
Robert sone of William Bateson and Jane dau. of
    Marmaduke Cockin of Newton ... ... 22 Febry
Anna & Ruth both daughters of John Robinson ... 23 Mar

1680.

Thomas sonne of Willm Smyth ... ... 4 Aprill
Elizabeth daughter of Willm Slater ... ... 18 ,,
Willm sonne of Willm Millers ... ... 25 ,,
Jennet daughter of Willm Gibson... ... ... 9 May
Agnes daughter of Edward Jackson ... ... 11 Juely
Alice daughter of Oliver North ... ... 29 Augst
Samuel sonne of Rowland Burrow... ... ... 5 Sep
Thomas sonne of John Shaw... ... ... 10 October
Elizabeth daughter of Geo. Charnley [1] ... ... 26 ,,
Richard sonne of Cuthbert Smythies ... ... 24 ,,
Ellin daughter of Mr. Oliver Dickonson ... ... 31 ,,
John sonne of Andrew Cue ... ... 13 February
Margaret dau. of Edward Crosfeild ... . 20 ,,

Ano Domini 1681.

Jane dau. of Richard Godsalfe ... ... 10 Aprill
Mary dau. of Mr. Thomas Brabin ... ... 27 ,,
James son of James Harris ... ... 5 June
Alice daughter of Myles Aykridge... ... ... 17 ,,
Agnes daughter of Robert Cockin ... ... 19 ,,
Ester daughter of Willm Bateson ... ... 26 ,,

[1] Interpolated.

Richard sonne of James Corner	10 July
Thomas sonne of John Robinson	31 ,,
Agnes dau. of Cuthbert Smithies	23 October
Elizabeth dau. of Richard North & Margaret dau. of John Corner ... ...both	30 ,,
Jane dau. of William Smyth	6 November
Edmond sonne of Edmond Burrow [1]	28 ,,
Jane daughter of Henry Johnson	28 Jany
William sonne of Edward Cockin	5 February

Ano Domini 1682.

Ellin dau. of Will Whitehead	23 April
Catherine dau. of Mr. Tho Brabin natus	12 October
Elizabeth daughter of Symon Dawney	18 June
Rowland son of Rowland Burrow	13 Aug
Ellin dau. of Robert Toppin	27 ,,
spur John son of John Brough & Isabell Vstison... ...	22 Oct
Katherine daughter of Richard Godsalfe	10 Decr

An'o dom'j 1683.

Mary dau. of Edward Jackson	1 Aprill
spur Richard sonne of Richard Taylor and Elizabeth Mansergh	15 July
William sonne of John Robinson	22 ,,
Elizabeth dau. of Richard North	7 Aug
John sonne of William Bateson	14 October
Elizabeth dau. of Rowland Burrow	4 Nov
Edward son of William Smyth and Richard son of John Corner ... ...both	18 ,,
Alice dau. of Robt Robinson	23 December
Stephen sonne of Cuthbert Smythies	10 Feb

An'o dom'j 1684.

Isabell daughter of William Slater	3 Aprill
Jane dau. of Edward Cocking	20 ,,
Margaret dau. of Richard North	18 May
Jane & Anne both daughters of Andrew Cue ...	25 ,,
Katherine dau. of Roger Moore Esqe.	10 June
Margret daugr. of Richard Godsalfe	7 Sep
Richard son of Oliver North	18 January
Thomas filius Richard Wright ... ... vicesimo secundo Martij	
Mary filia George Carus generosi	3 Nov

[1] Interpolated.

Anno primo regni Jacobi secundi regis, 1685.

Johannes filius Edwardi Cockin ... ... decimo septimo May
Jane spur: filia Gulielmi Slater & Agnes spur
    Johannis Hall & Agnis Harries ... ... octavo die July
Margereta filia Edmundi Burrow ... ... secondo die Augusti
Richard filius Johannis Mansergh... ... ... vicesimo die „
Mary dau. of Roger Moore Esq. ... ... 14 Sep
Richard son of James Bond ... ... 27 September
Samuell son of Rowland Burrow ... ... 4 October
Mary daughter of Thomas Brabin gentleman ... 10 „
Thomas son of Richard North Docker ... ... 8 Nov
Thomas son of John Robinson ... ... 3 January

Anno 1686.

Jane Tatham daughter of James Tatham ... ... 2 Aug
Alice daughter of Simon Batty ... ... 22 „
Katherine filia Georgi Carus ... ... 7 March
Jane daughter of James Harries ... ... 17 October
Margaret dau. of Edward Burrow ... ... 31 „
Richard son of William Slater ... ... 19 December
Ann daughter of Robert Greenwood ... ... 6 February

Anno domini 1687.

Thomas son of John Woodhouse ... ... 1 May
Anthony son of Thomas Bouch Rector... ... ... 19 June
Jenet dau. of Henry Chatburn ... ... 7 August
Ann dau. of Oliver North ... ... 14 „
Alice dau. of William Smith... ... ... 4 September
An dau. of Mr. Thomas Brabin natus ... ... 27 „
Richard son of Andrew Cue ... ... 19 February
John son of William Lawrence ... ... 26 „
An filia Georgi Carus de Sellat ... ... 10 „

Anno domini 1688.

Jane filia Richard North ... ... 27 May
George son of George Carus ... ... 12 March
Elizabetha filia Thomae Bouch Rectoris de Whit-
    tington ... ... 24 Junij
Elizabetha filia Roberti Towers ... ... 26 Augusti
Henricus filius Richj North de Dockr ... ... 9 Septembris
Jacobus filius Johis Robinson ... ... 13 Novembris
Richus filius Jacobi Tatham ... ... 12 Decembris
Johes filius Willmj Robinson... ... ... 17 February

Anno dom 1689.

Jane filia Thomas Bouch Rectoris de Whittington	5 Junij
Agnes filia Edmundi Burrow...	23 „
Thomas filius illegit Rowland Burrow	26 Septembris
Thomas filius Thomae Carus de Westhall generosi	15 Decembris
Henricus filius Johannis Leafielde...	23 February
Christopherus filius Willmj Laurence	9 March

Anno domini 1690.

Alicia filia Thomas Tatham de Newton	13 Aprilis
Judith filia Georgij Carus de Sellat hall generosi...	15 „
Richardus filius Edward Cockin	27 „
Jacobus filius Willmj Slater de Newton	25 Maij
John son of Henry Chatburn de Newton	8 June
Mary dau. of Thomas Bouch Rector de Whittington	16 „
John son of William Symth de Newton	22 „

[1690.]

Henry son of Robert Towers milln[r]·	26 October
Oliver son of Peter Cautley	24 November
Thomas son of Thomas North Jnr generosi... ...	28 Decembris
James son of Edmund Dodgson of Casterton	...primo die Marcij
Elizabeth daugr. of Jno Robinson de Docker ...	„ „

Anno domini 1691.

Eling daur. of William Robinson	24 May
John son of John Barraw Docker	21 June
Tho son of George Carus[1]	1 „
John son of John Woodhouse	16 August
Elizebeth daughter of Symon Batty	12 October
Eling daugr. of Richard North de Docker	17 „
William son of John Margisson	25 „
Timothy son of Tho: Thompson	8 November
Alice dau. of James Tatham	13 Decembr
Thomas son of Peter Cautley...	20 „
Jennet dau. of Robert Burrow	28 February
John son of Thomas Johnson of the West end of the Church natus erat vigissimo tertio die Februarij et bapt primo Martij	
Jane dau. of William Lawrence	6 March

[1] Interpolation.

Anno domini [1692.]

William son of Thomas North Jr generossi	13 November
Ann filia Elizabeth Burrow	13 „
Bridget filia Georgi Carus	23 June
Joan filia Jacobi Tatham	20 November
William son of Henry Chatburn	27 „
Robertus fillius Roberti Towers	3 February
Thomas filius Thomas Jamson et Margt Dawney	26 „

Anno domini 1693.

Anna filia Thomas Johnson	4 Maij
George & John both sons of James Downham (geminii) bap 15th die Junij Anno pdc[t]	
William son of William Robinson	23 Julij
Johannes filius Johannis Robinson de Docker ...	3 Decemb
Danielus filius Georgij Carus generossi natus erat	12 Novembris
Robertus filius Roberti Burrow	18 February
Wittmus filius Willmj Martin et Isabelle Taylor ...	18 „

1693.

Sarah dau. of John Towerson was born 28th March in anno 1675 and was bap. 16 day of January when aged 19

John son of John Towerson was born 4th day of January in anno 1677 and was baptised ye 16th of January when aged full 16 years. The said John Towerson their father being a quaker, brought them up after ye sect, but after his death the sd. children desired to be ingrafted into Christ Church by baptism of their own accord.

Anno domini 1694.

Thomas son of Thomas Cautley	28 March
Esthera filia Willm Lawrence	15 Aprilis
Agnes filia Willm Slater de Whittington	22 Julij
Jacobus filius Edwardi Cocking	19 Augustij
Thomas filius Oliver North de Newton...	26 „
Johnathanus filius Johis Burrow	nono die Septembris
Thomas son of Tho: Thompson [1]	23 „
Petrus filius Thome Thompson de Docker	30 „
Johanes filius Roberti Atckinson de Newton ...	14 Octobris
Richardus filius Richardi North de Docker ...	primo die Januarij
Elling filia Johannis Crampton de Whittington ...	13 Januarij
Sthephen filius Timothei Thompson de Docker ...	4 Februarij

[1] Written on erasure and added at a later date.

Anno domj 1695.

William filius Christopher Hodgson de Newton ...   3 Marcij
Mary filia Johannis Barrow Docker   ... ...   7 Aprilis
Johannes filius Thomae North de Newton Ju   ...   21 „
Thomas son of Willm Styth of Whittington born 1st bapt 4 August
James sonn of James Tatham born 19th bapt 25 August
John son of James Millers   ... ...   3 November
Agnes dau. of Wm Martin   ... ...   28 December
Agnes dau. of Robert Burrow   ... ...   29 „
Richard son of Robert Atckinson born 9th bapt 16 February
Alice daugr. of John Burrow born 7th bapt 16 February

Anno domini 1696.

Thomas son of Simon Batty ...   .   12 April
Dorothy dau. of Henry Robinson ...   .   10 May
Elizabeth dau. of John Heblethwaite   ... ...   26 July
Agnes dau. of John Blackburn   ... ...   13 September
Jane dau. of John Robinsou de Docker...   ... ...   20 „
Mary dau. of John Moore de Holmehouse   ... ...   29 Decr
Margret dau. of Robert Burrow   ... ...   31 Jany
Thomas son of Mr. Thomas Bouch Rect   ... ...   3 February
William son of John Styth ...   .   14 „
Christopher son of Christopher Hodgson   ... ...   14 March

Anno domini 1697.

John son of John Margison de docker ...   .   6 June
Agnes dau. of Thomas Heavisides...   ... ...   26 „
Agnes dau. of Luke Cornew ...   .   22 Aug
Thomas son of Walter Parke...   ... ...   5 Sep
Jane dau. of Thomas Peck   ... ,.. ... ...   3 Octr
Miles son of Thomas North de Newton   ... ...   18 „
Mary dau. of Thomas Cautley de Docker   .., ...   30 January

Anno domini 1698.

Henry son of Henry Chatburn   ... ...   27 March
Jane dau. of Edward Taylor ...   .   27 „
Jennet dau. of Richard Cocking   ... ,.. ... ...   2 Aprill
John son of William Styth ...   .   3 „
Elling dau. of Richard Todd...   ... ...   8 „
Margrett dau. of Will Burrow de Newt: ... ...   14 May
John son of Richard North de docker ...   .   15 „
Richard son of James Johnson   ... ...   25 June
William son of James Bordrigge ...   .   25 July
Susana dau. of Simon Batty ...   ... ,.. ... ...   14 Augst

Richard son of Richard Heblethwait de Moore ...	4 September
Thomas son of Henry Robinson	25 ,,
Robert son of Tho: North of Newton	29 Octr
Willm son of James Milners	11 Decr
Jane dau. of Bryan Dixon	1 Jany
Matthew son of Robt Atkinson	22 ,,
Elizabeth dau. of Wm Slater	22 ,,
Margaret dau. of John Burrow of Whittington ...	19 Febry
William son of John Moore of Whittington	21 ,,
Mary dau. of Thomas Bouch	11 March

1699.

Alice daughter of James Tatham	9 April
Thomas son of Robert Burrow	23 ,,
Mary dau. of Mary Johnson	13 Sept
Elizabeth dau. of Thomas Smith	17 Octr
William son of William Martin	11 Feby
Thomas son of Henry Robinson	24 March
Henery son of Thomas Cowtley	16 ,,

1700.

Agnes dau. of James Johnson	31 Mar
Myles son of Mr. Tho: North	21 April
Marmaduke son of Richard Cockin	21 ,,
Richard son of Richard Slater	28 ,,
Sarah dau. of Jamᵉ Stewardson	29 ,,
Thomas son of William Burrow of Newton	12 May
John son of John Hebelthwaite of Newton	23 June
John son of James Bordridge of Whittington ...	13 Octr
George son of Agns Tison of Whittington	19 ,,
Thomas son of James Tatham of Whittington ...	10 Novr
Jane dau. of Willm Overend of Whitt	18 ,,
Sarah dau. of Bryan Dickson of Whitt	8 Dec
Edward son of John Borrow of Whitt	12 Jany
James son of Willm Styth of Whitt	12 ,,
Dorothy dau. of Tho: Peck of Whitt	23 March

1701.

Susanna dau. of Simon Batty of Whitt	6 April
Margret dan. of Elizabeth Parsiball	19 ,,
Easter dau. of John Johnson of Newton	27 ,,
Margaret dau. of Richd Hebelthwait of Newton ...	4 May
Margaret dau. of Robert Atkinson of Newton ...	4 ,,
Richard son of Robert Burrow	7 July
Elizabeth dau. of James Lucas of Newton	2 August
William son of Walter Park of Docker	2 ,,

I

William son of John Nicholson of Newton ... ...   19 Sep
Michael son of Christopher Hodgeson of Newton...   5 Octr
Isaball dau. of Richard Cockin of Whitt   ... ...   12 „
Ann dau. of William Lawrence of Whittington ...   16 Nov
Ellen Hardy buried ye 18 day of December 1701 [1]
Margret Parcible [1]

Anno Domini 1702.

Francis son of James Johnson of Whittington   ...   26 April
Ellin dau. of William Willan of Westhall   ... ...   7 Aug
Richard son of James Millers de Whitt... ... ...   23 „
Agnes dau. of Richard Skirrow of Docker   ... ...   20 Sept
Ann dau. of James Bordrigge of Whitt... ... ...   29 Novr
Sarah dau. of Edward Cocking Junr. de Whitt ...   23 Jan
Thomas son of Bryan Dickson of Whitt   ... ...   31 „
John son of Richard North of Docker ... ...   14·Feby
Agnes dau. of William Martin of Whitt   ... ...   7 Mar

Anno Dom 1703.

Agnes dau. of John Johnson of Newton   ... ...   18 April
John son of James Lucas of Newton ... ...   25 „
Dorothy dau. of Henry Robinson of Whittington...   2 May
Septimus son of Mr. Thomas North Junr. of Newton   10 „
Ellen dau. of William Willan of Westhall   ... ...   20 „
Edward son of Robert Burrow of Docker   ... ...   1 Aug
Robert son of Tho: Toping of Whitt   ... ...   2 Jany

1704.

Ann dau. of Daniel Pearson of Whitt ... ...   26 March
John son of Francis Chipingdale of Newton... ...   20 May
John son of Henry Chatborn of Whitt... ... ...   28 June
Thomas son of Richard Hebelwhaite of Newton ...   6 Aug
Samuel son of Mr. Tho: North of Newton Junr....   16 „
James son of James Johnson of Whittington   ...   5 Novr
Ann dau. of Richard Cocking of Whitt... ... ...   1 Jany
Mary dau. of Robert Atkinson of New ... ...   4 Feb

Anno Domini 1705.

John son of John Burrow   ... ...   9 April
Oliver son of James Lucas of Newton ... ...   15 „
Bryan son of Bryan Dixon of Whitt   ... ...   13 May
Ellin dau. of James Bordrigge of Whitt   ... ...   10 June

---

[1] These two entries, apparently both entries of burials, seem to have been
inserted here by mistake.

James son of William Willan of Westhall ... ...   8 July
Margret dau. of James Barker of Holmehouse   ..   22 ,,
Ellinor dau. of Mr. Tho: Crowle of Whitt ... ...   30 ,,
George son of Thomas Ubank of Sellet... ... ...   9 Aug
Ann dau. of Edward Cocking of Whitt   ... ...   10 Sep
Jane dau. of Mr. Daniel Pearson ... ...   14 Oct
Nicolas son of John Croft de Docker ... ...   28 ,,
John son of John Johnson of Newton ... ...   2 Dec
Elizabeth dau. of Mr. Thomas North ... ...   7 ,,

Anno Domini 1706.

Henry son of John Millers ... ...   24 Nov
Mary dau. of Willm Styth ... ...   22 Dec
Ann dau. of John Cocking ... ...   12 Jan
Joseph son of Agnes Bland ... ...   22 Feb
Mary dau. of William Overend ... ...   23 ,,

Anno Domini 1707.

Isaball dau. of Fran Chipindale ... ...   6 April
George son of James Johnson ... ...   27 ,,
Margret dau. of Wiℍm Willan ... ...   23 May
Thomas son of Bray and Margret Dixon ... ...   15 June
Mary dau. of Mr. Thoms and Mrs. Ellin North ...   23 ,,
Margret dau. of James and Margret Ellis ... ...   6 July
Richard son of Myles and Isaball Willan ... ...   19 ,,
Jane dau. of Thomas and Jane Kue ... ...   20 ,,
Mary dau. of John and Hanah Burrow... ... ...   21 Sep
Jane dau. of John and Margret Croft ... ...   20 Dec
Alice dau. of James and Ann Bordrigge ... ...   4 Jan
Ann dau. of Mr. Thomas and Mrs. Ann Crowle ...   15 ,,
Robert son of Robert and Mary Atkinson ... ...   18 ,,
Elling dau. of James and Eliz. Barker ... ...   25 ,,
Paul son of John and Isaball Cocking ... ...   1 Feby
James son of Thomas and Alice Eubank ... ...   8 ,,

1708.

Alice dau. of Edward and Ellen Cocking ... ...   28 Mar
John son of Thomas and Agnes Willson ... ...   10 April
Jane dau. of Edward and Agnes Smyth of Newton   2 May
Ellin dau. of John Johnson of Newton... ... ...   27 June
Mary dau. of Richard and Ann Cocking of Whitt   22 Aug
Mary dau. of Mr. Thomas and Mrs. Ellin North ...   6 Sep
Thomas son of Eliz: Burrow bastard child ... ...   28 Dec
Alice dau. of William Overend ... ...   27 Feb

Anno dom⁹ 1709.

Elizabeth dau. of William Willan	16 April
Margret dau. of ffrancis Chippindale	1 May
Easther dau. of James Johnson	8 „
Agnes dau. of Henry Meale	8 „
Ann dau. of Richard Heblethwaite	31 July
Elizabeth dau. of James Thornton...	21 Aug
Barbary dau. of John Burrow	5 Nov
Richd son of Mr. Thomas North	5 „
George son of Thomas Crowle	10 „
Edward son of Edw: Cockin Junr.	13 Jany

Anno dom⁹ 1710.

Mary dau. of Edward Smyth	2 April
Elizabeth dau. of William Styth	18 June
Anne dau. of John Millers	16 July
Allice dau. of Bryan Dixon	23 „
Richard son of Richard Tatham of Newton	30 „
Mary dau. of John Tatham and Jane Gibson of Newton a bastard child	22 Oct
Ann dau. of John Cockin	29 „
Ann dau. of William Tompson	12 Nov
Thomas son of William Boardley	14 „
James son of Myles Willan	19 „
Francis son of Thomas Willson	25 Dec
Robert son of Robert Rackstraw and Mary Tode a bastard child	7 Jany
Thomas son of John Johnson Smyth	21 „
Robert son of John Willson of Newton...	4 Feby

Anno dom⁹ 1711.

Mary dau. of James Bordrige (deceased)	11 Apl
Ann dau. of James Ellis	24 June
Thomas son of Mr. Thomas Crowle	1 July
John son of Mr. Daniel Pearson	7 Oct
Willm and Elizabeth son and dau. of James Barker (born both at a birth)	20 Oct
Dorothy dau. of John Johnson	25 Nov
Myles son of Mr. Tho: North	27 „
Thomas son of Tho: Kue	23 Dec
Jonathan son of Richard Tatham	1 Jany
Elizabeth dau. of Edward Smyth	13 „
Ann dau. of Christopher Laurence	16 March

Anno dom⁹ 1712.

Ann dau. of Will Boardley	13 April
Margret dau. of Bryan Dixon...	4 May
Ellin dau. of Francis Chippindale	11 ,,
Thomas son of Mr. Thomas Crowle	14 June
Oliver son of Richard North of Newton	22 ,,
Ann dau. of John Lawrence	13 July
Allice dau. of William Thompson	26 Octr
William son of Edward Beetham	16 Novr
Elizabeth dau. of Thomas Huck	25 Dec
Jane dau. of Samuel Burrow	4 Jany
Edward son of John Cockin	31 ,,
John son of Richd Heblethwaite	8 March

Anno dom⁹ 1713.

William son of Willm Overend of Whitt	29 Mar
William son of Myles Willan...	6 Aprill
William son of Richard Batty	5 May
Isabell dau. of John Cornthwaite	16 ,,
William son of William Styth	18 ,,
Thomas son of John Woodhouse	30 ,,
Benjamin son of Mr. Thomas North	9 July
John son of Thomas Robinson	6 Sep
Ann dau. of Thomas Hodgson	4 Octr
Mary dau. of Mr. Thomas Crowle	18 ,,
Christopher son of William Boardley	31 Jany
Alice dau. of John Cockin	7 Feby
Mary dau. of Henry Clark of Killington a bastard child	7 ,,
Myles son of Hen. Eckridge	28 ,,

Ann dom⁹ 1714.

Ann dau. of Edward Smyth	30 May
Margaret dau. of William Slater	23 July
John son of Thomas Kue	25 ,,
Elizabeth dau. of John Johnson	1 Aug
William son of Christopher Lawrence	22 ,,
ffrancis son of ffran: Chippindale	24 Oct
Margret dau. of William Thompson	14 Nov
Jane dau. of John Lawrence	21 ,,
Hannah daugh. of Richd Batty	12 Dec
William son of Thomas Hodgeson...	9 Jany
Abigail dau. of Samuel Burrow	20 Feby
Alice dau. of Richd Tatham Senr	27 ,,
Joseph son of John Johnson weavr	20 Mar

Anno dom⁹ 1715.

Richard son of Richd Kue of Newton	8 May
Ellin dau. of Thomas Thompson	15 „
Ellin dau. of Thomas Huck	31 July
George son of Edward Beetham	14 August
William son of Henry Eckridge	18 September
James son of Bryan Dixon	25 „
Ann dau. of Richard North	4 December
Ann dau. of James Dickonson and Isabell Fryar (a bastard child)	27 „

Anno dom⁹ 1716.

Elizabeth dau. of Thomas Robinson	13 May
William son of Thomas Crowle Esqʳ	17 June
John son of Thomas Hodgson	17 „
Ellen dau. of Richard Batty	24 „
William son of William Slatter	29 July
James son of Richard Robinson	4 October
Alice dau. of John Johnson	9 December
Elizabeth dau. of Francis Chippindal	16 „
John son of William Tomson...	24 February

Anno domini 1717.

Elizabeth dau. of Richd Cew	9 June
Elizabeth dau. of Bryan Ward	21 „
Richard son of Tho: Tennison	7 July
Marry dau. of Samuel Borrow	20 „
Richard son of Thomas Crowle Esqʳ	27 Novbr
Ann dau. of Bryan Dixon	22 Decbr
John son of John Cockin	24 „
Charles son of Tho: Huck	5 Janr
Isack son of Edward Houghton	24 Feb

Anno domini 1718.

Matthew son of Wulfray Hopkin	30 March
Margrett dau. of Rich: Batty	6 April
Elizabeth dau. of Thomas Hodgson	1 July
John son of Thomas Nouel	12 „
Jane dau. of Christopher Lawrence carpiuter ...	10 August
Mary dau. of Wm. Moore, traveller of ye Parish Broad Church	14 „
Mary dau. of Thomas Robinson husbandman ...	16 October
Isabel dau. of Wm. Holme, miller...	28 „

John son of John Johnson, webster ... ... 1 January
Isabel dau. of Richard Tatham husbandman... ... 25 ,,
Jane dau. of Wm. Slater yeoman ... ... 25 ,,
Thomas son of Richard Robinson husbandman ... 1 February
John son of John Cockin, husbandman ... ... 8 ,,
Thomas son of Francis Chippindale, husbandman 1 March
Ann dau. of Bryan Ward yeoman ... ... 22 ,,

Anno Domini 1719.

Jane dau. of Edward Houghton husbandman ... 27 March
Thomas son of John Johnson, yeoman ... ... 12 April
Daniel son of Thomas Crowle Esqr ... ... 11 July
Alice dau. of Wm. Tomuson [?] ... ... 2 August
Richard son of Thomas Harrison ... ... 13 Sept
Elizabeth dau. of Richard Batty ... ... 15 November
Dorothy dau. of John Cowert ... ... 22 ,,
John son of Joseph Robinson ... ... 5 Decbr
Robert son of Edward France ... ... 28 Feb:
Margaret dau. of Ann Starnthait ... ... 13 March

Anno Domini 1720.

Wilson son of Mr. Thomas Carus ... ... 1 April
Wm. son of Thomas Noble ... ... 24 ,,
George son of Edward Cockin... ... ... 15 May
Alice dau. of Thomas Hodgson ... ... 28 August
John son of Franciss Guye ... ... 31 ,,
Elizabeth dau. of John Warriner ... ... 13 November
James son of Joseph Place & Elizabeth his daughter 20 ,,
Margaret dau. of Christopher Lawrence ... ... 27 ,,
Jane dau. of Thomas Robinson ... ... 29 January
Ann dau. of Christopher Hodgson... ... ... 2 February
Elizabeth dau. of John Johnson ... ... 5 ,,

Anno Domini 1721.

Mary dau. of Mr. Tho: Rawlisson... ... ... 31 July
George son of Tho: Carus Esqr ... ... 7 August
Richard son   }
Elizabeth dau.   } of Wm. Tomson... ... . 8 September
Robert son of Bryan Ward ... ... 10 ,,
Thomas son of Wm. Slater ... ... 14 ,,
Jane dau. of Joseph Robinson ... ... 13 October
Margaret dau. of Wm. Perkin ... ... 17 Novbr
Elizabeth dau. of Richard North of Newton... ... 17 December
Bryan son of Thomas Huck ... ... 24 February
William son of Thomas Harrison ... ... 18 March
Ann dau. of Thomas Noble ... ... 28 ,,

Anno Domini 1722.

Ellin dau. of Thomas Robinson of Whittington ...	15 April
Leonard son of William Martin	22 ,,
Christopher son of Thomas Hodgson	20 May
Rowland son of John Borrough	24 June
Elizabeth dau. of Joseph Place	29 July
William son of Mr. Thomas Carus...	7 August
William son of Christopher Hodgson	9 December
Thomas son of William Sclater	6 January
Richard son of Bryan Ward	24 March

Anno Domini 1723.

Richard son of William Holme	5 May
Thomas son of Edward Blackburn	5 ,,
Elizabeth dau. of Henry Chatburn	12 ,,
William son of Anthony Bird	2 August
James son of Thomas Robinson	25 ,,
Grace dau. of Tho: Carus Esqr	13 September
Brigate dau. of John Barrow	21 ,,
Matthew son of Richard Batty	22 ,,
James son of Franciss Guye	2 October
Anne dau. of John Johnson	3 November
James son of John Webster	8 ,,
William son of William Durham	15 ,,
Jane dau. of John Cockin	27 ,,
Michael son of Thomas Hodgson	8 December
Thomas son of Joseph Robinson	25 ,,
William son of Christopher Hodgson	25 ,,
Christopher son of Robert Heblewhaite	26 January
Edmund son of Thomas Noble	1 March
Ellin and Edmund dau. and son of Wm. Perkin ...	20 ,,
John son of Christopher Lawrence	22 ,,

Anno Domini 1724.

Agnes dau. of Edward Blackburn	19 Aprill
James son of James Garnet	22 May
George son of Thomas Kirby...	12 July
Joseph son of Joseph Place	13 December
Thomas son of Henery North	5 March
Henery son of Thomas Robinson	7 ,,

Anno Domini 1725.

John son of Edward France	27 March
Robert son of Richard Heblewhaite	23 May

Margret dau. of Wm. Holme	30 July
Robert son of Wm. Martin	30 ,,
John son of Christopher Hodgson...	3 October
John son of Wm. Sclater	15 ,,
Mary dau. of Bryan Ward	22 ,,
John son of Timothy Wardley	31 ,,
Mary dau. of Thomas Hodgson	17 Novmbr
Margret dau. of Jonathan Maison	17 ,,
Christiana dau. of John Barrough...	21 ,,
William son of William Perkin	28 January
John son of Edward Barton	30 ,,

Anno Domini 1726.

William son of Edward Blackburn	11 April
Alice dau. of Will Deeson	24 ,,
Will son of Joseph Robinson...	15 May
Edw. son of Henry Chathburn	18 ,,
Robert son of Richd Atkinson	1 July
Dorathy son of Tho: Kirby	14 August
Tho: son of Tho: Noble...	4 Septmr
Isabell dau. of John Cockin	11 ,,
Henry son of Henry Dickonson	5 Novr
Chris' son of Christoph' Lawrence	13 ,,
Jane dau. of Jōs Ireland	16 ,,
Mary dau. of Anthony Bird	18 Decembr
Alex: son of James Adcock	10 Febry

Anno Domini 1727.

John son of Thomas Croswhaite	22 May
Margaret dau. of Henry North	2 June
Mary dau. of Richd Trotter Esqr	7 ,,
Eliz: dau. of Willm Parkinson	12 July
Eliz: dau. of Thō. Yeadon	28 ,,
Henry son of Henry Brown	9 August
Willm son of Willm Martin	22 Septr
Hannah dau. of Thō. Hodgshon	5 Novr
Geō: son of Christophr Lawrence	12 ,,
Willm and Elizabeth son and dau. of Lawrence	
Tomlinson	25 ,,
Henry son of John Heblethwaite	3 Decembr
Ellin dau. of Richd Johnson	4 ,,
Bryan son of Thō. Robinson	10 ,,
Willm son of John Barrow	27 ,,
Margaret dau. of John Johnson	31 ,,
Willm son of John Hogart	1 Janry
Mary dau. of John Whittington	7 ,,
Willm son of Edward France	7 ,,

John son of William Holme ... ...   2 Febry
John son of Edward Blackburn ... ...   4 „
Mary dau. of Edward Barton... ... ...   11 „
Thō: son of Willm Armestead   ... ...   3 March

[1728.]

Ann dau. of Henry Chathburn   ... ...   7 April
Eilliner dau. of Will Perkin ... ...   14 „
Thos. son of Edward Tallan ... ...   21 „
Alice dau. of John Cornthwaite ... ...   6 Novemr
John son of James Adcock ... ...   26 Janry
Margaret dau. of Joseph Robinson ... ...   17 Febry
Thō. son of Rich. Attkinson ... ...   3 March

1729.

Eliz. dau. of Thos. Yeadale ... ...   30 Mar
Jane dau. of Christophr Lawrence... ... ...   20 April
Mary dau. of Thomas Noble ... ...   25 May
John son of John Webster ... ...   18 June
Ann dau. of Christopher Hodgshon   ... ...   3 Aug
Bryan son of Bryan Ward   ... ...   21 Sep
Hannah dau. of Mr. Tho: Dickson   ... ...   21 Nov
Mary dau. of John Hogart ... ...   1 Jany
John son of Will Martin... ... ...   8 Feby
Mary dau. of Mary Parker bastard child   ... ...   9 „
Alexr. son of Will Adcock   ... ...   20 Mar

Anno dom 1730.

Isabel dau. of Henry Chathburn ... ...   April
John son of John Carter   ... ...   26 „
Tho: son of Tho: Robinson ... ...   8 May
John son of Willm Armistead   ... ...   12 July
Robert son of John Dantan ... ...   15 Nov
Robert and Jennet son and dau. of Edw. Barton...   19 „
Edw. son of Edwd. Tallan ... ...   27 „
John son of Willm Parkin ... ...   27 „
Richd son of Edwd. ffrance ... ...   28 Dec
John son of Henry North   ... ...   30 Jany
Ellin dau. of Thos. Hodgshon... ... ...   19 Feby
Agnes dau. of Richd Heblethwait... ... ...   6 Mar

1731.

Joseph son of John Barrow ... ...   7 May
Ann dau. of James Adcock ... ...   6 June
Mary dau. of Christophr Hodgshon   ... ...   13 Aug

Margaret dau. of John Hogart	29 Aug
Lawrence son of John Millers	1 Jany
Parthania and Elizabeth daurs of William Gill ...	5 Mar
Susanna dau. of William Adcock	10 ,,
Ann dau. of John Cornthwaite	13 ,,

1732.

Henry son of Henry Chatburn	30 April
Dorathy dau. of Chrisr. Lawrence...	18 June
James son of Tho: Hodgshon	23 July
John son of Thos. Tatham	17 Octr
Willm son of Willm Armistead	26 Dec
Margaret dau. of Tho: Yeadale	27 December
Jane dau. of Edwd Barton	28 Jany

1733.

James son of Edward Tallan	27 May
Ellen dau. of John Whittington	10 June
Benjamin son of Thos. Hodgshon	8 July
Jane dau. of Henry North	5 Octr.
Robert son of Robert Gibson	11 ,,
Margaret dau. of Willm Martin	11 Novr
James son of Willm Parkin	9 Dec
Jane dau. of Christophr Hodgshon	9 ,,
Edmond son of Thos Kirby	29 Feb

1734.

Eliz[th] dau. of Edwd ffrance	30 Mar
Chrisr. son of Thos. Smith	5 July
Richd son of Tho: Gunson	16 Octr
Jane dau. of John Millers	10 Novr
Abraham son of Geo. Ginnings	6 Jany
Mary dau. of John Barrow	8 Feby
Henry son of Henry Gibson	16 ,,
John son of Henry Chatburn...	16 ,,
Margaret dau. of John Heblethwaite	16 ,,
Isabel dau. of Richard Johnson	23 March

1735.

Jane dau. of Geo. Nuby	29 March
Margaret dau. of Willm Armestead	18 May
Jane dau. of Willm Wilkinson	18 ,,
John son of William Adcock	1 June
William son of James Burton	9 Novr
John son of John Lonsdale	28 Jany

1736.

Alice dau. of Richard Cockin...	2 May
Ann dau. of Edward Tallan	30 ,,
Thos son of John Saul	1 Aug
Isabel dau. of Thos. Foxcroft	22 Sep
Hannah dau. of William Ernshaw...	4 Octr
Joseph and Benjamin sons of Christophr Hodgshon	10 ,,
Ellin dau. of Robert Gibson	25 Dec
Isack son of Willm Armistead	20 Feby

1737.

Robert son of John Millers	17 April
Elizabeth dau. of George Nuby	8 May
George son of George Ginnings	22 ,,
James son of Richd Johnson...	5 June
Jane dau. of Bryan Ward	26 ,,
Thō: son of John Barrow	21 August
Richard son of Henry North	24 ,,
Mary dau. of Robert Willson...	20 Novembr
Ellin dau. of Willm Harrison	22 January
John son of Robert Robinson...	5 March

1738.

Rachel w. of Edward Robinson	25 March
aged 26 years this 25th day of March	
Agnes dau. of Edward Robinson	25 ,,
Ralph son of Edward Tallan	17 Septembr
Miles son of Mr. Oliver North	9 Decembr
Thomas son of Robert Gibson	21 January
Sara dau. of Mary Conder, bastard child	25 ,,
Abraham son of Willm Armestead	11 Febry

1739.

Robert son of Edward France	8 April
Ellin dau. of Nicholas Croft	6 May
Sara dau. of John Saul	13 ,,
Myles son of John Knowles	22 July
Thomas son of John Denton	18 November
Henry son of Henry North	3 March

1740.

Ann dau. of Robert Chippindale	23 May
Mary dau. of William Harrison	3 August

William son of William Adcock	17 August
Dorathy dau. of Robert Robinson	7 September
John son of George Nuby	2 November
Willm son of James Balderstone	22 February

1741.

Ellin dau. of Robert Gibson	3 May
Judith dau. of Mr. John Sunderland	29 ,,
Ann dau. of Willm Lawrence...	1 January
Nathan son of William Armistead	17 March

1742.

William Green son of Robart Green	18 September
Robert Cheppendell son of Robart Chippendell ...	31 October
Henary Stackhows son of Henary Stakhows ...	2 January
Mathew Saull son of John Saul	20 March

1743.

Edman son of Richard Thompson	24 April
Cristofer son of Robart Robinson	1 May
Jane dau. of John Sanders	3 ,,
John son of Con Dolen	29 ,,
Margret dau. of Robt [?] Harrison...	11 June
James son of James Harries [?]	21 August
John son of Will Lawrence	16 October
Joseph son of Mils Eckridg	23 ,,
Agnas dau. of Will: Smeteh	25 December

1744.

Richard son of William Armistead	6 May
Thomas son of John Woodman	28 October
Thomas son of Mr. John Sunderland	1 December
Crestefar son of John Hodshon	25 ,,
Isabell dau. of John Johnson...	30 ,,

1745.

Joseph son of Henry Stackhouse	19 May
Henry son of Miles Ekridge	26 ,,
Margaret dau. of Edwd Thornber	30 June
James son of Richd Thompson	18 October
Edwd son of Wm Brown [1]	1 December

[1] Evidently an interlineation at a later day.

Stephen son of Geo: Nuby ... ... 12 January
Margaret dau. of Leonard Martin 9   „
Richd son of John Backhouse ... ... 22 February

1746.

Dorathy dau. of Willm Lawrence ... ... 29 June
Jane dau. of Allon Kirk... ... ... 6 July
Jane dau. of Richd Taylor ... ... 29 „
Eliz dau. of John Glover ... ... 30 November
Jane dau. of Myles Eckridge... ... ... 4 January
Thomas son of John Johnson ... ... 4 „
Hanna dau. of Richd Cockin ... ... 11 „
Willm son of John Hodshon ... ... 22 March
Robt son of Richd Thompson... ... ... 22 „

Ano dom 1747.

John son of William Smith ... ... 10 Aprill
Elizabeth dau. of Mr. William Fleemen ... ... 26 „
Crestophas son of Edward Thornbore ... ... 9 May
Jams son of Jams Bolderston ... ... 4 June
Richard son of Thomas Yeadon ... ... 15 Nov
Agnes dau. of William Brown ... ... 15 „
Jane dau. of William Doram ... ... 15 „
Meare dau. of Richard Telar ... ... 29 „
Isabell dau. of Goarg Nuby ... ... 21 February

In ye year of our Lord 1748.

John son of Joseph Johnson ... ... 15 April
Christopher son of William Laurence ... ... 4 May
Ann dau. of Henery Corner ... ... 19 June
Bryan son of John Glover ... ... 31 July
Catharine dau. of Allan Kirk ... ... 5 August
John son of Johnathan Batersby 15   „
John son of Mary Noble and John Taylor ... ... 16 Nov
Ann and Elizabeth daughters of Richard Thomson 19 „
Dorathy dau. of William Smith ... ... 4 Dec
Michaelle Fleming son of Sir Wm Fleming Bart... 21 „
Ellin dau. of Milles Eckridge... ... ... 29 Jan
James son of Thos. Brenan ... ... 12 Feb
John son of John Johnson of Docker ... ... 19 „

In the year of our Lord 1749.

John son of John Hodgson ... ... 26 March
Thomas son of William Brown ... ... 2 April
George son of William Durham ... ... 11 June

Jane dau. of Joseph Johnson...	9 July
Elinor dau. of John Bachouse	9 ,,
Thomas son of Richard Taylor	20 Aug
Henry son of John Court	10 October
Mary dau. of Jonathan Batersby	5 November

Anno Domini 1750.

Susanna dau. of the Revd. Mr. Nicholson	16 April
Mary dau. of Henry Corner	22 ,,
William son of William Laurence	7 Aug
Frances dau. of Francis Newton	21 October
Jane dau. of John Slater	4 December
Thomas son of John Court	16 January

In the year of our Lord 1751.

Richard son of Robert Heblethwaite	5 April
Ann dau. of Richard Thompson	7 ,,
Margret dau. of William Dorham	16 June
John son of Abraham Cowrall [?]	7 July
William son of John Johnson	6 October
Isabel dau. of William Smith...	20 ,,
Margret dau. of William Brown	17 Nov'
Elinor dau. of Miles Ekridge...	15 December

In the year of our Lord 1752.—*New Stile.*

John son of John Backhouse...	6 Jan
John son of the Rev^d Mr. Nicholson	28 ,,
William son of John Slater	13 March
Mary dau. of Joseph Johnson...	6 April
William son of Edward Robinson	24 May
John son of John Court	2 August
Jane dau. of Michael Hodgson	23 ,,
Francis son of Thomas Bradley ... ... [*sic*] 18 March
Thomas son of Thomas Richardson	1 July
William son of William Lawrence	23 Sep
Dorothy dau. of Abraham Collin	11 Nov
Charles son of William Haughton...	13 ,,
Mary dau. of George Newby	16 Dec
William son of William Durham	26 ,,
Benjamin son of Jonathan Batersby	30 ,,

In the year of our Lord 1754.

Mary dau. of John Adcock	6 June
Mary dau. of Thos. Nicholson clerk	11 March
William son of Wm. Birket	17 ,,

Christopher son of John Slater   ...   .   29 March
John son of James Bailief   ...   .   12 May
Thomas son of Thomas Chorley   ...   .   6 June
John son of Miles Eckridge ...   .   7 „
Elizabeth dau. of Michael Hodgson   ...   .   14 July
Elizabeth dau. of Chrisr. Hodgson   ...   .   21 „
James son of John Court   ...   .   1 September
Anne dau. of Tho: Heblethwaite ...   .   8 „
Mary dau. of William Brown   ...   .   1 December
Mary dau. of John Barker   ...   .   25 „
Ann dau. of William Richardson ...   .   28 „
James son of William Lawrence ...   .   29 „

In the year of our Lord 1755.

Jane dau. of John Wetherburn   ...   .   1 January
Jane dau. of William Smith ...   .   19 „
Elizabeth dau. of Margaret Chippendale a bastard
     child   ...   .   2 February
Jennet dau. of John Slater ...   .   16 March
Margaret dau. of William Houghton   ...   .   11 May
Elizabeth dau. of John Adcock   ...   .   18 „
Mary dau. of William Durham   ...   .   17 August
Ann dau. of Joseph Johnson ...   .   16 November
Thomas son of Thos. Nicholson clerk   ...   .   23 December
John son of John Hardy   ...   .   28 „

In the year of our Lord 1756.

John son of Christopher Hodgson...   ...   .   7 March
Isabel dau. of Thomas Addison   ...   .   4 April
Christopher son of John Lawrence   ...   .   9 May
Elizabeth dau. of Robert Heblethwaite...   ...   ...   11 July
Margaret dau. of Thomas Bradley...   ...   .   26 Sep
Robert son of James Speight...   ...   .   14 Nov
Christopher son of Abraham Colin   ...   .   21 „
Richard son of Thomas Chorley   ...   .   4 December
Richard son of Peter Houghton   ...   .   26 „

In the year of our Lord 1757.

William son of William Smith   ...   .   20 Feb
Christopher son of William Berkett   ...   .   27 „
Thomas son of Thomas Robinson ...   .   13 March
Agnes dau. of William Brown   ...   .   13 „
Mary dau. of Michael Hodgson   ...   .   3 April
Thomas son of John Slater ...   .   6 „
William son of William Durham ...   .   5 June
Thomas son of William Ratson   ...   .   10 August

James son of John Adcock ... ...   6 November
Isabel dau. of Thomas Addison ... ...   27 „
Elizabeth dau. of Ruth Breaks (a bastard) ... ...   18 December

In the year of our Lord 1758.

Alice dau. of Christophor Hodgson ... ...   29 Jan
Bryan son of Bryan Dixon ... ...   5 Feb
Thomas son of William Houghtou... ... ...   6 „
Nancy dau. of Richd Thompson ... ...   6 March
William son of James Willan... ... ...   12 „
Stephen son of Stephen Emely ... ...   14 May
John son of Miles Eckrigge ... ...   28 „
Benjamin son of Jonathan Battersby ... ...   2 July
Annas dau. of John Hardy ... ...   6 August
Edward son of Edward Cummin ... ...   22 October
Jane dau. of John Nicholson... ... ...   26 November

1759.

Robert son of Bryan Dixon ... ...   25 March
Agnes dau. of Robert Heblethwaite ... ...   13 April
William son of Christopher Hodgson ... ...   22 „
Daniel son of Thos. Robinson ... ...   29 „
Francis son of James Brennan ... ...   27 May
Margaret dau. of Thos. Chorley ... ...   18 June
Hannah dau. of Michael Hodgson... ... ...   11 November
Mary dau. of Abraham Collin... ... ...   9 December
Hannah dau. of John Hardy ... ...   28 „

In the year of our Lord 1760.

William son of Willm Brown... ... ...   13 January
Emmanuel son of Willm Durham ... ...   20 „
Christopher son of Thomas Nicholson ... ...   17 February
Joseph son of Peter Troughton ... ...   17 April
Elizabeth dau. of James Willan ... ...   27 „
Mary dau. of Richard Thompson ... ...   11 May
Elizabeth dau. of Stephen Emely ... ...   11 „
Margaret dau. of Bryan Dixon ... ...   18 „
Thomas son of Edward Cummin ... ...   21 Dec

In the year of our Lord 1761.

Isabel dau. of William Houghton ... ...   8 Feb
Thomas son of James Brennan ... ...   22 „
John son of William Willan ... ...   22 „
Mary dau. of Willm Durham ... ...   29 March

Nancy dau. of John Hardy ... ...   12 April
William son of John Adcock ... ...   6 Sep
Ellin dau. of Miles Eckrigge ... ...   18 Oct
Jane dau. of Thomas Robinson ... ...   18 „
Alice dau. of Christopher Hodgson ... ...   1 Nov
Elizabeth dau. of Richard Danson... ... ...   27 Dec

In the year of our Lord 1762.

Ann dau. of Thomas Chorley ... ...   17 Jan
Richard son of Ann Whittington (a bastard) ...   23 Feb
Thomas son of Thomas Bradley ... ...   13 June
Margaret dau. of Abraham Collin ... ...   18 July
Jane dau. of Thos. North of Docker ... ...   28 August
John son of Thos. Brennan ... ...   29 „
Isabel dau. of Ellin Cummin (a bastard) ... ...   3 October

In the year of our Lord 1763.

Ellin dau. of Robt Heblethwaite ... ...   16 Jan
Robert son of James Willan ... ...   20 March
Thomas son of William Durham ... ...   17 April
Robert son of John Heblethwaite ... ...   22 May
Ellin dau. of Thos. Nicholson ... ...   29 „
Richard son of Willm Smith ... ...   24 July
James son of James Rob. ... ...   24 „
Nancy dau. of Michael Hodgson ... ...   14 Aug
Edward son of John Blackburn ... ...   21 „
Elizabeth dau. of John Hardy ... ...   16 October
Agnes dau. of Christopher Hodgson ... ...   23 „
James son of James Brennan ... ...   13 Nov

In the year of our Lord 1764.

Richard son of James and Elizabeth Johnson ...   9 March
Isabel dau. of Thomas and Isabel North ... ...   29 May
Mary dau. of John and Agnes Thornborough ...   24 June
Isabel dau. of John and Ann Willis ... ...   14 October
William son of Jonathan and Elizabeth Battersby   18 „
Jane dau. of John and Ellin Court ... ...   16 December
John son of William and Mary Sewart ... ...   25 „
Ann dau. of Robert and Elizabeth Mawdesley ...   30 „

Burials.

[At the top of the first page of Burials—which is numbered "24," though that has no Agreement with the binding of the leaves—are written the words "Jesus:" "Jesus" "and Edward Corte."]

In the thirteenth day of December in the Yeare of our Lorde god A thousande fiue hundreth thirty and eyght and in the Reigne of our Soueringe lord Kinge Henry the eight Kinge of England and of france lorde of Irelande Defender of the faythe and in earth Immediatlye under God supreme heade of the Church: of this Realme of Englande thirty   This present booke prepard ordayned and made   Witnesseth recordeth and discribeth all and singular Names and Surnames of any person or parsons to be buried at the pishe Church of Whittington in Lonsdale as well unto the years end as from thence so furth with the date of the moneth and yeare for ever: 1538

Ano regni regis Henerici octaui xxxvii°: 1546.[1]

Richard Thornton ... ...   [2] Sepult 20° die Aprilis A° p°dict
Elzabeth vxor Richardi Thornton ... ...   24 Aprilis
John Pachet ... ...   4 Augusti
James Sighwike   7   „
Elzabethe dau. of Willm Burrow   12   „
Wiffe of Miles Bayliffe ... ...   13 Januarij
John son of Myles Bayliffe   20   „

1547.

Margret dau. of Myles Bayley   ... ...   20 Septembris
Margret dau. of James Thornton ... ...   9 Februarij
Willm son of John Ward   20   „
Jenet dau. of Allexander Atkinson   ... ...   12 Marcij

---

[1] As the years of the Kings and Queens have been given in printing the Christenings they have not been repeated in printing the Burials and the Marriages, although they are given in both in the Original. The commencement of each Civil year has been inserted here though it is seldom given in the Original.
[2] The words "Sepult" and "A° p°dict" attached to each Entry in the Original are not repeated in this Volume.

1548.

Richard son of Robert Robinson	20 Aprilis
Elsabeth wiffe of Richard Johnson	13 Julij
Mabell wiffe of Oliu⁵ Thornton	24 ,,
Edmund son of Christopher Burrow	28 Augustij
Elsabeth dau. of John Johnson	3 ,,
Cateryn wiffe of Willm Adcoke	13 ,,
Maude wiffe of Willm Heaton	20 ,,
Mabell wiffe of Richard Robinson	3 Septembris

1549.

An w. of Brian Hudleston	3 Maij
Elsabeth filia Johanis Banes	20 Junij
Richard Robinson	8 Augusti
John Claghton	3 Octobris
Elsabeth w. of Myles Godsalfe	13 Septembris
Bryan Borthrige	28 Octobris
Thomas Newton	17 Novembris
Richard Sigwicke	8 Decembris
Margret w. of Edward Vstonson	20 ,,
Margret Johnson	5 Januarij
Willm Garnet...	20 Februarij

1550.

Margret w. of George Sill	26 Aprilis
Margret w. of John Ward	14 Maij
Richard Adcoke	4 Junij
Gilbert son of John Ward	28 ,,
John Barker	11 Augustij
Rowland son of Christopher Burrow	7 ,,
Thomas son of Edward Gibson	10 ,,
An dau. of Allexander Atkinson	11 ,,
Willm son of Robert Robinson	11 ,,
Bryan son of James Thornton	12 ,,
An dau. of James Slater...	4 ,,
Thomas son of Richard Hirdson	14 ,,
Margret dau. of Edward Crofte	18 ,,
Bryan son of John Hewthson...	19 ,,
James son of Willm Nealson...	19 ,,
Thomas son of Allexander Adcoke	21 ,,
Oliu⁹ son of Gyls Hardy...	21 ,,
John son of Oliu⁹ Dicconson	23 ,,
Gilbert Thornton	29 Decembris
Agnes w. of George Lupton	19 Februarij

1551.

Jane dau. of James Sclater	9 Maij
Henry son of Andraye Wilson	12 ,,
Jenet Alrey	16 Junij
George Syll	20 ,,
John son of Willm Robinson...	29 ,,
Margere w. of Bryan Hudleston	24 Augustij
Robert Parcevell	24 Octobris
Mr. Bryan Hudleston	31 ,,
Margret Paupcula	30 Novembris
Willm Thornton	21 Decembris
John son of Peter Hine	27 Januarij
Alice dau. of Willm Heaton	8 Februarij

1552.

George Lupton	8 Maij
Margret w. of Reonold Whithead	16 Marcij

1553.

Jenet dau. of John Rydall	2 Aprilis
Margret w. of Richard Burrow	4 ,,
Jane w. of Allexander Adcoke	5 ,,
John Farleton	19 ,,
James Heaton...	29 ,,
Elsabeth dau. of Henry Sclater	18 Januarij
Richard Wilton	16 Februarij
Christopher Ward	12 Marcij

1554.

Richard Banes	8 Aprilis
Dorothy Bayēs	10 ,,
Allexander Adcoke	2 ,,
Jenet w. of Willm Wilson	11 Maij
John son of Allexander Adcoke	8 Junij
Jenet w. of Thomas Hartwood	...primo die Julij
Agnes w. of John Smyth	23 ,,
John son of John Sigwicke	18 Novembris
Jenet w. of Richard Robinson	5 Decembris
Jenet w. of Xpofer Dawson	2 Februarij
Ellyn dau. of John Haryson	21 ,,
Richard son of Gilbert North	22 ,,

1555.

Thomas Hartwood	25 Maij
Margret dau. of Renold Robinson	29 ,,

Agnes w. of Thomas Newton de Newtō	19 Junij
Agnes w. of John Alrey	28 Julij
Oliu⁹ Thornton	19 Novembris
Thomas Bland...	4 Decembris
Christopher Whithead	22 Februarij
Elzabeth Apley	24 ,,
Myles Hudleston pson of Whittington	27 ,,
Jenet dau. of James Slater	2 Marcij
Jenet dau. of Thomas Johnson	8 ,,

1556.

Thomas son of James Slater	16 Aprilis
Maud uxor Jacobi Slater	21 ,,
Jenet Dicconson	22 Maij
Gilbert Tatham	6 Julij
Thomas Robinson	12 Augustij
Agnes w. of John Dawson	28 Septembris
Ellyn Paupcula	21 Januarij
Agnes dau. of John Ridall	12 Februarij
Agnes w. of Xpofer Dicconson	18 ,,
Alice Wethman	12 Maij

1557.

Elsabeth Slater	28 Maij
Wiħm Burrow	28 ,,
Elzabeth Thornton	28 ,,
An Clagton	12 Aprilis
John Nealson	17 ,,
Jenet Adcoke	19 ,,
Oliu⁹ North	28 ,,
John Slater and Jane Johnson ... In vicem-ultimo die ,,
Edward Ashburne	18 Maij
Willm Whithead	28 ,,
Thomas Cort	12 Augustij
Reynold Johnson	16 ,,
Jane Whithead	12 Septembris
Elzabeth North	11 Novēbris
Mr. Richard Newton	16 ,,
Agnes Hirdson	18 ,,
Elzabeth Hirdson	16 Decēbris
Margret Backhouse...	14 ,,
Jenet Burrow	15 ,,
Jenet Robinson	27 ,,
Wiħm Claghton	28 ,,
Jenet Howson	11 Januarij
John Burrow	20 ,,
John Robinson	22 ,,

Esabell Hutton	...	...	...	...	...	...	...	28 Januarij
Renold Borthrige	...	...	...	...	...	...	...	18 Februarij
Thomas Backhouse...	...	...	...	...	...	primo die Mcij
Thomas Robinson	...	...	...	...	...	...	4	„
James Thornton	...	...	...	...	...	...	24	„
Jenet w. of Thomas Newton Gent...	...	...	...	24	„

1558.

Richard Banes	...	...	...	...	...	...	...	5 Aprilis
Willm Thorneton	...	...	...	...	...	...	26	„
Elsabeth Newton	...	...	...	...	...	...	7 Maij
Robert Ashburne	...	...	...	...	...	...	16	„
Ellin Southworth	...	...	...	..	...	...	28	„
Thomas Vstonson	...	...	...	...	...	primo die Julij
Anthony Rimer	...	...	...	...	...	...	24	„
Jenet Simpson	...	...	...	...	...	...	8 Augustij
Agnes Sigwicke	...	...	...	...	...	...	16	„
Agnes Howson	...	...	...	...	...	...	17	„
Richard Jackson	...	...	...	...	...	...	22 Septembris
Margaret Ridall	...	...	...	...	...	...	2 Novembris
Elsabeth Hirson	...	...	...	...	...	...	16	„
Jane w. of Willm Heaton	...	...	...	...	19 Februarij
Christopher Ridall ...	...	...	...	...	...	24	„

1559.

Alice Heaton ...	...	...	...	...	...	...	14 Junij
Edmund Tatham	...	...	...	...	...	...	2 Novēbris
Henry Robinson	...	...	...	...	...	...	8	„
Christopher Burrow	...	...	...	...	...	19	„
John Ashburne pauper ...	...	...	...	...	21	„
Jenet Corte ...	...	...	...	...	...	...	2 Decembris
Willm Burrow	...	...	...	...	...	...	14 Februarij
Agnes Johnson	...	...	...	...	...	...	16	„
Mabell Robinson	...	...	...	...	...	...	26	„

1560.

Willm Burrow	...	...	...	...	...	...	...	14 Aprilis
Alice Godsalfe...	...	...	...	...	...	...	18 Maij
John Slater	...	...	...	...	...	...	...	24	„
John Smyth ...	...	...	...	...	...	...	4 Julij
Thomas Smyth	...	...	...	...	...	...	16 Septēbris
John Wilkinson	...	...	...	...	...	...	22 Octobris
Alice Ashburne	...	...	...	...	...	...	24	„
Xpofer Dicconson	...	...	...	...	...	14 Novēbris
Agnes Harrison	...	...	...	...	...	...	18	„
Mabell Robinson	...	...	...	...	...	...	26 Decēbris

Agnes Cansfeild ... ... 19 Januarij
Alice Whithead ... ... 8 Februarij
Thomas North ... ... 10 „
Alice Heaton... ... ... 18 „

1561.

Thomas Heaton ... ... 25 Maij
Thomas Slater... ... ... 16 „
Elsabeth the wiffe of Willm Thornton ... ... 3 Junij
Renold Robinson ... ... 17 „
Willm Slater ... ... 13 Septembris

1562.

Thomas Jackson ... ... 17 Maij
John Slater ... ... 8 Junij
Elsabeth Heaton ... ... 8 „
Richard Bailey ... ... 8 Augustij
Phillip Frearman ... ... 5 Septēbris
Jon Nealson ... ... 26 „
Vxor Ricardi Bannes ... ... 16 Novēbris
Vxor Ricardi Hardy ... ... 18 Decēbris
Richard Cansfeild... ... ... 11 Februarij
Mabell North ... ... 24 Marcij

1563.

John Smyth ... ... 5 Aprilis
Johannes Bannes de Sellet generosus ... ... penvltimo die Maij
Rowland Dodgeson... ... ... 20 Septembris
Vxor Johānis Slater ... ... 20 Decembris
Relict Reginalld Johnson ... ... 14 Januarij
John Robinson ... ... 10 „
The sone of Xpofer Hewtson... ... ... 3 „
John Adcoke ... ... 20 Februarij
Tho: Hirdson filius Johanis Hirdson ... ... 24 Marcij
Milo Bayliffe ... ... 3 „

1564.

Jane Hutton ... ... 18 Julij
The sone of Willm Backhouse ... ... 5 Septembris
Ric: Cort the sone Ricardi Cort ... ... 6 „
Michaell Johnson fillius Ric Johnson ... ... 12 „
Alice Bayliffe ... ... 13 Novembris
Elyn Slater widow ... ... 28 „
Elyn Burton vidua ... ... 20 Januarij
Bryan Cansfeild ... ... 21 „

Agnes Harrison vidua	24 Januarij
John Ridall	26 „
Vidua Waller	16 Februarij
Uxor Johanis Burrow	17 „
Relict Christopher Burrow	24 „
Isabell Cansfeild	16 Marcij

1565.

Anthony fillius pauperis...	primo die Aprilis
James sone of Thomas Johnson	13 Septembris
James Thornton	18 Novembris
Eldred dau. of Antony Frearman	3 Decembris
Mabell dau. of Robert Burrow	5 „
Ellyn dau. of Mr. Thomas Newton	23 „
Willm son of Ric: Johnson	3 Januarij
Leonard son of Willm Ewan	5 „
Miles son of John Burrow	8 „
Elsabeth w. of Willm Adcoke	25 „
Sibell w. of Antony Frearman	17 Februarij
Margaret Cort dau. of Ric: Cort	27 „

1566.

Bryan Robinson	8 Aprilis
Vxor Ricardi Wethman	14 „
Peter Hine	ultimo die „

1567.

Alice Relict Johanis Adcoke	22 Aprilis
Edward Gibson	27 Septembris
Relict Edward Gibson	27 „
Vxor Johanis Dowson	30 „
Edward Thornton	primo die Octobris
Marmaduke Cort	20 „
Johne doughter of Henry Patchat	2 Novembris
Thomas Dawney	14 Decembris

1568.

Robert Leaminge et Willm Robinson	5 Aprilis
Relict Edmundi Tatham...	8 Maij
Relicta Thome Dawney	10 „
Thomas sou of Oliuᵖ Dicconson	4 Junij
Alice w. of Richard Godsalfe	16 Decembris
Stephen fillius Gulielmi Johnson	16 „
James Toluson	4 Februarij
Willm Kinge	12 Marcij
Lawrance Cansfeild	8 „

1569.

John Heaton	2 Aprilis
Willm Nealson	2 „
Margret w. of Richard Tatham	3 Maij
John the sone of Willm Adcoke	20 „
Jenet w. of Willm Bortbrige...	10 Junij
Bryan Bland	20 „
The wiffe of Rowland Heaton	24 „
The doughter of Rowland Heaton...	27 „

1570.

Antony son of Thomas Bayliffe	10 Maij
Jane uxor Ricardi Willye	10 „
Thomas Bayliffe	12 „
Relict John Robinson	5 Junij
The doghter of Giles Hardy	5 Augustij
Robert Gurnell alias Croft	22 „
Elzabeth w. of Miles Bayliffe...	16 Januarij
Richard North	17 „
Uxor Jacobi Awrey	21 „
Uxor Thomae Johnson	23 „
Richard Robinson	11 Februarij
Robert son of Xpofer Skyrreth	7 Marcij
Uxor Jacobi Sigwicke	20 „

1571.

Alice Bayliffe dau. of Thomas Baliffe	5 Octobris
Alice dau. of John Harries	9 Decebris
Wiffe of Lawrance Casfeild	22 Februarij
John the sone of Renold Whithead	26 „
Thomas Clarkson	22 Marcij

1572.

Elzabeth w. of Robert Robinson	9 Julij
The sone of Edmund Whithead	10 „
Elsabeth w. of Thomas Hall	13 „
Elsabeth w. of Simond Sill	23 Novembris
John son of Richard Thornton et Ellin his wiffe...	18 Decembris
Margaret w. of Richard Johnson	6 Februarij
Wiffe of Renold Thornton	24 Januarij
Wiffe of Robert Cort	25 Februarij
Xpofer Mellinge	8 Marcij

1573.

Wiłłm Vstonson	12 Maij
Wiffe of John Robinson	20 Novēbris

1574.

Elzabeth Stones	28 Marcij
John Robinson	26 Junij
Vxor Wiłłm Ewan	8 Octobris
Elsabeth Whithead	27 Januarij
An Pachet dau. of Robert	14 Februarij
Uxor Renold Borthrige	24 Marcij

1575.

Uxor John Wilton	26 Marcij
Uxor Jacobi Slater	24 Aprilis
An dau. of Bryan Dawney	26 „
filia Bryan Dawney	3 Maij
Elsabeth Harryson	6 „
Wiffe of James Robinson	3 Junij
Vxor Jacobi Thornton	7 Julij
Miles son of Rowland Whithead	12 „
Richard son Edmundi Whithead	16 Septēbris
Wiłłm son Rowland Whithead	18 „
Allexander son of Gilbert Atkinson	28 „
John Allanby	5 Novembris
Myles Johnson	20 „
John Johnson	9 Januarij
Thomas Bland pson of Whittington	16 Februarij

1576.

John Robinson	28 Marcij
Margret dau. of Myles Hudleston	27 Aprilis
John Robinson	28 Marcij
Vxor Persevell	28 Maij
Vxor Thome Smyth	14 Junij
John son of Thomas Gibson	21 Augustij
Thomas Dawney	15 Novembris
Willm Johnson	10 Decembris
Egidius[1] Hardy	28 Februarij
Thomas son of Edward Dicconson	4 Marcij
Daughter of Marmaduke Hutton	12 Marcij

[1] Giles

1577.

Uxor Willm Burrow	4 Aprilis
Thomas Johnson	26 ,,
Jenet dau. of Thomas Smyth	2 Augusti
Mr. Myles Hudleston [1]	26 Julij
Vxor Edwardi North	27 Augusti
filia Thome North	13 Decembris
Thomas son of Xpofer Hewtson	20 Januarij
filia Marmaduk Robinsone	8 Februarij

1578.

Richard Hirdson	20 Aprilis
Rowland Banes	2 Maij
James Johnson	27 Augustij
Caterin Hudleston	28 ,,
Relict Renold Robinson	primo die Septembr
Edmūd Heysem	28 Novembris
M^{tris} Cateran Hudleston	20 Februarij
Relict Thomae Johnson	8 Marcij
Bryan Godsalfe	4 ,,

1579.

John Harryson	4 Aprilis
Allan Sigwicke	19 Junij
Willm Lupton ⎱	7 Julij
Uxor Richard Tatham ⎰	
Syls wiffe...	24 Octobris
Edward Tayler	12 Novēbris
Vxor Henrici Pachet	16 Decembris
John son of Thomas Robinson	29 ,,
Sone of Willm Barrow	5 Januarij
Vxor Roger Harrison	15 Februarij
Agnes Bland	24 ,,

1580.

Mary Thornton	28 Marcij
Sone of John Keysby	3 Junij
Vxor John Sigswicke	...primo Augustij
Xpofer Hewtson	2 Septembris
Relict Willm Nealson	primo die Octobris
Relict John Harryson	9 ,,
filius Elizabethae Harryson	14 ,,

[1] This entry is repeated at the bottom of the page on which it occurs, but the page has been turned upside-down when the second entry was made.

Richard Richardson	29 Octobris
filia Renold Johnson	6 Novembris
Thomas Batty...	18 Januarij
Allexander Atkinson	26 ,,
Bryan Dawney	10 Februarij
John Sigswicke	24 Marcij

1581.

Renold Thornton	25 Marcij
Relict Renold Johnson	28 ,,
Rilick Marmaduke Robinson	22 Maij
An dau. of Richard Knight	28 Junij
Thomas Johnson	20 Augustij

1582.

Uxor Martyn Croft	6 Aprilis
An dau. of John Sigswicke	10 ,,
Relict Richard Wilton	16 ,,
Jenet Robinson	19 Junij
Relict Brian Cansfeilds	7 Julij
Gilbert Atkinson	10 Septembris
Jane filia Gilbert Atkinson	26 Octobris
Thomas Hall	2 Januarij
Richard Wilkinson	10 Marcij
Alizander Slater	23 ,,

1583.

filia Gilbert Atkinson	25 Marcij
Elsabeth filia Ricardi Cort	13 Aprilis
Vxor Johanis Ridall	22 ,,
Elsabeth filia Johanis Keysby	12 Maij
Thomas son of Marmaduke Robinson	...primo die Julij
Rallinge Heaton	17 Octobris
Richard Tatham	18 ,,
Uxor Brani Godsalfe	30 Januarij

1584.

Relict Toluson	24 Maij
Xpofer Holme...	23 ,,
Renold Slater	5 Augustij
Simond Sill	16 Septembris
Willm Backhouse	8 Novembris
John son of Richard Thornton	6 Decembris
Elsabeth dau. of Gilbert Atkinson...	10 Januarij
An Paupcula	24 Marcij

1585.

WiHm Borthridge	9 Augustij
Thomas North	26 Decebris
Renold Johnson	11 Januarij

1586.

filia Thomas Nealson	22 Maij
Oliu⁹ Dicconson	28 Augustij
Au dau. of Richard Sigswicke	24 Septembris
Elsabeth wiffe of Robert Burrow	8 Octobris
Margret uxor Mr. Thomae Newton	24 ,,
Elzabeth w. of Robert Pachet	20 Januarij
Relict Jacobi Heaton	15 ,,
Elsabeth Adcoke	12 Februarij
Robert Robinson	7 Marcij
Willm Sigswicke	9 ,,
Robert Whithead	21 ,,

1587.

Henry Slater	27 Marcij
Thomas Dicconson	5 Aprilis
Ellin dau. of Edward Dicconson	5 ,,
Wiffe of James Cort	25 ,,
Thomas Cansfeild	12 Maij
Vxor Gilberti Heaton	25 ,,
Anthony Whithead	23 Octobris
WiHm filius Gulielmo [sic] Sigswicke	ultimo die Augustij
Uxor Johannis Lynckolne	24 Octobris
Mr. WiHm Hudleston	17 Novembris
Margret wiffe of John Johnson	eodem die ,,
Vxor Roberti Robinson	21 ,,
Vxor Gulielmi Herod	28 ,,
John Cokynge	8 Januarij
Katheryne Noble	21 ,,
Richard Tayler	28 ,,
Relict Borthrigg	30 ,,
Agnes w. of George Toppinge	8 Februarij
Jenet w. of John Pachet	14 ,,
Gilbert North	20 ,,
Jane dau. of Thomas Sigswicke	ultimo die ,,
Edmund Burrow	4 Marcij
Jenet uxor Gulielmi Slater	21 ,,

1588.

Jane uxor Edmundi Burrow	20 Maij
Mr. Robert Banes de Selloth	7 Junij

Ellynge uxor Thomae Mellinge ... ... 18 Junij
Wiffe of Oliu⁹ Dicconson ... ... 18 Julij
Elsabeth uxor Gilberti North... ... ... 5 Septebris
Uxor Ricardi Hirdson ... ... 6 Novembris
Alice filia Henrici Brabin 5   „
Uxor Gulielmi Ewan ... ... 16 „

1589.

Spurria Johannis Ewan ... ... 27 Novembris
James et John children of Marmaduk Sclater ...5 & 7 Decembris

1590.

Richard son of John Johnson ... ... 21 Maij
Uxor Gulielmi Heaton ... ... 22 Julij
Uxor Johannis Bland ... ... 8 Septebris
John Dowson ... ... 22 Decembris
James Batty ... ... 15 Januarij
Esabell uxor Briani Dicconson ... ... 25 „
Spurria Katheryne filia Edwardi Cansfeild ... ... 13 Februarij
Jenet dau. of Brian Dicconson ... ... 14 „
An dau. of John Johnson ... ... 10 Marcij

1591.

Jane Hall dau. of Thomas Hall ... ... 30 Marcij
Jenet w. of Richard Robinson ... ... primo die Aprilis
Margret wiffe of Thomas Dicconson ... ...   „   „
Symond son of Renold Godsalfe 25   „
Elsabeth uxor Xpoferi Mellinge ... ... 7 Maij
John Godsalfe... ... ... 12 Augustij
Elsabeth dau. of Marmaduke Sclater 22   „
Thomas Thornton ... ... 3 Septembris
Richard Knight ... ... 6 Octobris
Elsabeth uxor Ricardi Hall ... ... 13 Novembris
Isabell Moore... 20   „
Rilict Harlinge vidua ... ... 6 Januarij
Thomas son of Leonard Carter 9   „

1592.

George son of John Harrison ... ... 28 Marcij
Rallinge Whithead ... ... 27 Augustij
Margret Lupton Pauparcula ... ... 3 Septembris
Margret w. of Richard Godsalfe 4   „
Ellinge dau. of Thomas Hirdson ... ... 30 „
Wilłm Heaton ... ... 11 Octobris
An dau. of Thomas Heaton ... ... 14 „

Margret dau. of John Barrow... ... ... 11 Novembris
An w. of Richard Hudleston ... ... .3 Decembris
Elsabeth w. of Willm Backhouse 13   „
Margret Relict Plummer   ... ...primo die Februarij
Margery w. of Willm Jackson   ... ... 8 Marcij
James Cort   14   „
John son of John Heaton   23   „

1593.

Margret Robinson ... ... 6 Maij
An uxor Johannis Johnson ... ... 5 Junij
Jane dau. of Symond Hutton   ... ... 10 Augustij
Thomas Smyth   ... ... 26 Septembris
John son of Richard Hardy ... ... ultimo die   „
John son of Aethare Fouscroft   30   „
Agnes Relict Bryan Bland   ... ... 5 Decebris
Agnes dau. of George Backhouse ... ... 4 Februarij
Elsabeth w. of John Dowson 17   „

1594.

Ellinge dau. of John Barrow ... ... 3 Aprilis
Willm son of Thomas Newton gent 3   „
John Hodgeson   ... ... 20 Augustij
Margret w. of John Hodgeson   22   „
Tristram Sill... 29   „
Isabell dau. of Mr. Lambert ... ... 19 Octobris
John son of Anthony Hewtson   21   „
Richard Godsalfe ... ... 14 Novembris
Elsabeth Awrey 21   „
John son of Willm Ewan   ... ... 7 Januarij
Sibell dau. of John Harries 21   „
Thomas son of Christopher Stors ... ... 15 Februarij
Christopher Nealson   ... ... 17 Marcij

1595.

Willm son of Christopher Hewtson   ... ... 13 Maij
Johne dau. of Athure Fouscroft   ... ... 14 Septembris
Robert son of John Dawney 19   „
Adam son of Willm Lonsdale   ... ... 16 Octobris
Edward son of John North ... ... 10 Novembris
John Godsalfe... 14   „
John Johnson... ... ... 4 Decembris

1596.

Myles Bayliffe son of John ... ... 10 Aprilis
Jenet dau. of John Bayliffe ... ... 2 Maij

Wiłłm Carter	2	Augustij
Athure Fouscroft	11	Decembris
John Willton	12	„
Alice Bayliffe	12	„
Elsabeth dau. of Wiłłm Sclater	16	„
Elsabeth Cansfeild	20	„
Ellynge dau. of Mr. John North	23	„
Jenet w. of Christopher Vstonson	26	„
Elsabeth w. of John Burrow	22	Januarij
John son of Mr. John Newton pson	3	Februarij
Edmund Miars gent	6	Marcij
Jane w. of Mr. John Banes	17	„
Mabell dau. of John Johnson...	24	„

1597.

Thomas Newton gent	26	Marcij
An dau. of Richard North	6	Aprilis
Wiłłm Bland	13	„
Elsabeth Batty	13	„
Elling w. of Edmund Whithead	16	„
Richard son of Edmund Myars gent	26	„
Jane dau. of James Blackburne	5	Maij
Thomas son of Richard Hall	27	„
Wiłłm son of Thomas Whithead	7	Junij
Jane dau. of Marmaduke Sclater	8	„
Wiłłm son of Thomas Heaton ... ...ultimo die		„
Isabell dau. of James Blackburne	5	Julij
Elsabeth w. of Francis Toluson	19	„
Margery dau. of Mr. John North	3	Augustij
Jane Laborey	3	Septembris
Robert Stephenson	24	Augustij
An dau. of John Bland	13	Septembris
George son of Athure Fouscroft	23	Octobris
Elling w. of John Ewan...	3	Novembris
John son of Wiłłm Jackson	20	„
John son of Richard North	20	Decembris
Myles Johnson	2	Januarij
Alice w. of Willm Robinson	9	„
Margret w. of Willm Bland ... ... ultimo die		„
Paupcula...	15	Februarij
Paupcula...	16	„
Thomas Sigswicke	3	Marcij
Christopher Vstenson	4	„
James son of John Toluson	7	„

1598.

Thomas son of Bryan Nealson	13	Aprilis
Jane dau. of Willm Slater	24	„

L

Alice w. of Richard Robinson ... ... 17 Maij
Jane w. of Thomas Godsalfe ... ... 24 „
John Dawney ... ... 5 Junij
Alice Backhouse ... ... 6 „
Margret dau. of Wiłłm Sclater ... ... 19 „
Richard son of Thomas Bland ... ... 6 Julij
Isabell w. of Wiłłm Ewan ... ... 7 „
Richard Bannes gent ... ... 22 „
Ellinge w. of Wiłłm Sclater ... ... 30 „
Elsabeth w. of Thomas Whithead ... ... 5 Augustij
Jenet et Elsabeth daughters of Richard Hall ... 5 Novēbris
Elsabeth w. of Thomas Robinson ... ... 16 Decembr.
John son of Richard Robinson ... ... 10 Januarij
Willm son of John Heaton ... ... 21 Februarij

1599.

An w. of Wiłłm Lupton ... ... 6 Junij
John son of Richard Robinson ... ... 14 Julij
Bryan son of Jams Bland ... ... 15 „
Christopher son of Bryan Nealson ... ... 11 Octobris
James Awrey ... ... 10 Novembris
Renold Whithead ... ... 21 Januarij
Agnes w. of Edward Ashburne ... ... 22 „
Dorothe w. of George Backhouse ... ... 6 Februarij
John son of John Johnson ... ... 14 „
Augnes Belks... ... ... 2 Marcij
Richard son of John Beley ... ... 17 „

1600.

Wiłłm¹ Margeson ... ... 2 Maij
Jane w. of Wiłłm Vstenson ... ... 7 Junij
Elsabeth dau. of Robert Dicconson ... ... 28 Augustij
Jenet w. of John Barrow ... ... 12 Octobris
James Backhouse ... ... 4 Novembris
Margret Wilton ... ... 17 „
Isabell w. of Edward Skyreth ... ... 18 „
Marmaduk Newton, gent ... ... 26 Decembris
Richard son of John Knight ... ... 27 „
Sone of James Heaton ... ... 27 „
Wiłłm son of John Johnson ... ... primo die Januarij
Thomas son of Robert Cansfeild ... ... 14 Marcij
Thomas Sclater ... ... 15 „

1601.

Wiłłm Sclater ... ... 14 Aprilis
Margret Whithead ... ... 15 Maij

¹ Willm over Richard struck through.

James son of Thomas Bland ... ... 8 Augustij
Alice w. of Thomas Tayler ... ... 3 Septembr
Elsabeth w. of Thomas Hirdson ... ... ultimo die „
Wiffe of Thomas Nealson ... ... 20 Octobr.
Dorothe dau. of Mr. Lambert ... ... 20 Januarij
Jenet w. of Richard Sigswicke ... ... 7 Februarij
Ellinge w. of Thomas Sigswicke ... ... 10 „
Thomas Nealson ... ... 23 Marcij

1602.

Marmaduke Robinson ... ... 28 Marcij
John son of Edward Atkinson ··· ... ... 29 „
James son of James Heaton ... ... 6 Maij
Thomas son of James Bland ... ... 11 Junij
Bryan son of Symond Dawney ... ... 26 Octobris
Alice dau. of John Johnson ... ... 13 Novembr
Alice w. of Symond Dawney ... ... 29 Decembris
Wiłłm Heaton ... ... 5 Januarij
John Burrow ... ... 27 „
Thomas Mellinge ... ... 13 Februarij
Gilbert Heaton ... ... 14 Marcij

1603.

Margret dau. of John Godsalfe ... ... ultimo die Marcij
George Overend ... ... 5 Aprilis
Spurrius Francis Russell sone of Tho: Russell ... 9 „
Elsabeth Sharpe ... ... 10 „
Wiłłm Robinson ... ... 16 „
Jenet w. of Rallinge Heaton ... ... 23 „
Wiłłm Patchet ... ... 24 „
Alice w. of Thomas Bland cum filio Johane... ... 25 „
Alizander son of Bryan Nealson ... ... 7 Maij
Margret w. of Renold Dodgeshon ... ... 20 „
An late wiffe of Thomas North ... ... 24 Junij
An wiffe of Marmaduke Hutton ... ... 28 Septembr
Jane dau. of Francis Hirdson ... ... 12 Decembr
Bryan son of Francis Hirdson ... ... 17 „
Richard Cort ... ... 19 Februarij
Alice w. of John Buser ... ... 27 „
Ellinge dau. of Francis Hirdson ... ... 4 Marcij

1604.

Wiłłm son of John Barrow ... ... 23 Junij
Jenet Relict Thomae Johnson ... ... 25 Septembris
Edward North gent ... ... 2 Novembr
Wiłłm Robinson ... ... 28 „

Jenet Relict Thomae Mellinge ... ... ultimo die Januarij
Robert Burrow ... ...ultimo die Decembr
James son of Thomas Tayler ... ... 7 Februarij

1605.

Marmaduke Sclater prish clarke ... ... 24 Aprilis
Alizander Atkinson ... ... 27 Junij
Doughter of Mr. Thomas Carus ... ... 7 Septembr
Thomas son of Bryan Nealson ... ... 10 Octobris
Thomas son of Willm Brabin gent ... ... 8 Januarij

1606.

Willm son of Richard Robinson ... ... 10 Marcij
Robert son of Samuell Lambert gent ... ... 21 „
Jenet dau. of Richard Godsalfe ... ... 7 Septembris
Bryan Dicconsou ... ... 14 Novembr
John son of Richard Robinson ... ... 7 Februarij
Jenet dau. of Richard Robinson ... ... 12 „
Elsabeth uxor Johanis Cokin... ... ... 17 Marcij

1607.

John Bland ... ... 22 Aprilis
Thomas son of John Smyth ... ... 4 Maij
John son of Thomas Whormby ... ... 25 Novembris
Richard Hudleston gent. ... ... 5 Decembris
Richard Johnson ... ... 14 „
Ellinge dau. of Leonard Ewan ... ... 15 „
Willm son of Willm Whithead ... ... 4 Februarij
Doughter of Mr. Thomas Carus ... ... 24 „
Alice uxor Henrici Patchet ... ... 2 Marcij
Roger son of Willm Cansfeild ... ... 5 „
Alice dau. of Richard Cort ... ... 7 „
John son of Richard Robinson ... ... 14 „

1608.

Jenet dau. of James Heaton ... ... 13 Junij
Willm Adcoke... ... ... 22 „
Elsabeth uxor Roberti Stephenson ... ... 11 Januarij

1609.

Jane uxor Renoldi Whithead... ... ... 11 Junij
Jenet Relict Willm Heaton ... ... 6 Octobris
Thomas Thornton ... ... 13 „
Ellyn Relict Richardi Thornton ... ... 14 „

James North	3 Novembris
Jane uxor Jacobi North...	9 Decembris
Elsabeth Mellinge	10 Februarij
John Cansfeild	20 Marcij

1610.

Agnes uxor Lenardi Cansfeild	19 Aprilis
Elsabeth dau. of Richard Dawney...	29 ,,

1611.

William Whithead	4 Aprilis
Henry Pachet	20 Maij
James Sigswicke	26 Septebris
An dau. of Richard Knight	21 Octobr
Margret w. of Marmaduke Margeson	17 Novembr
Elsabeth dau. of Thomas North	18 Decembr
Trystram Bourdall	18 Januarij
Barbara Wilton	17 Marcij

1612.

Thomas son of Myles Bayliffe	18 Julij
Willm son of Thomas Tayler...	4 Januarij
An dau. of Willm Burrow	7 ,,
Elsabeth Fabat	17 ,,
Alice Relict Rowlandi Godsalfe	27 ,,
An dau. of Edmund Tatham	19 ,,
Francis Toluson	25 ,,
Elsabeth w. of Henry Eykrige	20 Februarij
Marmaduke son of John Robinson	21 Marcij

1613.

Thomas Hobson	5 Julij
Oliu⁹ North	primo die Octobris
Thomas Jenyngs	9 ,,
James son of James Russell	15 Decembr
Thomas Borthrige	7 ,,
John son of James Haryes	8 ,,
Marmaduke Hutton	4 Januarij
Alice Eykrige	3 Februarij
Elsabeth w. of James Awrey	22 Marcij
Em: w. of Thomas North	23 ,,

1614.

Anthony Hewtson	14 Julij
An uxor Gulielmi Brabin gent	17 ,,

Thomas Godsalfe	19 Octobris
John son of Henry Eykrige	5 Novembris
John son of Thomas Keysby	2 Januarij
Margret w. of George Backhouse	23 ,,
Thomas North	2 Februarij
John son of Richard Dawney...	6 Marcij
John son of Bryan Widder	6 ,,
Gilbert Dicconson	13 ,,

1615.

Margret w. of James Blackburne	5 Aprilis
George son of Richard Robinson	17 Maij
John Robinson, tanner	16 Marcij
Wiłłm Johnson de Docker	vicessimo primo die Octobris
Agnes w. of Leonard Ewan	19 Novembris
Thomas son of John Balye	8 Decembris
Elizabeth w. of Henrye Eykrigge	15 Januarij
Jenet w. of John Caysbie	21 ,,
Thomas son of Leonard Ewan	12 Marcij
Agnes Relict ould Wiłłm Borrowe	14 ,,

1616.

Isabell w. of Bryan Bland	decimo die Aprilis
Elizabeth w. of Richard Hutton	12 Maij
Margret Relict John Godsalf de Newton	24 ,,
Alice Relict Richard Robinson	decimo die Junij
Jenet Relict Thomas North minor	6 Julij
Margret w. of Richard North de Docker	25 Septembris
Jenett Relict Richard Knight	19 Octobris
Ann dau. of Richard Cansfild	27 ,,
Jane dau. of James Johnson	...tertio die Novembris
Agnes Relict Anthonye Huitson	...quinto die ,,
Alice dau. of Bryan Bland	...sexto die ,,
Anne Rigge spinster	...decimo nono die ,,

From the xix daye of December 1616 unto the iiij[th] day of November
1617 next ensuinge it pleased God to visit this pish of Whittington with a dangerous diseasse or contagious sicknes within
the which time and space afforsaid there was sicke in this said
pish about twoe hundred in which tyme there deseased as
followeth vid.:

Xpofer Mellinge	11 Januarij
James Mellinge	17 ,,
James Bland de Newton	24 ,,
Wiłłm Genings	quarto die Februarij
Dorethie w. of Renold Bordrigge	...decimo die ,,

Mr. George Brabin ... ... undecimo die Fedruarij
John Johnson senior ... ...decimo tertio „
Anne Edmundson servant to Mr. Brabin ...decimo quarto „
Mabell Relict Thomas Hebson ... ... „ „
Wiłłm Lansdall ... ... „ „

1617.

Uxor Paupcula ... ... 29 Marcij
Elizabeth Relict Wiłłm Adcocke ... ... primo die Aprilis
Mr. Wiłłm Brabin ... ... tertio die „
Freeis Hutton Relict Symon Hutton ... ... eodem die „
Mabell Relict Wiłłm Gennings ... ... quinto die „
Jane w. of Marmaduke Cockin ... ... septimo die „
Agnes Relict Wiłłm Lansdall ... ...decimo sexto „
Edward Scayffe ... ...ultimo die „
Mabell w. of James Heaton ... ... 8 Maij
Robert Dowthwaite ... ... 12 „
George son of Richard Hutton and Mrs. Toppin ... 13 „
James Bland de Docker... ... ... 15 „
Katherin w. of John Johnson younger ... ... 21 „
Thomas son of Robert Bethem ... ... 20 „
Relict ould Richard Johnson... ... ... 31 „
Isabell w. of Thomas Caysbie ... ... 4 Julij
Thomas Caysbie ... ... 11 „
Willm son of Xpofer Mellinge ... ... 8 Octobris
Richard Halle ... ... 4 Novembris

The end of the sicknesse afforsaid.

Jane w. of James Dodgson ... ... 16 Novembris
Margret w. of John Johnson ... ... 26 „
John Caysbie ... ... 3 Januarij
Leonard son of John Carter ... ... sexto die „
Elizabeth Bordrigge ... ... 8 „
Agnes Relict Xpofer Huitson ... ... 17 „
Alice w. of John Harries ... ... ultimo die „

1618.

Elizabeth Bewser ... ... 2 Aprilis
Mabbell Bland ... ... 3 „
John son of John Hardye ... ... 15 „
Jane dau. of Wiłłm Kidd ... ... 16 „
Isabell w. of John Bland ... ... 20 Junij
Catherin dau. of Richard Dickonson de Docker ... 21 „
Richard Baliffe ... ... undecimo die Augustij
Edward Atkinson ... ... quinto die Septembris
Alice w. of Mr. Henrie Brabin ... ... 8 „

Leonard Cansfeeld ... ... 25 Octobris
Richard North gent ... ... 12 Decembris
John Harries de Newton ... ... ultimo die „
Ellin w. of Thomas Hirdson ... ... 27 Januarij
John Heaton de Docker... ... ... 2 Marcij
Elizabeth w. of Wiłłm Kempe ... ... 8 „
Richard Robinson alias Robins ... ... 11 „
M'gret Relict Richard Robinson p'd ... ... 19 „

1619.

Marye Relict Richard Baliffe ... ... quarto die Aprilis
Elizabeth Clarkson ... ... 25 „
Isabell w. of Edmund Whitehead ... ... 21 Maij
Wiłłm son of Leonard Carter ... ... 25 „
John Lickbarrowe [1]... ... ... 28 „

1620.

Elizabeth Relict John Sigswicke ... ... 9 Aprilis
Marmaduke Robinson ... ... 23 Maij
John Ewan ... ... 26 Novembris
Richard Vstenson ... ... 20 Decembris
Elizabeth dau. of Willm Kidd ... ... 6 Januarij
Edmund Adcocke ... ... 2 Marcij

1621.

John Townson ... ... 21 Aprilis
Relict Marmaduke Robinson ... ... 31 Augustij
Ann dau. of Thomas North minor ... ... eodem die „
Dorothie fillia John Carter ... ... 2 Septembris
John Slater ... ... 16 „
Thomas Gibsou ... ... 20 Novembris
Anne fillia Thomae Bland ... ... 21 „
Jane uxor Leonard Carter ... ... 25 Januarij
Thomas Whitehead... ... ... 28 „
Jenet uxor Thō: Gibson ... ... 21 Februarij
Margret uxor Oliver Dickonson ... ... 26 „
Relict Edmund Nealson... ... ... 20 Marcij

1622.

M'grett Relict Edward Atkinson ... ... 20 Maij
M'grett uxor James Newton ... ... 12 Augustij
Wiłłm Vstenson ... ...

[1] A blank has been left at top of this page of original large enough to contain two entries.

John Wilson ... ... primo die Januarij
Vxor Thomas Carter 2   „
Jane Gibson 5   „
Wiłłm son of Wiłłm Slater ... ... 2 Marcij
A poore man of Bolton 3   „
A youth drowned in a well 6   „

1623.

A poore boy of Sedbridge ... ... 9 Aprilis
Edmund Burrowe .. .. 12 Maij
Francis Hirdson ... ... 19 „
Marye Bower ... ... 29 Junij
John Harrison ... ... 4 Julij
Mr. Baynes ... ... 30 „
Ellin Cockeram ... ... 6 Augustij
Leonard Ewan 16   „
Thomas Dawnie ... ...primo die Septembris
Agnes fillia James Bordrigge... 13   „
Edmund Whitehead 16   „
Rowland Burrowe ... ... eodem die „
Rowland Johnson ... ... 23 Octobris
Wiłłm Cirkbryd ... ... 20 Novembris
fillius Edwardi Barrowe ... ... eodem die „
Thomas son of Richard Hale 30   „
John Hodgson alias Moresyde ... ... decimo die Decembris
Symon Dawnie ... ... quinto die Januarij
filia John Hardie 11   „
Ellin uxor John Morsyde 14   „
Ellin uxor Richard Knight 20   „
Uxor John Dickonson ... ... 7 Februarij
John Dickonson 8   „
Richard Knight ... ... decimo die „
Jenet uxor Bryan Gibson 15   „

1624.[1]

Lenard Carter ... ... 13 Maij

1630.

Myles son of Henry Ayckrigge ... ... 16 Aprilis
Alice dau. of Rowland Whithead 19   „
John Newton, gent., parson of Whittington... undecimo die Julij
* * son of Wiłłm Bordrigge ... ... primo die Augustij
Michaell Bordrigge... ... ... quinto die   „

[1] The remainder of the page—about a third is left blank, as is also the top
    of the next page—about one-eighth of it. It will be noted there are no
    entries of Burials from 1624-1630.

Margrett Johnson widdowe ... ... 11 Augustij
Elizabeth fillia Randall Kewe... ... ... 2 Februarij
Richard North de Whittington 11   „
Agnes w. of Wittm Whitehead 26   „
Henrie son of Thomas Johnson ... ... 24 Marcij

1631.

Robtt son of Richard Manserge ... ... 23 Apprilis
John Vstenson poysened himselfe... ... ...quinto die Junij
* * son of Richard Backhouse ... ... 26 Augustij
Thomas Carter de Newton ... ... 17 Septembris
Alice dau. of Robtt Robinson ... ... primo die Octobris
spuria Margrett filia Edwardi Baliffe ... ... 8 Novembris
Richard Johnson Senior... ... ... 8 Decembris
Jane dau. of Thomas North de Whittington... ... 5 Januarij
Anne w. of Wittm Townson 30   „
Agnes w. of John Johnson ... ... ultimo die   „
John son of Rowland Whitehead ... ... 18 Februarie
Jane w. of Johann Dickonson ... ... ultimo die   „
Margrett Pachett ... ... septimo die Marcij
John son of Thomas Carter 20   „

1632.

Alice Lupton ... ... 8 Aprilis
spurria Margrett dau. of Francis Brockherste and Margrett
       Pachett ... ... 16 Junij
Elizabeth w. of Rowland Ewan ... ... 21 Augustij
Alice Blande, widdowe, Relict James Blande ... 6 Septembris
Jane filia Edwardi Burrowe ... ... 12 Octobris
James son of George Sigswicke 27   „
* * dau. of John Hardie ... ... secundo die Novembris
Jane Sands widdow of age about four score and
       twelve yeares 20   „
Elizabeth Relict Francis Hirdson ... ... 20 Decembris
Anne filia Edwardi Cockin ... ... vicessimo sexto Februarij
George Sigswicke ... ...decimo quinto Marcij

1633.

James Dodgson ... ... 27 Aprilis
Jane Dowthwait widdowe ... ... 4 Maij
Margrett dau. of Marmaduke Margeson ... ... 17 „
Jane w. of Thomas Bland ... ... 25 „
Elizabeth filia Wittm Harries ... ... 10 Junij
John Johnson ... ... 16 „
Marie filia Wittm Maddison ... ... 3 Julij
Jane w. of Thomas Brabin gent ... ... 19 „

Richard Newton, gent, vicar of Mellinge	... ...	8 Augustij
George Backhouse		19 Septembris
Margery ye wife of Thom Johnson		
Ann dau. of Thom Blackburne		20 November
Margret dau. of Brian Dickonson and Ann Dawny		eodem die
Agnes w. of Robt Jackson of Newton		27 November
John son of Robt Robinson		4 December
Margery w. of Thom Johnson		14 ,,
Isabell Jackson al's Woodhous of Newton		23 ,,
Dorothy dau. of Ric Taylor		25 ,,
Edw: Crosbie late of Tybie		5 Februarij
Margret w. of Robt. Robinson		11 ,,
Mabell w. of Bryan Nealson		10 Marcij
A daughter of John Dawny		21 ,,

1634.

Agnes w. of Olyr Kyrkbride		28 Marcij
John Knight		6 Maij
Willm Burrow		22 Julij
Isabell Sill widdow...		7 Augustij
Willm Harrison		24 ,,
Ann Dowthwaite		26 ,,
Willm Whitehead		30 ,,
Dorothie Knight, widdow		22 September
Margret Melling Relict		24 Januarie
Willm son of John Hardie		2 Februarie
A sonne of Thom Dowthwayte		16 ,,

1635.

Ric son of Thom Johnson Junior		12 Aprill
Ellen Relict John Harrison		23 ,,
Ric son of John Lonsdall		2 Maij
Willm Maddison		11 ,,
Ric: Bordrick		17 ,,
Thom son of John North gent		25 ,,
Ellen dau. of Willm Harrison		13 June
A daughter of Willm Brabyn gent		27 ,,
Jennet w. of John Smith		21 November
Ellen w. of Edw: Dowthwaithe		18 ,,
Elize Hudleston		20 March
Willm son of Richard Dawney		21 ,,
Eliza: dau. of Robt Bethom		24 ,,

1636.

Ric. Hardie		25 March
Willm son of John Whitehead		15 Aprill

Dorothy dau. of Ric. Bordrick	21 Aprill
Ellen dau. of John Whitehead	26 ,,
Robt son of Ric Dawny ...	28 ,,
Willm son of Willm Bordricke	16 Maij
Elzabeth dau. of Row Whitehead ...	eodem die
Isabell dau. of John Dawny ...	23 Maij
Geo: Toppin ...	25 ,,
Ja: wife of Ran: Kew ...	6 June
Dorothy Relict Wm Harrison	21 ,,
Isabell dau. of J: Padget	22 Aug
Eliza: dau. of Wm. Stithe	10 Sep
Jenet w. of Thom Blackburn	2 Octob
Jane dau. of Ric Cocking	3 ,,
Dorothy dau. of Ric. Bacchus	29 ,,
John son of Thom Dowthwayte	28 Novēb
Margrett Pratt	14 Decemb
An Relict Thome Heaton	3 Janua
Jenet Moore widdow	5 ,,
Thom son of Bryan Bland	26 ,,

1637.

Margrett w. of John North gent[1] ...	5 Aprill
A dawghter of Ric Bordrick ...	7 May
Gulielmus Gregg ...	25 ,,
Johes filius Gulielmi Melling...	8 Junij
Roulandus filius Rici. Godsalfe	13 ,,
Elizabetha Whitehead spinster	19 ,,
Richard Bordrick de Newton	20 July
Roulandus Whitehead de Newton...	22 Octobris
Bryan Dawny de Newton	...primo die Novembris
Johes Smithe de Newton	11 ,,
An infant of Randall Kew	25 ,,
Jane ye daughter of Ja: Melling ...	2 Decembr
Johes Padget de Whittington	5 ,,
Ellen Hewgill uxor Willm Hewgill	9 ,,
Margret ye daughter of Bryan Dickonson	22 ,,
Ellen Dawny w. of Tho: Dawny de Newton	23 ,,
Jenet the wife of Gilbert Atkinson	28 ,,
Christofer the sonne of Ric: Tayler	25 January
John Godsalfe the sonne of Ric Godsalfe	10 February

1638.

Ric: son of James Godsalf	3 Aprilis
Dorothy dau. of Tho: Tayler...	10 Maij
Mr. Willm Brabyn of Docker Hall	26 ,,
John Betham of Whittington	5 Junij

[1] A hand drawn on left margin of page seems to point to this entry.

Robt son of Willm Brabyn gent	19 Julij
Isabell w. of Cuthbert Feray	21 Augustij
Cuthbert Feray	1 Septembr
Johīs Asheton alias Poulton	6 ,,
Infante of Mr. Henry Brabyn of Docker	10 ,,
Elsabeth Lonsdall	27 ,,
Thomas Sidgswicke of Whittington	10 October
Two infants of Ric: Tayler	15 ,,
Agnes w. of Richard Tayler	2 Novemb
Mr. Thomas Brabyn of Whittingtō Hall	5 ,,
Ellen the wife Sander Adcock	6 ,,
Robt Fayrey	2 December
James Johnson of Whittington	7 ,,
Ric: son of Tho: Milner...	22 ,,
9 ¹ Alexander Adcock	3 January
Isabell w. of Willm Burrow	8 ,,
Jane dau. of John Harries	30 ,,
Elzabeth w. Willm Kempe	14 March
Bryan Nealson of Whittington	17 ,,

1639.

Ann Carter dau. of Leonard Carter	13 Aprilis
Ann Dawny dau. of Ric: Dawny of Newton... ...	6 August
Willm Ayckrigge son of Henry Ayckrigge	8 Septem
James Melling of Whittingtō	17 Novemb
Katherine w. of Tho: Barker of Whittingto... ...	28 ,,
John Barker son of Tho: Barker ,..	2 Decemb
Thomas Whitehead son Rawlyn Whitehead... ...	ultimo Januarij
Jennett Harries of Newton	7 February
Elzabeth w. of James Bordrigge	11 ,,
Chr: Cort son of Richard Cort	18 ,,
Jane w. of John Burrow...	11 March
Edward Tayler son of Tho: Tayler	29 ,,

1640.

Robt Parker	4 Maij
Marmaduke Marginson	14 Aug
Mr. Daniell Maiers late parson of Whittington died the first day of October at Thornes, and was buryed in the pishe church of Sedber the third day of October following Anno Dni 1640	
John Barrow of Docker	11 October
Richard Patton of Whittington	12 ,,
Isabell dau. of Ric: Patton	3 December
James Bordrigge	2 Marcij
Wilfrid Moore	10 ,,

¹ Date in original as here, in margin of leaf.

1641.

Bryan Garnet servant to old Bryan Bland	7 Aprilis
George Blande	24 Junij
* * son of John Cockin	quinto die Julij

Mr. Jackson entered to the Rectori of Whittington 26° die Julij

John Miller de Newton ... ...secundo die Augustij
Ellin filia John Cockin	tertio die Octobris
Thomas Cantsfeeld	2 ,,
* * son of Richard Tayler...	16 Novembris
Dorethie dau. of Wiłłm Godsalfe	20 Februarij
Anne w. of James Boones	24 ,,
Alice dau. of Wiłłm Harlinge	4 Marcij
Agnes Burrowe	13 ,,

1642.

spuria Thomas son of John Dickson and Grace Robinson	11 Aprilis
Henrie son of John [1] ... ...
Jenett dau. of Richard Patton	12 Junij
Luke Garnet clerke	17 Julij
Jenett Phillipson widdowe died at Margesons of
Docker ... ...ultimo die ,,
Isabell Harelinge	tertio die Augustij
Edmund son of Alexander Adcocke ... ...primo die Septembris
Wiłłm Kempe...	24 Octobris
Elizabeth dau. of Richard North	eodem die
Marie dau. of Mr. Richard Jackson pson of Whit-
tington	4 Decembris
Willm Myers clerck	2 Marcij
Henrie Aykrigg	21 ,,

1643.

Doughter of Robertt Jackson de Newton	26 Marcij
Isabell w. of Bryan Bland	24 Junij
Katherine w. of John Hardie	27 Julie
Margrett w. of Edmund Adcock	22 Octobris
Doughter of Robertt Robinson ... ...
Edward Cockin sepult xij die Julij [2]

It will be observed that there are no entries of Burials for 1644, 1645, and 1646.

1647.

Anne w. of Thomas Robinson	27 Januarij
The wiff of Thomas Nealson ... ...quarto die Februarie

[1] Struck through and Surname illegible.
[2] The whole of this entry is struck through in original.

Grace Myers vidua ... ... nono die Februarie
Ewan Dimsdall [?] ... ... 10 Marcij

1648.

Dorethie Relict John Newton	26 April
Henrie son of Mr. Thomas Brabin	...quarto die Maij
Henrie son of Thomas Robinson	...quinto die „
Ellin w. of Henrie Pattison	3 October
Willm Margison	vicessimo die „
Elin w. of Robtt Bethom	„ nono „
John Tompson	decimo tertio Decembris
Agnes Rydall vidua	14 „
Rowland son of Willm Godsalf	27 „
Alice Relict Tho: Harling	ultimo die „
Jane dau. of Mr. Rich: Jackson	eodem die

1649.

Margrett Cockin	... septimo die Januarij
Alis uxor James Johnson	19 Septembris
John son of Thomas Smith	eodem die
Nichalas Bunnell [?]	22 Septembris
Margrett uxor Mr. Luke Garnett	decimo sexto Decembris
Ellin w. of Christopher Foster	eodem die
Grace Robinson de Docker	decimo die Marcij
Richard Dickenson	12 „
Margrett dau. of Tho: Johnson junior	10 „

1650.

Rowland Godsalff	18 Aprilis
ye sone of Bryan Cantsfeild	quinto die Maij
Marmaduk Cockin	16 „
Isabell dau. of Rich: North	23 July
Francis Styth Mabell Bordrigg	

Here follow some words which cannot be made out as the bottom of the leaf is worn away.
Here in original follow the Baptisms commencing 1538.

Mr. Thomas Brabin [1] ... ... 14 January

It will be noted that no Burials are entered for the years 1651, 1652, 1653, and 1654.

1655.

Thomas Jackson uxor Roberti Jackson de Newton
    obit undecimo die Aprilis et sepult erat ... 12 Aprill
Cristapher Barrow obit 23 Aprill et sepult ... ... 24 „

[1] This entry in original immediately follows the Grants of Pews printed at end of this volume. It is written at extreme top of page, the remainder of which is left blank.

James Godsalfe son of James Godsalfe ... ...   3 May
Annas Peck obit 23 October et sep erat viginta
    quatuer dies ... ...   October
Elizabeth w. of Robert Battersebe obit 15 day of
    November et sep erat ... ...   eodem die
Richard North de Docker obit triginta dies et sepul
    erat ... ...   31 December
Bryan son of Bryan Dawny ... ...   14 February

1656.

Walter Myres ... ...   15 Aprill
Robert Jackson ... ...   30 June
John son of Thomas Taylor waller ... ...   3 Sept
John son of Widdow Allan ... ...   21 ,,
Alice dau. of Thomas Smyth ... ...   5 October
Dorothy dau. of Thomas Taylor waller ... ...   15 ,,
Francis son of Wittm Stith ... ...   18 ,,
An dau. of John Cort ... ...   29 ,,
Alice w. of John Eshton ... ...   last day December

1657.

Isabell, widdow, which had been wife to Edward
    Cocking ... ...   6 Aprill
Henry Harris ... ...   29 ,,
Isaac son of Bryan Dawny ... ...   6 July
John son of Wittm Johnson and   *   *   Vstonson   16 ,,
An dau. of James Blackburne ... ...   18 ,,
Willm Harris ... ...   15 August
Mr. Richard North ... ...   28 ,,
Brian Bland son of James Bland ... ...   9 Septr
John son of John Johnson and An Walker ... ...   2 October
Richard Corner ... ...   7 ,,
Bryan son of Thomas Smyth carpinter ... ...   28 ,,
*   * Robinson of Towne End yeo: ... ...   9 November
Thomas Taylor which came from Milthrope ... ...   24 ,,
Willm Towers ... ...   27 ,,
Thomas Barker ... ...   4 December
Robert Johnson, borne in Bentham, servant to John
    Johnson ... ...   14 ,,
Thomas Johnson North west of the church ... ...   1 January
Richard Backhouse of Newton ... ...   24 ,,
James son of Thomas Newby of Docker ... ...   20 February
Henry Robinson ... ...   24 ,,
Isabell Bings widdow ... ...   25 ,,
Annas w. of Wittm Bordridge Junior ... ...   19 March
Richard Whithead son of Wittm Whithead of Burton
    in Kendall ... ...   23 ,,

1658.

Isabell Robinson	28 March
Jane Thatham spinster	17 Aprill
Richard Dawny	26 ,,
Alice dau. of Wiłłm Slater of Whittingto.	28 ,,
Mary King	22 May
Thomas son of John Dawny of the yet of Newton	28 ,,
Jane Slater dau. of Wiłłm Slater of Whittington	30 June
Jane dau. of John Dawny of the yeat of Newton...	5 July
Willm son of Richard Dicconson of Docker	4 September
Agnes w. of Thomas North of Docker	16 ,,
Thomas North of Docker	4 October
An Lonsdale spinster	17 ,,

1659.

Elizabeth w. of Willm Johnson webster	17 Septem
Willm Stith showmaker...	19 ,,
Elizabeth w. of John Margison	11 December
Dorothy w. of Richard Tatham	26 ,,

1660.

Thomas Nealson of Newton	4 Aprill
Wiłłm Bordridge son of Rowland Bordridge ...	6 ,,
Jennet dau. of John Newton, gent, and wife of Thomas Johnson	27 ,,
Jennet late wife of John Bethome of Whittington	5 Octob
Katherine dau. of James Hardy blacksmith ...	11 January
Alice Burrow widdow old of the Beckside in Whittington	27 Aprill
Elizabeth w. of Robert Blackburne taylor	2 May
Alice Adcocke spinster	3 ,,
Dorothy w. of Robert Burrow	24 ,,
Edward son of James North farmer of Docker hall	17 July
James Godsalfe of Newton	4 September
Thomas Mason	8 ,,
Richard son of John Dawny of Newton	5 December
Henry son of Robert Burrow...	22 ,,
Thomas Smyth of Newton carpenter	1 January
Margret dau. of Bryan Nealson shoomaker	3 ,,
Margret dau. of Wiłłm Adcocke	4 March

1662.

Willm son of Wiłłm Margison of Dockʳ	17 June
Thomas Douthwaite webster...	5 July
John Dawny, thacker	15 October

M

An Harris, widdow	23 Aprill .
John son of Bryan Manser	2 June
Leonard son of John Troughton	25 ,,
Alice Harris, widdow	7 August
Jane dau. of John Newton Rector and late wife of	
Willm Maddison	30 Sep
Thomas Carter	8 October
Isabell Relict Willm Kidd	12 November
Willm son of Francis Dooleman	14 ,,
Willm son of Robert Burrow...	12 January
Katherine w. of John Harris of Newton	18 ,,
Alice Harris an old woman never married	20 ,,
Richard Hodgon and John Hall	12 February
Margret dau. of Thomas Johnson	15 March
James Northe...	20 ,,

1664.

Willm Vstonson	28 March
Marmaducke Robinson	4 Aprill
Agnes dau. of Thomas Taylor, waller	2 June
Richard son of Richard Johnson	4 ,,
Elizabeth w. of Samuell Garnet	19 July
Richard Tayler	20 ,,
Thomas Robinson of Churchland	21 September
Katherine late wife of Willm Bordridge	11 October
An dau. of Henry Pattison	22 ,,
An Eikridge, widdow	10 November
Willm Bordridge	14 December
Alice Relict Robinson	30 ,,
Elizabeth Cocking spinster	27 January
Jenet puera daughter of Thomas Robinson of	
Churchland	8 Feb
Robert son of Robert Burrow and } both buried...	1 March
Elizabeth Dawthwaite	
Mary Relict Barrow	5 ,,
Edward son of Willm Burrow	10 ,,

1665.

Willm Melling, tyler	8 May
An dau. of Bryan Dawny	30 ,,
Jane Melling, spinster	14 July

[*Volume II. of Original Register.*]

It will be noted that the Burials from 1661 to 1665 inclusive are now
repeated. They are found so repeated in the second Volume of the
Original Registers, but as many different items of interesting inform-
ation are found in each set of entries it has been thought well to
print both.

The word "sep" or "sepult" is repeated in the original, but has been omitted
in the transcript.

1661.

Elizabeth wife of Robert Blackburne taylor sep the second day of May An° p°do	
Alice Adcocke spinster	3 May
Dorothy wife of Robert Burrow	24 ,,
Edward sone of James North	17 July
James Godsalfe of Newton	4 Septr
Thomas Mason	8 ,,
Richard son of John Dawny of Newton	5 Dec
Henry son of Robert Burrow...	22 ,,
Thomas Smyth of Newton carpinter	1 Jany
Margret dau. of Brian Nealson	3 ,,
Margret dau. of Willm Adcocke	4 Mar

1662.

Willm son of Willm Margison	7 June
Thomas Douthaite webster	5 July
John Dawny thatcher	15 Octr

1663.

An Harris widdow	23 Apl
John son of Brian Manser	2 June
Leonard son of John Troughton	25 ,,
Alice Harris widdow	7 August
Jane wife of Willm Maddison and dau. of John Newton Rector	30 Septr
Thomas Carter	8 Octr
Isabell Relict of Willm Kidd...	12 Nov
Willm son of Francis Dooleman	14 ,,
Willm son of Robert Burrow base borne	12 January
Katheraine wife of John Harris	18 ,,
Alice Harris an old woman never married	20 ,,
Richard Hodgon and John Hall ... ... both	12 Febry
Margret dau. of Thomas Johnson	15 Mar
James North	20 ,,

1664.

Willm Vstenson	28 March
Marmaducke Robinson	4 April
Agnes dau. of Thomas Taylor	2 June
Richard son of Richard Johnson	4 ,,
Elizabeth wife of Samuell Garnet	19 July
Richard Taylor	20 ,,
Thomas Robinson of Churchland	21 Septr
Katheraine late wife of Willm Bordridge	11 October
An dau. of Henry Pattison	22 ,,
An Eykridge widdow	10 Nov
Willm Bordridge next to the psonage	14 Decr
Alice Relict Robinson	31 ,,
Elizabeth Cocking spinster	27 Jany
Jenet dau. of Thomas Robinson	8 Feb
Robert son of Robert Burrow and Elizabeth Daughwaite ... ... both	1 Mar
Mary Relict Barrow	5 ,,
Edward son of Willm Burrow	10 ,,

1665.

Willm Melling tiler	8 May
An dau. of Bryan Dawny	30 ,,
Jane Melling	14 July
Willm Slater of Whittington...	27 August
James son of John Bland tanner	27 ,,
An wife of Thomas Nuby of Docker	1 Octr
Elizabeth Hunter widdow	3 Decemb
Jane dau. of James Melling	9 Feb
Jenet dau. of Richard Johnson carp.	9 March

1666.

Jane dau. of Thomas Taylor waller	6 June
Agnes wife of Willm Manser	14 ,,
Francis Manzer tayler	18 July
Bryan Nealson shoomaker	28 ,,
John Hardy of Newton	3 Aug
Isabell late wife of Richard Backhouse	4 Septr
John son of Willm Slater of Newton	23 Octr
Mathew son of Brian Nealson	8 Novr
Alice late wife of Richard North of Docker	15 ,,
Willm Toluson	16 ,,
An late wife of John Carter	5 Dec
Bryan son of Bryan Nealson shomaker	14 ,,
Jane late wife of Thomas Cansfeild	24 ,,

Elizabeth late wife of Richard Manser	14 Jany
Alice dau. of James Curteous	17 „
John son of Richard Taylor	6 Febry
Thomas Johnson opsite psonage	10 March

1667.

Jane wife of Willm Tayler	9 Aprill
John son of Christopher Lawrence	28 „
John son of Bryan Dawny	6 June
Marmaducke Slater	24 August
Elizabeth daur. of Thomas Towerson	7 Novr
Isabell daur. of John Shawe...	4 March

1668.

Richard North	16 Aprill
Elling Adcock spinster	29 July
Margret wife of John Shaw	25 Septem
Edward son of Marmaducke Cocking	27 „
Elling w. of John Wildman Jun:	11 Oct
Jane dau. of Willm Hall spinster...	4 Novem
Margret dau. of Robert Kellett spur:	24 „
Jane Johnson widdow	1 Jany
John Melling sometime slater	23 Feb
Jenet Jackson widdow and Thomas son of John	
Dawny of North Yeat in Newton	22 „

1669.

An dau. of Willm Adcocke	31 Mar
Marmaducke son of Thomas Hutton	5 May
Margret w. of Thomas Miller...	10 „
Alice dau. of Bryan Dawny	19 „
James Fletcher	15 Aug
Willm Burrow	2 Sept
Thomas son of Willm Hall	24 Novr
John son of Edmond Burrow...	15 Decem
Mary Cu spinster	Febry
Jenet w. of Randolfe Cue	25 „
Elling w. of John Lonsdale	2 March

1670.

John son of Henry Meales	22 Apl
John son of Robert Toppin	17 May
Robert son of Robert Toppin...	24 „
Isaac son of John Stoory	27 „
Rebecca dau. of John Stoory...	4 June

Wiłłm Dicconson	18 August
Elizabeth Dawny widdow	4 Sept
Ann dau. of Bryan Dicconson	13 ,,
John son of Richard Robinson	5 Decr
Wiłłm Adcock	17 Febry
Wiłłm Slater of Newton	26 ,,

1671.

Edward Dicconson	3 Aprill
Dorothy dau. of Richard Tatham Sen:	29 ,,
Thomas Miller	23 May
Robert Robinson	2 July
Agnes Beck spinster	18 ,,
An w. of John Cocking	29 ,,
John Cocking	3 August
Esther dau. of Andrew Cue	4 ,,
Esther Benson virgo	5 Sept
Thomas son of Thomas Stith	8 Novr
Elizabeth w. of Thomas North of Docker	16 Decem
James Harris carp:	26 Jany
Jane Melling widdow	31 ,,
Wiłłm Cumerland puer spurius	17 Feby

1672.

Wiłłm Harling	3 May
An Harling widdow	9 ,,
Thomas Taylor waller	20 June
John son of Rowland Braithaite	29 July
Wiłłm son of Wiłłm Margison	28 Sept
Alice wife of John Harris	18 Novr
Jane dau. of John Johnson	14 Jany
Edmund son of Richard Tatham Sen	19 ,,
James Denby	14 February

1673.

Elizabeth late wife of Robt Robinson	11 Aprill
John Hall taylor	2 May
Thomas Blackburne of Docker	25 July
Francis Booth	29 August
Reginald Whithead	13 Sept
Alice dau. of Wiłłm Lonsdale	4 Oct
Randolf Cue	18 ,,
Wiłłm son of Robert Toppin	1 Decr
Elizabeth dau. of John Shaw	1 Jany
Mabell Patchet spinster	17 ,,
Elizabeth w. of Henry Pattison	16 Feb

Henry Pattison	26 Feb
Wiłłm Lousdall	7 March
Jenet w. of Wiłłm Bond	13 ,,
Thomas Beck	18 ,,

1674.

Mathew Bethome batchler	30 March
Alice w. of Richard Beck	7 July
Bryan Barker batchler	23 ,,
Isable dau. of Wiłłm Slater	7 Oct
John Lonsdall Senior	17 ,,
Thomas Robinson	16 Dec
Mary dau. of Mr. Thomas Brabin	20 Jany
Richard Tatham Senior	8 Feby

1675.

Robert Robinson	25 March
Richard son of Robert Cornthaite	15 May
An w. of Richard Procter	9 June
John Bland tanner	27 ,,
Elizabeth Gibson	19 July
Catheraine Adcocke widdow	2 August
John son of Robert Toppin	...last day of ,,
James son of Edward Douthwaite	10 Sept
Alice dau. of Mr. Christopher Parkinson	26 ,,
Thomas son of Thomas Bland mason	27 ,,
John son of Thomas Smyth carp:	14 Oct
Henry Mires	18 Novr
Jenet w. of Edmund Burrow	22 ,,
Margret Benson spinster	26 ,,
John Petty batchler	28 ,,
Margret Nealson widdow	30 ,,
Jane Robinson of Capenwray widd :	25 Decr
Jenet Vstinson widdow	3 Feb
Thomas son of Symon Dawny	20 ,,
Robert son of Richard Robinson	4 March

1676.

Johane w. of James Melling	22 May
Thomas Hodgon	...last day of ,,
Wiłłm Taylor	6 June
Jane dau. of John Cort	8 ,,
Jane Cansfeild, bēng aged eighty 84 years, most of her time a true servant in divers good houses, some few years in her old age had her Reliefe out of the parish poore stock never married	16 ,,

George son of Thomas Watson ... ...   5 July
Mary dau. of Mark Bentom ... ...   9 „
Elizabeth dau. of John Robinson and George son of
    Edmund Burrow ... ...   23 „
Isabell Bradeley ... ...   1 Septemb
Jenet w. of John Bland ... ...   10 „
Mr. William Newton ... ...   24 „
Mary wife of Thomas Dowthwait ... ...   2 October
John son of Thomas Bland ... ...   13 Decr

1677.

Isabell dau. of John Robinson ... ...   9 Aprill
Elling dau. of Mr. Oliver Dickonson ... ...   19 „
Edward Holden schoolmaster ... ...   20 „
Ellin w. of Bryan Dikonson ... ...   9 May
Ellin dau. of Edward Dowthwaite... ... ...   13 July
Mr. Thomas Carus Esq ... ...   10 Septemb
Jane Godsalf spinst· ... ...   12 Oct
Thomas Bland freemason ... ...   19 Novr
Isabell dau. of Marmaduke Cocking ... ...   22 „
Ellin daughter of Bryan Dickonson ... ...   23 „
Bryan Dickonson ... ...   26 „
Jenet dau. of James Harris ... ...   3 Decr
Jane dau. of Thomas Watson ... ...   14 „
Rihard [sic] son of Thomas Taylor ... ...   25 „
Thomas Manserge ... ...   6 Jany
John Cort ... ...   8 Feb
Joanna w. of Mr. Oliver Dickonson ... ...   19 „
Dorothy Bromley widdow ... ...   9 March

1678.

William Hall ... ...   24 May
Richard Robinson Jun' ... ...   28 June
Margret dau. of Robert Wilson ... ...   25 October
Thomas son of Christ' Tailer ... ...   10 Feb
Richard Beck ... ...   21 „

1679.

Agnes Collison, Docker ... ...   16 April
Robert Burrow ... ...   23 „
Jenet Wildman, Newton ... ...   17 May
Elizabeth Towerson, Whittington ... ...   24 June
Anne dau. of John Robinson Whitt: ... ...   19 Sep
Thomas Mires, Whitt: ... ...   19 „
John Godsalve, Newton ... ...   13 Oct
Agnes Whitehead, Newton ... ...   29 Dec

| Agnes Madison, Whitting : | .. | ... | ... | ... | ... | 19 Jan |
| Edward Burrow, Whitting : | ... | ... | ... | ... | ... | 18 March |

1680.

Elisabeth Neuby, Neuton	...	...	...	...	...	11 May
George Chamley, Mendic :	...	...	...	...	...	11 Nov
John Bland, Neuton	...	...	...	...	...	12 Dec
Richard Corner, Docker...	...	..	...	...	...	21 Mar

1681.

Elizabeth dau. of John Millers	...	...	...	...	1 Apl
Margret Melling	...	...	...	...	...	...	29 ,,
Agnes Robinson Whittington	...	...	...	·...	15 May
Jane Robinson spinster ...	...	...	...	...	...	22 June
John Dickonson Docker...	...	...	...	...	...	9 Jany
Alice dau. of Sam : Garnett	...	...	...	...	..	7 March

1682.

Agnes Burrow, Whittington ...	...	...	...	...	6 Apl
William Robinson, Whitting ...	...	..	...	...	5 June
Alice Hodgon, Neuton	...	...	...	...	...	14 Aug
William Patison, Neuton	...	...	...	...	...	24 ,,
Bryan Dauney, Whittington ...	...	...	...	...	19 Oct
Dorathy Dauney, Whittington [1]	...	...	...	...	30 Mar
Anne Burrow, Whittington [1] ...	...	...	...	...	3 Apl
Rowland Burrow, Docker	...	...	...	...	...	4 Jany
Elizabeth Dauney, Whittington	...	...	...	...	26 Feby
Thomas Dauth[et] Neuton	...	...	...	...	...	2 Mar
Thomas Neuby Docker ...	...	...	...	...	...	11 ,,

1683.

Edmund Adcock Whitting	...	...	...	...	...	29 Apl
Betteras Jackson Neuton	...	...	...	...	...	13 May
William Johnson Whitting	...	...	...	...	...	24 June
John Dauthwait Neuton	...	...	...	...	...	22 July
Thomas Taylor Whittington ...	...	...	...	...	7 Aug
Mrs. Mary Carus widdow	...	...	...	...	...	8 Oct
Mrs. Lucy North Docker	...	...	...	...	...	29 Nov
Margret Johnson Whitt :	...	...	...	...	...	6 Feb
Eline Whitehead Docker	...	...	...	...	..	14 ,,

1684.

| John Dauney Neuton | ... | ... | ... | ... | ... | ... | 31 Mar |
| Jane dau. of Edw : Cockin | ... | ... | ... | ... | ... | 25 June |

[1] Probably these are meant for 1683.

Alice dau. of Rich Johnson ... ...   6 Dec
Richard Tathem Neuton   ... ...   23 ,,
James Corner Docker   ... ...   5 Feb
Margret ye wife of Oliv' Birch   ... ...   15 ,,
Richard son of John Corner Neuton   ... ...   23 ,,

1685.

Margereta Cort vid :   ... ... secundo Aprilis
Elisabetha Wilson vid : ...   .   vicessimo septimo May
Samuel filius Rowlandi Burrow   ... ...   decimo nono July
Mabill vxor Thomae Slater   ... ...   vicessimo primo .,
Margereta filia Edmundi Burrow ...   ... decimo septimo Augusti
Isabell Relfe dau. of Tho : Relfe ...   ... decimo quinto Septemb
Rowland Briggs   ... ...   20 Oct
John Burrow ...   .   29 Nov
Alice Smith   ... ...   18 Dec
Elizabeth Backehouse   ... ...   19 Jany
Jane Overen   ... ...   3 Feb
Jane Slater   ... ...   16 ,,

1686.

John Ginyon ...   .   25 Aprill
Alice Cockin ...   .   28 ,,
Robert Toppin...   ... ...   4 May
Catherine Tayler   ... ...   3 June
Elizabeth Tayler   ... ...   28 ,,
Thomas Tayler   ... ...   2 August
Henry Greenfield   ... ...   30 ,,
Thomas Hutton   ... ...   10 October
James Whitehead ...   .   15 ,,
Mabill Gouthrop   ... ...   21 Nov
Ann Blackburn   ... ...   29 ,,
Thomas Styth ...   .   29 Jany
Mathew Overend   ... ...   14 March

1687.

Mrs. Ruth Jackson ...   .   30 Mar
John Dawney of high green in Newton   ... ...   15 Aprill
Marmaduke Cockin   ... .   4 June
Alice Cockin ...   .   17 ,,
Anthony Bouch   ... ...   20 ,,
Jane Hardy dau. of Richard Hardy   ... ...   21 ,,
William son of John Robinson   ... ...   12 July
Isabell Whitehead ...   .   16 ,,
Thomas Blackburn ...   .   6 Nov
James Melling and Margret Sanders   ... ...   19 Decr

Abigell dau. of James Bond	2 Jany
An dau. of Thomas Brabin Esq	4 ,,
Jane dau. to James Hardy	19 ,,
Edward Whitehead	18 Feby
Alice Tathum	19 ,,
Richard Cort Junior	22 ,,
Agnes Harris	6 March
Willmus fillius Jacobi Hardy	19 ,,

1688.

Johannes Dawney de Newton	17 May
Jane filia Richi North de Whittington	21 July
Margarita Hodgson vid de Newton	29 Augusti
Johes Corner de Newton	7 Septembris
Christopherus filius Thomae Carus genosj de West-	
hall	2 Decembris
Jacobus filius Georgij Backhouse de Newton ...	30 Januarij

1689.

Thomas Grainsworth de Dockershall spur	19 Aprilis
Thomas filius Mariae North de Newton vid	28 July
Petrus Burrow Senr	26 Septembris
Symon Dawney	19 Octobris
Bryanus filius Johis Wildeman de Newton	20 Novembris
Robt^{us} filius Robt^i Burrow de Whittington	23 ,,
Robertus filius Oliveri North de Newton	24 ,,
Margareta filia Richj Godsalve	27 ,,
Margareta ux Franc Slater de Whittington	20 Marchij
Henricus Postlethwaite[1]	nono die May

1690.

Henricus Postlethwaite	nono die May
Mary dau. of Thomas Bouch Rector	19 Junij
James son of William Slater de Newton	21 ,,
James Melling de Whittington	1 August
Alice dau. of Richd North de Whittington	7 Sept
Richard Robinson de Whittington Ag^n	16 Septembris
Robert Blackborne de Newton	25 ,,
Tho: son of Richd North de Whittington	24 Octobris
John Cornthw^{te} de Whittington	27 ,,
Richard North de Whittington	2 Novembris
Alice Atckinson dau. of Tho: Atckinson	23 ,,
Oliver son of Peter Cautly de Newton	25 Decembris
Mary dau. of Thos. Carus generos:	primo die Marcij

[1] This struck through in the original but repeated following year.

1691.

Dorothy Robinson ux	... 28 Marcij
Thomas Slater de Whittington	15 Junij
Margret Dawny of Newton widd:	17 ,,
Elling Greenfield	5 August
Elizebeth w. of Wittm Millers	12 ,,
John son of Henry Chatburne	31 ,,
Thomas Harries de Newton	8 Novr
Richard Johnson	nono die ,,
John Harries de Newton	9 Decemb
Alice w. of Edward Jackson de Newton	10 ,,
Ann w. of John Johnson	18 ,,
Alice daughtr of James Tatham	2 Jany
Thomas son of Peter Cautley	23 Febry

1692.

Ester Mansergh w. of Brian Manser of Newton ...	3 July
John Wildeman of Newtown	28 ,,
Richard Cornuer of Whittington	25 Oct
John Sanders of Whittington	21 Decembr
Anthony Greenfield de Docker parke	21 ,,
Miles Eckridge de Whittington	9 Jany
Elizabeth Myres vid :	3 Febry
Marmaduke Cocking de Whittington	5 ,,
John Woodhouse	nono die ,,

1693.

Isabell Robinson de Whittington	14 April
James Bond of Newton	18 ,,
Jane Styth de Whittington vid : ... ···	17 May
Judith filia Georgij Carus generosi	quarto die Junij
Mary w. of James Downham de Whittington ...	15 ,,
Anna filia Thome Johnson Senr	primo die Augustij
Anna ux Petri Burrow de Whittington...	3 ,,
Auna ux Roberti Skirrow de Docker	11 Septembris
Georgius filius Jacobi Downham de Whittington ...	30 ,,
Isabella Styth de Whittington vid : ...	octodecimo die Octobris
Rebekah Hackforth	decimo die Decembris
Thomas Johnson de Whittington Senr	...sexto die Jany
Jana uxor Christopheri Lawrence	25 ,,
Bridgeta Dawney de Newton	...quarto die Feby
Johes filius Jacobi Downham	octavo die Marcij
Petrus Burrow	...nono die ,,
Willielmus Margisson de Docker	19 ,,

1694.

Anna Harries ... ...decimo	primo die Aprillis
Agnes Mansergh de Newton	21 ,,
Laomi a bastard child fathered on Val Ormerod de	
Burton ... ...primo	die Maij
William Whitehead de Newton ... ...decimo	die ,,
William Robinson de Whittington and William	
filius ejusdem Wiħmj Robinson	21 Maij
Margareta uxor Wiħmj Slater de Newton	22 July
Thomas Thompson de Docker	20 Septembris
Thomas Thompson Ju :	19 Octobris
Alice dau. of Thomas Tatham	27 Decembris
Stephen Margisson de Docker ... ... postremo	die Januaris
Jhonnathon Borrow filius de John Borow de Whitt :	20 Febru
John Preston of Cansfill...	15 March
Mary North de Newton vid :...	16 ,,

1695.

Mary Scott Pochae de Slaidburn	26 Aprillis
Francis w. of John Preston de Whitt :	19 May
Mrs. Jane Jackson de Whittington	23 August
James Hardy Whittington	7 Septr
Chathrine Slater of Whitt :	17 ,,
Ann uxor Edwardi Tayler	19 December
Maud Margison de Docker	14 Februari
Elisabeth Cockin of Prest Huton	15 ,,
Agnes dau. of Robt Burrow	23 March

1696.

Christopher Lawrence of Whitt :	29 April
Francis Slater of Whitt :	30 July
Anne Adcock wid : of Whitt :	4 November

1697.

Francis Myers of Whittington	29 April
Isabell Martin de Whitt	10 May
Agnes dau. of William Martin	23 ,,
Jenet Newby of Newton haveing reliefe out of the	
parish poor stock	18 July
John Barrow of Docker	23 ,,
Dorothy dau. of Henry Robinson	25 ,,
William Barker of Whittington	15 August
James Gifferd de Newton	23 March
Robert Battersby of Newton	2 ,,

1698.[1]

Mary Gifford de Newton	19 May
Margret dau. of Wiłłm Burrow	29 „
John son of Richd North de Dock'	9 June
Catherine Douthwhait de Newton...	27 Septr
Ellen dau. of Richard Todd	23 October
Ann Cortice de Dock'	5 Septr
Wiłłm son of WiłłmMarton	9 Decemb
Susana dau. of Simon Batty	28 „
Lydia w. of Richd Hardy	7 January
Thomas son of Thomas Bouch Rector	12 „
Dorothy w. of Joseph Johnson	2 February
Jane w. of Thomas Watson	27 „
Thomas son of Henry Robinson	11 March

1699.

Mary dau. of Thomas Bouch Rector	30 March
Alice dau. of James Tatham	1 May
John Carlile	2 June
Ellen Toppam...	14 „
Agnes w. of John Cort	21 „
Miles son of Mr. Thomas North Junior	30 „
Agnes dau. of Luke Corney	18 July
Ann dau. of Oliver North	25 „
Ann w. of William Gibson	30 „
Mary dau. of Mary Johnson	24 Septembr
Agnes w. of Richard Johnson de Whittingto : ...	10 „
Mary Johnson...	22 „
Bryan Mansergh	1 February

1700.

Mary dau. of Thomas Smith of Newton	1 Apr
Robert Wilson of Newton	29 „
Jane w. of William Willan	4 June
Marmaduke son of Richard Cockin	16 „
Agnes w. of Will: Overend of Whitt:	21 Novem
Jane dau. of Will: Overend of Whitt:...	27 „
Margret Whithead of Newton	28 „
John Butterfield of Newton	11 Decem
John Walker of Newton...	15 „
George son of Agnes Tyeson of Whitt:	19 „
Thomas Atkison of Whittington	21 „

---

[1] Four Baptisms entered here by mistake and crossed out in original are
duly entered in original under their proper date among the Baptisms.

Myles North of Newton	5 February
Matthew son of Robert Atkinson of Newton... ...	5 „
Ann w. of Tho: Nuby of Docker	7 March

1701.

Jane w. of John Styth of Whittington	15 August
Margret dau. of Elizabeth Parcivle	10 January
Ellen Hardy of Whittington	18 Dec
Ann dau. of William Lawrence of Whitt	22 Feb
Thomas son of Oliver North of Newton	13 March

1702.

Myles son of Mr. Thomas North of Newton... ...	2 May
Robert Greenwood of Newton	10 „
Ellen dau. of William Willan of Westhall	23 Aug:
Agnes Atkinson of Newton	8 November
Richard Hardy of Whittington	1 January
Isabell Petty of Whittington	10 „
Margaret w. of John Heblethwait of Newton ...	14 „
Rose Bond of Newton	8 February
Edward Wilson of Whittington	7 March
Jane Dickson of Whittington	12 „

1703.

Thomas son of Richard North of Docker	9 September
Mabbel w. of William Slater of Newton	4 Octo:
Margaret Wildman of Newton	13 Nov.
Agnes w. of Tho: Newby of Newton	29 Decembr

1704.

Margret Meal of Whittington	14 April
Henry Williamson of Docker...	23 „
Richard son of James Millers of Whittington ...	25 „
Henry Hutton of Whittington	13 May
Joseph Johnson of Whittington	11 July
Dorothy Hardy of Burton in Lonsdale	12 „
John son of Henry Chatborn of Whitt:	27 August
Samuel son of Mr. Tho: North of Newton Junr ...	29 „
Allis Robinson of Manser	29 October
John Margieson of Docker	30 „
John son of James Bordridge of Whitt:	30 „
Isaball Denney of Westhall	4 November
Elizabeth Taylor of Newton	19 January
Ann Newton of Whittington...	5 February

George Gurnal of Whittington   ...   .   12 February
John Millers of Whittington...   15   ,,
Agnes w. of Hue Mittyson of Whitting: ...   ...   3 March

1705.

Dorothy dau. of Tho: Peck of Whitt: ...   .   28 March
Jenet Taylor of Whittington ...   .   6 June
Christopher Taylor of Whittington   ...   .   25 ,,
Mary w. of Richard Tatham of Newton...   ...   ...   4 August
Ellinor dau. of Mr. Tho: Crowle of Whittington ...   7   ,,
Will: Burrow who was found drowned within the
    Liberties of Hornby or Arckholme at Whit-
    tington   16   ,,
Ellin dau. of Mr. Daniel Pearson ...   .   28 Octo.

1706.

Will: son of Christʳ Holme of Cansfield   ..   ...   29 March
Francis Garnet of Whittington   ...   .   10 Aprile
William Millers of Whittington   20   ,,
Eliz: dau. of John Heblethwaite ...   .   15 June
Thomas son of Bryan Dicxon of Whitting: ...   ...   26 July
John Wildman of Newton   ...   .   9 August
Agnes Holden of Whittington   ...   .   11 Octobr
Henry son of John Millers of Whittington ...   ...   6 Decembr
Ann dau. of John Cocking   ...   .   31 January

1707.

Margret w. of Richard Tode ...   .   18 May
Mary dau. of Mr. Thomas North ...   .   1 August
John Tompson of Whittington   ...   .   18 Octobr
John Croft of Docker: Hall ...   .   20 Decembr
Henry Robinson of Whittington ...   .   2 January

1708.

Jane dau. of Thomas Kue   ...   .   10 Aprill
Robert Skirrow of Dallton   19   ,,
Elizabeth Millers of Whittington ...   .   6 July
Jane Bland of Newton ...   .   15 Septemb.
James Styth of Whittington ...   .   15 Octob.
Joana dau. of James Tatham...   ...   .   12 Jan:
Ann Kue of Newton   20   ,,

1709.

Elizabeth w. of John Nickolson   ..   ..   2 June
Jane Willson of Newton...   ...   .   19 August

Elizabeth Nelson of Newton ... ... 20 Septembr
Ellin dau. of Edward Cockin ... ... 18 January
Margret Eckridge of Whittington ... ... 26 „
Richard Cockin of Whittington ... ... 12 March

1710.

Ann Lindale a bastard child ... ... 21 May
James Johnson of Whittington ... ... 10 June
Margret w. of James Ellis ... ... 28 „
Christopher Peck of Whittington ... ... 24 Octobr
James Bordrigge of Whittington ... ... 6 Novembr
Alice dau. of Bryan Dixon ... ... 9 February

1711.

Thomas Willson of Whittington ... ... 8 April
Thomas Toping of Whittington ... ... 26 „
Elizabeth dau. of James Bark{r} ... ... 9 January
Elizabeth dau. of William Styth ... ... 21 February
Mr. Thomas North Senr of Newton ... ... 6 March
Jane w. of Tho: Foster ... ... 23 „

1712.

Agnes Townson of Whittington ... ... 5 Aprill
Thomas son of Mr. Thomas Crowle ... ... 9 „
Margret Sill spinster ... ... 8 May
John Nickolson of Newton ... ... 25 June
Margrett Harris of Newton ... ... 2 Septem :
William son of Edward Beetham ... ... 17 Novem :
John Mansergh of Newton ... ... 18 „
Thomas Cockin of Whittington ... ... 7 February
Edward son of John Cockin ... ... 4 March
Jane Medcalf of Whittington... ... ... 18 „

1713.

Jane Burrow of Whittington... ... ... 2 Aprill
Henry Meal of Whittington ... ... 7 „
Ann dau. of William Boardley ... ... 7 „
George Backhouse of Newton ... ... 30 June
William Slater of Newton ... ... 9 July
James son of William Styth ... ... 18 Octobr
Ann Cockin the younger ... ... 14 Novem :
Andrew Kue of Newton... ... ... 16 „
William Overend ... ... 21 „
Margret w. of Christoph{r} Cartmall of Farleton ... 28 „

Easter dau. of James Johnson ... ... 25 February
Jenet Labourah of Newton ... ... 23 March

1714.

Elizabeth Cockin of Whittington ... ... 26 March
Thomas son of Mr. Daniel Pearson ... ... 2 April
Rowland Burrow of Docker ... ... 13 May
Elizabeth w. of Henry Chatburn ... ... 14 „
Margret w. of Edmund Burrow ... ... 16 „
John Cornthwaite of Sellet Hall ... ... 10 August
John Johnson Senʳ of Whittington ... ... 4 Novemb
Alice dau. of Wiłłm Thompson ... ... 11 January
Richard Tode of Whittington ... ... 8 March

1715.

Edward Taylor of Whittington ... ... 24 Aprill
Isabell dau. of ffrancis Chippindale ... ... 28 May
Richard Cortt of Whittington ... ... 11 Aug
Thomas Foster of Whittington ... ... 7 Nov
Ellen wife of Frances Chapman ... ... 6 Jany
John Jackson of Whittington... ... ... 20 „
Elizabeth wife of William Slater ... ... 18 Mar
Thomas Dawney of Newton ... ... 23 „

1716.

John Woodhouse of Whittington ... ... 27 May
Thomas Bouch Rector of Whittington ... ... 31 Aug
Mary wife of Richard Robinson ... ... 4 Octr
ffrancis Chapman of Holmshouse ... ... 6 „
Ann the wife of Edward Cocking ... ... 14 Nov:
Judith the wife of Richard Godsalve ... ... 8 Jany

1717.

Ellen Robinson of Whittington ... ... 24 Ap
William Lawrence ... ... 26 May
Elizabeth dau. of Bryan Ward ... ... 28 June
Elizabeth wife of Edward Crosfield ... ... 3 Nov
Margret wife of Willm Brumley ... ... 6 „
Mary Tatham ... ... 10 „
John son of John Cockin ... ... 24 Dec
Wm Borrough ... ... 14 Jany
Elizabeth Adcock... ... ... 20 „
Isack son of Edward Houghton ... ... 25 Feb
Elizabeth dau. of John Johnson ... ... 21 Mar

1718.

Wm son of Elizabeth Overin	25 Mar
Edward Borrough	26 ,,
Katherine Johnson...	29 ,,
William Slater of Whittington	20 April
Julian Croft widdow	6 Jany
Luke Cornwell husbandman	6 Feb
Isabel wife of Thomas Tatham	21 Mar

1719.

Elizabeth wife of Thomas Peck husbandman ...	9 Aprill
Mary dau. of Sarah Morrah traveller	6 July
John son of Mr. Tho: North of Newton	29 Octr
Alice Patteson widdow	2 Mar

1720.

Thomas son of Franciss Chippindale	23 June
Franciss son of Elizabeth Johnson widdow	7 Aug
John son of Franciss Guye	5 Sep
Catherine wife of Richard Heblewhaite	7 ,,
Jane Gibson	21 Nov
Dorothy Johnson	11 Mar
James son of Joseph Place	22 ,,

1721.

Elizabeth wife of Thos Smith	30 May
Elizabeth dau. of Joseph Place	30 ,,
Margaret Towerson widdow	21 July
Thomas son of Wm Sclater	15 Sep
Jane w. of Wm Tomson...	29 ,,
Abigail Borrough widdow	11 Octr
Richard Robinson	23 Nov
Robert son of Bryan Ward	6 Mar
Jane wife of Edward France	14 ,,

1722.

Bryan son of Thomas Huck	6 Aprill
Elizabeth dau. of Richard North	28 May
Rowland son of John Borrough	6 Nov
Richard Johnson	13 Jany
Elizabeth dau. of Wm Tomason	16 ,,
Elizabeth dau. of Joseph Place	29 ,,
Elizabeth Borrough	3 Feb

Jane dau. of Christopher Lawrence ... ... 8 Feb
Jane dau. of Joseph Robinson ... ... 11 ,,
Ellin dau. of John Millers ... ... 14 ,,
William son of Christopher Hodgson ... ... 23 ,,
William Brumley ... ... 2 Mar
Ann dau. of Christopher Hodgson... ... ... 15 ,,
Ann wife of Christopher Hodgson ... ... 19 ,,

1723.

Alice North, widdow ... ... 7 May
Thomas Peck ... ... 21 ,,
Thomas son of Edward Blackburn... ... ... 10 June
Richard son of Bryan Ward ... ... 29 Aug
Ann Tomuson widdow from Tunstal parish ... ... 3 Sep
William Gibson ... ... 10 Dec
John Millers ... ... 27 ,,
Richard Heblewhaite ... ... 11 Jany
Oliver North ... ... 25 ,,
Margaret wife of Edward Crosfield ... ... 15 Mar

1724.

Margaret wife of Edward Houghton ... ... 27 May
Edward Cockin Sen' ... ... 1 June
Ann Eckrigg ... ... 11 ,,
Ellin dau. of Thomas Tomson ... ... 12 ,,
Hannah wife of William Daubikin... ... ... 4 July
William son of Christopher Hodgson ... ... 4 Dec
Thomas Klaif ... ... 20 Jany

1725.

George son of Thomas Kirby... ... ... 7 Oct
Ann dau. of John Johnson ... ... 16 ,,
Thomas son of Joseph Robinson ... ... 21 ,,
Elizabeth dau. of John Johnson ... ... 22 ,,
Wm Wardley ... ... 19 Nov
Wm Marsden ... ... 2 Dec
Ellin dau. of William Perkin... ... ... 12 ,,
Wm Nicholson ... . 13 Mar

1726.

Will Hunter ... ... 13 April
Mary wife of James Harris ... ... 28 July
Chris' son of Christoph' * * ... ... 27 Nov
Robert Attkinson of Newton ... ... 4 Decr
Will : Styth ... ... 6 Jany

Robert son of Edward France   ...   .   7 Jany
Ellin Robinson   ...   .   15 ,,
James Robinson   ...   .   5 Feb
Will : Millers ...   .   20 ,,
Frances wife of Mr. Daniel Pearson   ...   .   6 Mar

1727.

Richd Godsalve   ...   .   6 Aprill
Alex son of James Adcock   ...   .   29 ,,
John son of Tho: Croswhaite...   ...   .   28 May
Jane wife of Willm Smith   ...   .   21 June
Joseph Eskridge   ...   .   9 Sep
Richard Backhouse...   ...   .   20 Octr
Mary Barrow ...   .   18 Novr
Alice Robinson   ...   .   28 ,,
Mr. George Carus ...   .   27 Dec
Willm Dowbigin   ...   .   17 Jany
Jane wife of William Slater ...   .   20 ,,

1728.

Henry Dickonson ...   .   17 April
John Hardy   ...   .   24 ,,
Jane dau. of Nicholas Fisher ...   .   27 ,,
Isabel dau. of John Cockin   ...   .   3 May
Eliz: dau. of Thos Yeadon   ...   .   9 ,,
Ellin Mansergh widdow ...   .   13 ,,
Simon Batty   ...   .   22 Aug
Tho son of William Slater   ...   .   11 Oct
Will Tompson   ...   .   4 Dec
John Townson...   ...   .   8 ,,
John son of Christophʳ Hodgshon ...   .   21 ,,
Easter Styth widdow   ...   .   29 ,,
Will: Martin ...   .   1 Jany
Mary wife of James Coward ...   .   1 ,,
Eliz: Barrow ...   .   6 ,,
Benj: Cornthwaite ...   .   6 ,,
John Marshall   ...   .   11 ,,
John Willson ...   .   20 ,,
Isabel Backhouse ...   .   30 ,,
James Tatham   ...   .   1 March
Christopher son of Robert Heblethwaite   ...   ...   6 ,,
Margaret Martin widdow   ...   .   9 ,,
Ann Tatham widdow   ...   .   16 ,,

1729.

Bryan son of Tho: Robinson ...   .   7 May
Geo: son of Christophʳ Lawrence ...   .   21 ,,

Alex: Adcock	22 June
Jennet North	30 Aug
James Garnet	9 Nov
Isabel Cornthwaite...	5 Jany
Eliz: dau. of Thos Huck	21 ,,

1730.

Thos Attkinson	26 June
Ellin wife of Richard Johnson	1 Sep
Jennet dau. of Edwd Barton	21 Nov
John Styth	10 Dec
Mary Todd	22 Jany

1731.

Henry Eckridge	17 May
Ann Lawrence	20 Aug
Christopher Hodgshon	31 ,,
Margaret Cort...	9 Sep
Benjamin Holme son of John Holme	27 ,,
Ellin Atkinson	11 Oct
Mary Bordrigge	24 ,,
Martha wife of Richd Tatham	26 ,,
Ann wife of John Cornthwaite	13 Mar

1732.

Willm Smith of Newton	9 June
Agnes wife of Thos Tatham	17 Oct
Ann Relph	27 Nov
Willm Eckridge	21 Dec
Margaret Robinson...	11 Jany
Thos son of Tho: Rooklay	28 Feb

1733.

Willm son of Willm Slater	7 April
Willm Parkin...	21 ,,
Richd Gunson...	5 June
John Burrow	28 July
Eliz Noble	13 Sep
Willm son of Willm Martin	29 ,,
John Robinson	20 October
Ellin dau. of John Whittington	28 ,,

1734.

Margaret wife of John Heblethwaite	3 Sep
Edwd Crossfield	15 October

Mrs. Vigessima Bouch ... ...   16 November
Margaret dau. of Willm Willson ... ...   21 Feb

1735.

John Lonsdale   ... ...   18 May
Mary dau. of John Barrow ... ...   3 June
Mary w. of Edward Cockin ... ...   3 August
Richard Tatham of Newton ... ...   24 ,,
Margaret wife of John Johnson of Newton ... ...   1 March

1736.

John son of Henry Stackhovse ... ...   4 May
Margaret dau. of John Heblethwaite ... ...   24 ,,
Agnes dau. of Tho: Foxcroft ... ...   25 ,,
Ann dau. of William Dickonson ... ...   15 August
Isabel w. of Thos Foxcroft ... ...   22 September
Hannah dau. of William Ernshaw... ... ...   8 October
Ellin w. of William Earnshaw ... ...   19 ,,
Benjamin son of Christoph^r Hodgshon ... ...   19 ,,
John Tatham of Newton ... ...   25 ,,
Isabel w. of Thomas Tompson ... ...   8 November
John Heblethwaite Elder of Newton ... ...   7 January
Abraham son of George Ginnings ... ...   30 ,,
Mary Nealson ... ...   4 February
Margaret w. of Richard North ... ...   18 March

1737.

Henry Chatburn ... ...   17 July
Ann w. of John Saul ... ...   14 January
Mary dau. of Robert Willson ... ...   28 ,,
John Carter son of Agnes Harrisson ... ...   16 February
William Tompson ... ...   2 March
Hannah Burrow ... ...   17 ,,

1738.

Agnes dau. of Tho: Kirby ... ...   1 May
Richd son of William Tompson ... ...   5 ,,
Barbary Burrow ... ...   7 ,,
Tho: Smith of Newton ... ...   23 July
Agnes dau. of John Cornthwaite of Kear Lain in ye
    p^{sh} of Burton ... ...   29 October
Margaret Armestead of Clapham ... ...   26 ,,
Alice w. of Oliver North ... ...   16 December
Jane Millers widow ... ...   29 January
Elizabeth Taylor widow ... ...   23 March

1739.

Thomas Millers	27 March
Robert Willson	15 June
Elizabeth dau. of William Chatburn	28 ,,
Ann Cockin widow	4 Sep
Francis Chippindale	27 Oct
James Bland, Newton	22 Dec
Jane Bland wife of James Bland of Newton... ...	29 ,,
William Batty	9 Feb
Sara dau. of John Saul	19 March

1740.

Richard son of Edward France	12 April
Robert son of Robert Gibson	23 ,,
Margaret dau. of Henry Stackhovse	1 July
Ann Adcock widow	6 ,,
Ellin dau. of Robert Gibson	3 August
John Robinson	8 ,,
Mary Atkinson of Newton widdow	16 ,,
Thomas Gunson of Holmehovse	16 November
Margaret wife of John Barrow of Docker	6 March
Agnes Margisson widow of Docker	19 ,,

1741.

Christiana dau. of John Barrow	20 May
Thomas son of John Barrow	25 ,,
Isabel dau. of Thomas Yeadon	13 July
William Slater of Newton	22 November
Richd son of Richd North of Docker	9 December
Richd North of Docker	15 January
Richard North of Whittington	21 ,,
Alice wife of Edward Blackburn	22 ,,
Margret wife of John Johnson	23 March

1742.

John Johnson...	8 May
Robart Marting	20 August
Richard North	29 October
Edmand Kerby	20 November
Doaraty Robson	10 December
Joseph Hodghan	12 ,,
Ann Lowrans	2 January
Elizabeth Huck of Docker	5 ,,
William Adkock	9 ,,

John Robison ... ...   13 January
William Nowball of Newton ... ...   7 February
James Bolderston of Newton   9   ,,

1743.

Elizabeth Watkings widdow ... ...   6 April
Isabell Thompson weddow of this town   30   ,,
Jane w. of John Johnson ... ...   10 May
Margrat Dekson wife of Brian Dekson   14   ,,
Daniall Pearson of Whitington   22   ,,
Margret dau. of Will: Harreson ... ...   20 June
Thomas son of Rob: Gibson ... ...   8 July
Agnes dau. of Will: Smith ... ...   13 January
Margret Chippindal weadow ... ...   7 February
Robert son of Edward Barton   21   ,,

1744.

Alice dau. of John Cockin ... ...   7 May
John Stithe ... ...   18 July
John Hodgson ... ...   2 October
Thomas Thompson ... ...   19 February

1745.

Mary Wilson ... ...   7 July
Wm Armystead ... ...   15 September
Margaret Martin ... ...   15 November
Robert Robinson   20   ,,
James Adcock ... ...   19 December
Jane Gunson ... ...   17 January

1746.

John Holm ... ...   3 November
Ann Adkinson ... ...   17 January
Edmand Chatburn   18   ,,

1747.

Isabell Allen ... ...   16 May
George Hornby clerk late Rector of Whittington...   19 November
Robert Thompson   25   ,,

1748.

John son of Joseph Johnson ... ...   17 April
Ellin Greenwood widdow ... ...   6 May

Edward Blackburn ... ...   3 July
Alice Thomson widdow ... ...   23 August
Elizabeth dau. of Richard Thomson   ... ...   14 January

1749.

Elinor dau. of Miles Ekerigg ... ...   9 June
Alice w. of Wm Chatburn ... ...   26 ,,
Robert Helme ... ...   13 September
Samuel Burrow ... ...   14 ,,
Elizabeth w. of John Cockin ... ...   20 ,,
Ann Bordrigg wid* ... ...   10 December
Ann dau. of Richd Thompson ... ...   17 January
Edward Houghton ... ...   30 ,,
Mr. Thomas North ... ...   17 February
Bryan Dickson ... ...   14 March

1750.

Ann mother of Joseph Bland ... ...   27 May
Mary w. of William Laurence ... ...   7 Aug
Mary dau. of Jonathan Battersby ... ...   13 ,,
Joseph Holme ... ...   31 Sep
Thomas Noble of Newton ... ...   14 Nov
William son of Wm Laurence ... ...   16 Feb.
John Whittington ... ...   19 March

1751.

Jane dau. of John Slater ... ...   10 June
Jaine Noble widow ... ...   1 Aug
Elizabeth wife to Edward Barton ... ...   21 Sep.

1752.—*New Stile.*

Jno. son of the Reverend Mr. Nicholson ... ...   1 Feb..
William Martin ... ...   30 Oct

1753.

Isabella Skirrow ... ...   15 Jan
James Dowthwaite ... ...   5 June
Jane dau. of Henry North ... ...   7 Oct
Edward Robinson ... ...   29 Nov
Jane Adcock ... ... [*sic*]   19 Sep

1754.

Benjamin son of Jonathan Batersby ... ...   8 Jan
John Margisson of Docker ... ...   2 March

Christopher son of John Slater	7 April
William son of William Durham	12 May
Ellin dau. of Miles Eckridge	24 June
Mary dau. of John Adcock	3 July
Richard Cockin of Newton	16 Sep

1755.

Elizabeth Huck	5 Jan
Ann w. of Miles Eckrigge	22 Feb
John son of Miles Eckrigge	16 April
Thomas Hodgson	4 May
Margaret w. of Robert Chippendale	1 June
John Towers	29 Sep
Catharine Eckridge	30 Novr

1756.

Thomas son of Thomas Nicholson clerk	5 Jan
William Penny	6 Feb
Mary dau. of William Durham	17 March
Jane dau. of William Smith	7 April
Agnes dau. of William Browne	9 ,,
Susanna dau. of Thomas Nicholson clerk	27 ,,
Ann dau. of Richard Thompson	23 May
Isabel dau. of Thomas Addison	1 August
Dorothy w. of Robert Gibson	20 ,,

1757.

Alice Overen	4 Feb
Mary dau. of William Smith	5 ,,
Richard Mansergh	27 March
Ann w. of Richard Procter	27 ,,
William Chatburn	26 Nov
Ellin Tomlinson	6 Dec

1758.

Charles son of Willm Houghton	8 March
Alice dau. of Christ: Hodgson	30 April
John son of Miles Eckrigge	25 June
Mary Penny	7 Novr
Richard Procter	14 ,,

1759.

Ruth Meals widow	22 May
William Robinson	9 Aug
Hannah dau. of John Hardy	29 Dec

1760.

Elizabeth Hodgson widow	27 Jan
Ralph Capstick	29 ,,
Mrs. Ellin North widow...	4 Feb
Ann wife of Rich⁹ North...	10 ,,
Emmanuel son of Willm Durham...	18 ,,
William Bordrigge	30 June
Edward France	10 Nov

1761.

Robert son of John France	15 Feb
Oliver North	20 March
Mrs. Elizabeth Rawlinson widow	26 ,,
Elizabeth Greenhow	9 May
William Margison	27 Sep

1762.

Henry North of Docker	22 Jan
Margaret dau. of Sarah Fell	23 March
John Millar	6 Sep.
Jane Stythe	6 ,,
Mary Brennan...	19 ,,
William Willan	25 Oct
Mary dau. of Rich⁹ Thompson	23 Nov
Alice dau. of Christopher Hodgson	8 Dec

1763.

Edward Thornborough	17 Jan
Thomas Kirby	24 ,,
Elizabeth w. of John France	7 March
William son of John Adcock	8 ,,
Margaret w. of Thos Huck	12 ,,
Thomas Robinson	13 ,,
Elizabeth dau. of Thos Nicholson	29 ,,
Richard Taylor	1 April
Nicholas Hallstead...	5 ,,
Richard Johnson	13 ,,
Elizabeth Johnson	18 ,,
George Newby	3 May
Thomas Robinson of Hutton Roof...	12 ,,
Joseph Johnson	29 ,,
Richard Whittington	22 June

John Cockin ... ... 10 July
Thomas son of Richard Hardy   ... ... 15 „
Thomas son of Willm Durham   ... ... 28 Aug

1764.

Dorothy dau. of Abraham and Margaret Collin ... 29 Feb
Richard son of James and Elizabeth Johnson   ... 10 March
Richard Tatham ... ... 18 April
Isabel dau. of Ann Newby ... ... 22 June
Isabel dau. of John and Agnes Thornborough   ...   2 Aug.
Edward Barton   ... ... 25 Sep.

Weddings.

[1558.]

Thomas Smyth   Jane Ridall ...   .
Thomas Smyth   Margaret Whithead   ...

[1559.][1]

Willm Aplegarthe   Elizabethe Johnson nupt.
Gyles Towne   Elzabeth Robinson   ,,   22 Novem.

[1560.]

Reynold Dodgeson   Margaret Thornton nupt. 26 [2]
Edmunde Loydge   Jane Smythe vidua   ,,   8 Jan.

[1561.]

*   *   *   [3]   13 Junij
*   *   *   [3]   14 Octobris
*   *   *   [3]   nupt. 18   ,,

[1562.][1]

*   *   * aupland [3]   *   *   *   son   ... nupt. 27 Juniij

[1563.]

*   *   * [B ?]rabin [3]   *   *   *   es ...   ... nupt. 17 Januarij

[1564.]

*   *   * [3]   *   *   * dge   ... nupt. 20 Novembris
[Christ]opher [Ni]chollson*   *   * [3]   ...   ,,   8 Decembris
Thomas Mellinge   Ellinge North   ...   ,,   14   ,,

1565.

Martine Crofte   Jenet Slater vidua   nupt. 13 Octobris
John Godsalfe   Margaret Thornton   ,,   6 Novembris
John Owesman   Dorathye Banes nupt. penultimo   ,,

---

[1] Leaf torn.   [2] Month torn off.   [3] Torn away.

1569.

Thomas Robinson	Elizabeth Blaude... nupt.	28 Januariij
John Preston	Jane Corte ... ... ,,	penultimo [1]

[1570.]

Anthony Frearman	Elzabeth Johnson	nupt.	11 Augustiij
Brian Dicconson	Elzabeth Johnson	,,	20 Januariij
Richard Sidgwicke	Jenet Toluson...	,,	5 ,,
Mr. Miles Hudleston	M^{tris} Catering Coyĕs	,,	12 ,,

1571.

John Harrison	Ellinge Mellinge...	nupt.	4 Maij
Gilbert Atkinson	Jenet Dicconson...	,,	11 ,,
Robert Robinson	Elzabeth Bayliffe	,,	2 Juliij
* * * and	* * * son [2] ...	,,	8 Novembris
Willm Hodgeson	Issabell North ...	,,	16 ,,

1573.

Henry Geslinge	Ellinge Vstonson...	...[3] primo Januarij
Thomas Johnson	Alice Robinson	2 Maij
John Robinson	Agnes Tomson	14 Novebris

1578.

Willm Holme	Emrey Hine	14 Agusti
Christopher Holme	Jenet Hine	14 ,,
George Toppinge	Agnes Robinson ... ...[4]	
[Ne ?]wton Rector	Dorathy Crosbie	7 Septembris

1579.

Thomas Sclater	Mabell Harrison	27 Januarij
Christopher Dicconson	Agnes Allamby	27 ,,
Francis Hirdson	Elzabethe Dawney ...	20 Novĕbr
Richard Hardy	Ellinge Geslinge	27 ,,

1580.

John Sigewicke	Elzabethe Stons	20 Januarij
* * * Bland [1]	* * * Richardson ...	30 ,,
James Mellinge	Jane Johnson	2 Julij

[1] Edge of leaf torn off.
[2] Torn away.
[3] All the Marriages being entered in similar form the word "Nupt." has henceforward been omitted.
[4] Date torn off.

1581.

Marmaduke Robinson	Mabell Wetheman ...	19 Novēbris
George Lupton	Essabell Johnson ...	14 Maij
John Speight	Alis Sill	28 ,,
Martin Croft	Jenet Slater vidua ...	12 Augusti

1582.

Marmaduke Robinson	An Powe	24 Novēbris

1583.

Roger Whithead	Agnes Nealson	28 Novēbris
Richard Atkinson	Maud Crofte	3 Februarij

1584.

John Euan	Margret Towne	24 Novembris
Tristram Sill	Isabell Corte	12 Februarij
John Linkcolne	Elzabeth Sidgwicke ..	14 ,,
Richard Deny	An Tasker	14 Novēbris

1585.

Edmund Adcoke	Margret North	13 Novēbris

1586.

Richard Blackburne	Alis Adcocke	9 Februarij
James Blackburne	Margret Adcoke	9 ,,
Symond Hutton	Frysis Sharpe	14 Augusti
Willm Heaton	Jenet Robinson	21 ,,
John Hodgson	Alis Hall vidua	16 Octobris

1587.

Leonard Carter	Jane Blande	28 Januarij
George Willm	Margeret Dodgson	... ultimo ,,
James Bond	Elzabeth Hall	,, ,,
Reonold Godsalfe	Alis Heaton...	15 Aprilis
Robert Burrow	Agnes Tatham	25 Junij
Thomas Bland	Alice Johnson	14 Julij
Renold Tatham	Alice North	13 Octobris
Thomas Whithead	Elzabeth Holme	19 ,,

1588.

Gilbert Thornton	Joane North	21 Novēbris
Wiħm Burrow	Isabell Pachet	26 Januarij
Giles Towne	Jenet Borthrige	2 Februarij
John Johnson	Margret Pachet	28 Januarij
John Burrow	Jenet Heaton	9 Februarij
Thomas Hirdson	Elsabeth Roneson ...	26 Octobr
John Toluson	Margret Lupton	2 Novēbris

1589.

Mr. Thomas Carus	Mrs. An Hudleston ...	26 Novēbris
Willm Ewan	Isabell Brockbancke ...	9 Februarij
Miles Bayliffe	Alice Tomson	10 ,,
Thomas Burrow	Ann Hodgson	12 ,,
Rodger Garnet	Jane Reminton	15 Novēbris

1590.

Henry Jackson	Eldred Harrison	19 Novembris
Edward Corte	Jenet Whithead	27 Junij
James Crofte	Elsabeth North	1 Octobris

1591.

Thomas Chatburne	Jane Laifeild	17 Novēbr
Willm Sharpe	Elsabeth Newton ...	6 Februarij
Arthure Fousecroft	Mabell Robinson... ...	7 Maij
John Buser	Alice Johnson	7 ,,
Richard Hall	Catherin Adcoke... ...	28 ,,
Wiħm Barker	Elsabeth Bland	2 Julij
Thomas Wilson	An Atkinson	26 Octobris
Robert Thornborrow	Dorothye Moyses ...	20 ,,

1592.

Christopher Mellinge	Margret Johnson... ...	3 Februarij
Leonard Lucas	Elsabeth Johnson ...	29 Aprilis
John Hodgson	Margret Tomson... ...	17 Junij
Christopher Walker	Ellinge Johnson	24 ,,

1593.

Christopher Manser	Jenet Jacson	14 Decēbris
Edmund Burrow	Margret Crosby	16 Janij

1594.

Wiłłm Whithead	Agnes Ewan	9 Februarij
Richard Knight	Ellyn Hall	16 ,,

1595.

Tristram Bowerdale	An Hewtson	8 Junij 1596
Edward Bowerdall	Margret Hewtson ...	8 ,, ,,

1596.

John Midleton	Ellinge Jackson ...	...30 Januarij 1596
Thomas Blackburne	Jane Brabin ...	... 7 Decembris ,,
Wiłłm Tomson	Elsabeth Hutton...	...27 Julij ,,
Addam Stors	Ellin Mellinge ...	... 8 Augusti ,,
Robert Hine	Elsabeth Hewtson	...22 Septēbris ,,

1597.

Marmaduke Cokinge	Jane Robinson	4 Decembris 1597
John Yeat	Elsabeth Toppinge ...11 ,,	1595
Christopher Holme	Ellin Parrate ...	...16 Februarij ,,
Richard Robinson	Margaret Guy ...	...11 Augusti 1596
Wiłłm Sands	Jane Myars vidua ...29 ,, [1]	,,

1598.

Edmund Whithead	Isabell Barrow ...	...21 Januarij 1596
Renolod Borthrige	Dorothe Thornton	...11 ,, ,,
Edward Atkinson	Margret Dowson...	...18 ,, ,,
John Johnson	Kateryn Dawney	...19 ,, ,,
Thomas Pearson	An Cokeram ...	...13 ,, ,,
Thomas Whithead	Jane Nealson ...	...18 Februarij ,,
Brian Nealson	Mabell Cort... ...	...28 Aprilis
Richard Cort	Margret Mellinge	... 20 Maij
Henry Ewan	Jenet Jackson ...	...14 Junij
James Bland	Alice Cowper ...	...23 ,,
Thomas Wildinge	Elsabeth Tomson	...25 ,,
John Knight	Dorothe Rondson	...11 Augusti
Edward Wilson	Alice Witton ...	...20 Septēbris
Wiłłm Maddison	Jane Newton ...	...22 ,,

1599.

Richard Johnson	Jane Harries	18 Novembris
Wiłłm Curtisse	Elsabeth Woodhouse ...	18 Januarij

[1] These dates appear in original as printed here.

Allan Winder	Isabell Diconson... ...	8 Julij
Thomas Robinson	Elsabeth North	28 ,,
Thomas Covell, gent	Dorothy Watson vidua	14 Augusti

1600.

| Bryan Gibson | Jenet Wilkinson ... ... | 22 Decēbris |
| Christopher Baines | Isabell Hutton ... ... | 15 Novēbris |

1601.

| Wilfrid Brockhouse | Isabell Dicconson ... | 29 Novēbris |
| Thomas Carter | Margret Backhouse ... | 28 Januarij |

1602.

| Richard Dawney | Jane Heaton ... ... | 23 Januarij |

1603.

| Stephen Atkinson | Margret Robinson ... | 8 Decēbris |

1604.

| Stephen Walker | Margeret Awrey... ... | 17 Junij |

1605.

Olyver Dicconson	Margret Husband ...	15 Julij
Edward Bainbridge	An Robinson	11 Augusti
Thomas Toppinge	An Hodgson	5 Marcij

1606.

Thomas Waller	Elsabeth Garnet	17 Augusti
Olyver North	Agnes Hirdson	24 ,,
George Sidgwicke	Katheryn Ewan	2 Octobris
Wiłłm Johnson	Catheryn Syll ...ultimo die Novembris
John Hardy	Margret Johnson... ...	25 Octobris
Wiłłm Gynnings	Mabell Fowscroft vidua	2 Novembris
James Harries	Jenet Dawney ...	primo die Februarij
Bryan Bland	Isabell Patchet	4 ,,
Hēry Eygrige	Elsabeth Thornton ...	8 ,,
Robert Jacson	Jenet Hardy	10 ,,

1607.

| Richard Kitchin | Jane Dodgson ... ... | 19 Aprilis |
| Danyell Hodgson | Margret Johnson ... | 17 Maij |

Thomas Harlinge	Alice Slater...	7 Junij
John Smyth	Jenet Conder	14 „
Edmund Burrow	Alice Godsalfe	28 „
Richard Manser	Elsabeth Hirdson	ultimo die Novēbris

1608.

| Thomas Widder | Jane North... ... ... | 8 Maij |

1609.

John Tayler	Margery Wyldder ...	7 Junij
Leonard Walker	An Heaton	18 „
Wiłłm Slater	Alice Hirdson	14 Januarij
John Bethome	Jenet Burrow ...penultimo die „

1610.

James Johnson	Alice Harlinge	9 Maij
Thomas Hodgeson	Mary Waydson	8 Julij
Richard Cansfeilde	Elsabeth Clarkson ...	4 Augusti

1611.

Wiłłm Smyth	Ellyn Burrow	11 Augusti
Lenard Newton, gent	An Banes, gentw. ...	15 Decembris
Henry Robinson	Alice Awrey	7 Februarij

1612.

| John Slater | Jenet Godsalfe ... ... | 18 Octobris |
| John Turner | An Bayliffe... ... ... | 11 Januarij |

1613.

John Dodgeson	Ellyn Ashburner ...	9 Octobris
John Wallmsley	Jane Hodgson	16 Novembris
John Brize	Dorrothie Hudleston ...	23 „

1614.

| Thomas Northe | Mabell Godsalfe ... ... | 17 Julij |

1615.

| James Newton | Margret Heaton ...quinto die Novembris |

1616.

Leonard Ewan	Agnes Bland	23 Julij
James Dickonson	Tomesin Harrison ...	17 Februarij
Robert Robinson	Margret Bland	23 ,,
Wiłłm Towers	Annie Barker	26 ,,
John Carter	Aune Newton	27 ,,
Robert Jackson	Agnes North vidua	... primo die Marcij

1617.

Xpofer Baitson	- Elin Stors vidua	21 Octobris
Renold Godsalfe	Jane Heaton	14 Decembris
Wiłłm Kidde	Isabell Margerison ...	17 Januarij

1618.

Bryann Bland	Isabell Scayffe vidua ...	14 Maij
John Eisston [?]	Margerie Cansfeeld ...	25 ,,
James Atkinson	Alice Prockter vidua ...	24 Augusti
Rowland Whitchead	Margaret Godsalfe ...	30 Januarij

1619.

Richard Dickonson	Grace Atkinson	2 Junij
James Borowes	Ann Margeson	5 Septembris

1620.

Thomas Barker	Katherine Bland ...	21 Maij

1621.

Bryan Smith	Elizabeth Beyly	26 Augusti
Wiłłm Smith	Elizabeth Fortune	quinto die Novembris
Thomas Smith	Margrett Adcocke ...	2 Decembris
Xpofer Bourdell	Elizabeth Conder ...	7 Januarij
Arthur Midleton	Elizabeth Burrow ...	19 Februarij

1622.

James Harries	Maude Townson	16 December

1623.

Henrie Harries [1]	Agnes Ewan vidua ...	12 Januarij

[1] It will be noted that hereabouts are many defects in the Register.

1627.

Thomas Johnson   Jenet Newton   ...   ...   secundo April

1628.

Francis Turner   Margrett Hutton   ...   25 Novemb⁹

1629.¹

John Wilkinson   Isabell Vstenson ...   ...   14 Novembris

1630.

John Eshton   Alice Wright   ...   ...   7 Novembris
Edward Burrowe   Anne Robinson   28   ,,

1631.

John Witton   Jane Burrowe   ...   ...   14 Maij
Wiłłm Adcock   Katherin Dawnye   ...   23 Junij
Richard Patton   Alice Nealson   ...   ...   11 Augusti
Richard Cornthwayte   Ann Johnson   ...   ...   9 Octobris
Thomas Johnson   Margerie North ...   ...   14 Novembris
Brian Nealson   Mabbell North widdowes   7 Februarij

1632.

Wiłłm Mellinge   Rebeckae Maddison   undecimo die Julij
Edward Thornburrow   Elizabeth Yeate ...   ...   13 November
John Lonsdale   Ellin Dawnie   17   ,,
Abraham Nealson   Anne Carter   ...   ultimo die Februarij

1633.

Wiłłm Hall   Jane Daunie   ...   ... secundo die Maij
Bryan Battie   Isabell Hutton   ...   ...   26 Septembris
Ric Tayler   Ann Cocking   ...   ...   20 Octobris
Wilfryde Moore   Isabell Bacchus ...   ...   16 Januarij

1634.

John Bland   Jennet Ostcliffe ...   ...   14 Juliij
Johes Harries   Katherine Bland...   ultimo die Augustij
Geo: Ward   Agnes Shaw   ...   quinto die Februarij

¹ Between 1628 and 1629 about a quarter of the page is left blank.

1635.

Thomas Robinson	Ann Hutton	19 Aprilis
Willm Hewgill	Ellen Smorthwayt ...	6 Maij
Willm Stithe	Elza: Robinson	18 Augusti
Francis Greenbank	Ann Deanj [? Dean] vid	28 ,,
Bryan Dickonson	Ellen Sidgswick	10 Decembris

1637.

Edw: Dowthwayt	Agnes Scamle	27 Aprill
Randall Kew	Jennet Douthwait ...	6 Julij
James Godsalfe	Alice Ewan	5 Octobris

1638.

Johes Bland	Alicia North	18 Junij
Robtus Jackson de Newton	Agnes Sidgswick ...	25 Februarij

1639.

Geo: Moone	Elizabeth Wilkenson ...	duodecimo Maij
Thomas Robinson	Ann Pow	undecimo Julij
Nicholas Dowthwate	Jane Wallen	30 Julij
Thom: Johnson	Jane Padget	10 Augusti
Willm Butterfell of ye pishe of Mitton Isabel Maiers of ye pishe of Bolton by ye Sands at Whittington		3 September
John Stamper	Agnes Batty	2 Februarij

1640.

Marmaduke Slater	Agnes Whithead... ..	10 September
Richard Jackson	Tomsin Futhergill ...	13 Octobris
Robt. Eyskrigge	Hellen Bordridge ...	23 Novembris
Ricd. Tayler	Katherine Darbie ...	25 ,,
Nicholas Brumell	Dorothie Greenewood ...	8 Februarij

1641.

Willm Harlinge	Anne Saule	quarto Julij

Mr. Jackson entered to the rectori of Whittington xxvito Julij anno p'dj.

Richard Kewe	Isabell Moore, vidua ...	17 Januarij

1642.

John Gibson	Agnes Miller	... ...	12 Junij
Wiłłm Godsalfe	Jane Dawnye	... ...	21 Augustij
Edmund Lodge pochie de Bolton	}	... ...	eodem die
Jenett Seele pochie de Halton vidua			

1643.

Bryan Dawnie	Dorothe Carter ...	...	29 Aprillis

1644.[1]

1645.

Edward Dowthwayt	Ellin Jackson	... ...	26 Augustij
John Hardie vidu[r]	Elizabeth Bowerdall vid		2 September
Mr. John Middelton	Mrs. Marie Coles...	...	9 October
Wiłłm Styth	Isabell Pow ...	decimo sexto Decembris

1646.[1]

1647.

Mr. Richard Jackson	Janue Carter	vicessimo sexto Januariij
Christopher Burrow	Marye Smith	29 „
Bryan Mansergh	Ester Dickonson	12 Februarie

1653.

William Townson	Jane Vstenson	... ...	7 Julij
Henry Loudg	Jenet Mahan	... ...	4 October 1654
Robert Burrow	Dorothy Betham...	...	17 March „

1655.

Thomas North of Docker	}		
Elizabeth Willson of Ouer Kellet		... ...	28 Aprill
George Willson of Newton	}		
Dorothy Harlin of the same towne		... ...	24 Maij

1656.

Thomas Smith of Arram of the pishe of Melling	}
Elizabeth [2] Dicconson of Newton	3 May

[1] The numerous blanks in the Original will be noted.
[2] This is written over "Isabell" struck through.

Edward Douthwaite of Newton Kathrain Melling of Whittington	}	29 July
Thomas Hutton of Whittington Jenet Postlthaite of Hutton Roofe	}	17 ,,
Henry Myres Elizabeth Grunwell (both servants at Whittington Hall)	...	18 October
Robert Blackburne Elizabeth Mires widdow		28 ,,
Willm Slater son of Willm Slater of Whittington Anas Smyth of Arram	}	7 January

1658.

Thomas sone of Willm Atkinson of Geesgil of the Prish of Orton in Wesmerland and Agnes North daughter of Richard North of Docker of this Parish, the banes of matrimony betwixt the said Thomas and Agnes wear published thre sabbath dayes and after married the third day of June aᵖᵖᵈ registered by me Willm Newton clerk and Register Whitt:

Thomas Turner sone of Willm Turner of the towne and parish of Melling and Margret North doughter of Richard North of this parish, the banes of matrimony betwixt the said Thomas and Margret wear published thre sabbath daies and imediatly after married the five-and-twenteth day of August A° pᵈ by me Willm Newton clerke and Register Whitt:

1662.

Thomas Croft worker at coole mines Agnes Bow	}	1 June
James Dickonson, miller Elizabeth Talens...	...	30 Novem
John sone of Willm Cort Jane Tayler daughter of Robert Tayler (both of Arram)	}	29 January

1663.

Edward Holden gent: and schoolemaster and Agnes Carter by vertue of a Licence granted and given by Sr Joseph Cradock, Commissary dated the 4th day of June, married the sixteenth day A° pᵈ and mens: pᵈ

1664.

John Rallison of Dalton and Margret Crosfeild of Holm both within the parish of Burton wear published the severall Sundaies within the Chappell of peston patrick nupt in our Church the xᵗʰ day of Novemb: Anno pᵈ

[*Volume II. of Original Registers.*]

1663.

Edward Holden gent. schoolmaster, and Agnes
    Carter[1] ...   .   nupt. 16 June

1664.

John Rallison of Dalton and Margret Crosfeild of
    Holme[1] ...   .   10 Novr

1665.

Miles Eykridge and Margret Slater   ...   .   18 Oct
                 by vertue of a License
Thomas Nuby and Jenet Hirdson   ...   ... nupt.   9 January
                 by vertue of a License
John Wildman and Elling Whithead   ... nupt.
                 Banes pub.   4 Feb
James Curteous and Margret Taylor...   ... nupt.
                 also Banes pub.   3 Feby

1666.

Thomas Denny of Halton and Isabell Bordridge
                 License   30 April
Richard Claughton of Holme and Jane North of
    Docker widdow   ...   .   Banes   1 May
Oliuer Birch and Margret Barker...   ...   .   8 „
    Banes being published according to the Cannon
Robert Skirrow and Ann Dicconson   ...   .   4 July
    Banes being published according to the Cannon
Thomas Taylor and Elizabeth Battersby   ...   ...   9 „
    Banes being published according to the Cannon
Thomas Towerson and Jane Cocking ...   .   11 Aug
    Banes being published according to the Cannon
Richard Crt and Margret Denison   ...   .   18 Septr
Jarret Skaife and Elizabeth Harrison ...   .   9 Octr
                 by vertue of a License
Robert Lawson and Jenet Slater...   ...   Banes   11 „

1667.

Henry Brogten and Alice Robinson   ...   ...Banes   16 April
Robert Toppin and Elling Cort ...   .   „   20 June

---

[1] It will be noticed that these two entries have occurred already with
    fuller particulars.

Robert Burrow and Margret Fairay ... ...Banes   22 June
Mr. Edward Richardson of Kirckby Lonsdale and
   Mrs. Isabell Carr   ...by vertue of License   29 Aug
John Robinson of Dent and Agnes Wilson of
   Newton... ... ...Banes   3 Septr
John Widder of Arram and Jane Eskrigg License   29 Octr
William Slater of Newton and Katheraine Taylor
   widdow ... ... License   23 January

1668.

Edward Ward in the county of Yorke and Alice
   Bayley in the county of Westmer... License   26 March
Thomas Shaw of Belrige in the townshippe of
   Scotforth and psh of Lancaster and Alice
   Dooleman widdow... ... ... License   14 April
Thomas Bland and Jenet Smyth, both of Newton
                           Banes   18 Octr
Richard North batchler and Alice Slater widdow
                       License   26 Jany
Nicholas Collison and Margret Robinson... Banes   6 Febry

1669.

Peter Burrow and An Jackson ... ... Banes   22 April
John Ridding of Midleton and Alice Dodshon of
   Barbron... ... ... License   9 June
Edward Allenby and Mary Setle both of parrish
   of Cartmell ... ...   23 ,,
   Banes being pub. according to the Cannon by
   certificat of the Minister of the said Cartmell

1670.

Thomas Chorlee and Isabell Wildman ... Banes   17 April
Andrew Cue and Agnes Croft... ... ... ,,   24 ,,
Edward Dicconson, webster, and Jane Wilson,
   spinster ... ... Banes   30 June
Richard Walker of the pish of Kirby Lonsdale and
   Alice Battersby of this pish by virtue of License   19 July
Thomas Watson and Jane Robinson ... Banes   25 ,,

1671.

John Towerson and Margret Cocking ... ...   30 June
   by virtue of License from the Lord of Chester
Willm Gibson and An Bradley ... ... Banes   2 July
Oliuer North and Jenet Jackson... ... ,,   6 ,,

Willm Lonsdale and Johanna Wilson   ...   Banes   26 August
John Wildman and Margret Dicconson   „   7 February
Banes pub. out upon the 28th January according
to the Cannon

1672.

Edmond Adcocke and Elizabeth North...   Banes   7 Novr

1673.

Christopher Taylor and Jane Jackson...   Banes   22 May
John Gawthrope and Alice Bland of Newt   „   17 June
Willm Slater and Margret Dicconson ...   „   26 „
John Cort and Agnes Slater w   ...   ...   „   22 Novr

1674.

Brian Waller and Jane Killner   ...   ...   Banes   21 April
John Lancaster w. and Agnes Bethome spinstr...   1 May
    License
Thomas Widder of Hornby w. and Agnes Taylor
    widdow ...   .   Banes   1 Septr
John Cockeram and Jenet Cocking   ...   „   29 „
Willm Whithead and Margret Allenby   „   22 Octr
Thomas Slack of the Parish of Lancaster and
    Judith Bland   ...   .   „   8 Novr

1675.

Oliuer Dicconson and Joane Lonsdalle vid License   30 March
Thomas Richardson of Kendall and Au Flemin Banes   3 June

1676.

Bryan Watson and Mary Hardy ...   ...   Banes   22 April
Richard Stors and Sarah Margison   ...   „   27 „
Giles Alcock and Sarah Widder of Chapenwray nupt.   4 May
John Nuby and Magdalen Procter   ...   License   19 Novr
Rowland Burrow and Abigaile Jackson   „   26 February

1677.

Bryan Johnson and Jane Dawney   ...   License   8 Septr
Willm Bateson and Briggit Manserge...   Banes   3 Novr

1678.

John Corner and Isabell Dickonson   ...   Banes   4 June
Willm Patison and Alice Whitehead   ...   „   26 Novr

1679.

Willm Brumley and Margret Gilpin ...	Banes	21 April
Thomas Newby and Jane Troughton ...	,,	9 June
Willm Smyth and Agnes Ullacke ...	,,	6 July
Thomas Wattson and Jane Ullacke ...	License	14 Augst
Edward Crosfeild and Elizabeth Betham	Banes	4 September

1680.

Willm Redded and Elizabeth Rawnson	Banns	22 May
Edward Townson and Jane Readhead...	,,	24 June
Edmond Hodgson and Alice Gawthroppe	License	17 August
John Robinson and Elizabeth Godsalfe	Banns	18 Octobr
Edward Cockin and Alice Towneson ...	,,	21 ,,

1681.

Thomas Turner of Nether Hutton and Mary Turner of Mellin	License	14 April
Richard North and Margret Greenefeild	,,	30 Novr
William Batty and Margret Nicholson...	,,	1 Decr
John Manserge and Ellin Jackson ...	...Bans	25 Jany

1682.

Thomas Newby and Ann Booth	...Bans	19 Febry

1683.

William Midleton and Mary Leece ...	...Bans	19 April
Richard Tatham Jun and Mary Heblethwaite	,,	29 May
Mathew Overend and Jane Adcocke	,,	12 Feb

1684.

Edward Tayler and Anne Hackforth ...	...Bans	19 May
Francis Slater and Margret Docker	,,	19 ,,
Richard Cort and Jane Turner	...nupt.	22 Jany
by License to Mr. Key, Vicar of Melling		
Thomas Wilson and Agnes Fauthet		12 Feb
by virtue of License		

1685.

James Bland and Jane Pearson		4 June
License to Mr. Jackson		
Edward Jackson and Alice Slater... ...	...Bans	21 Sept

James Tatham and Ann Melling... ... ... ,,   10 Octr
Simon Batty and Ellin Sill ... ... License 14 Novr
Peter Robinson and Merjery Miller ... ...Bans 16 January

[16]86.

Andrew Noble and Sarah Inmond ... Lycence 27 May
John Cort and Jane Rigg ... ...Bans 1 June
John Newton and Elizabeth Robbinson ... ,, 14 Nov
John Woodhouse and Margret Slater ... ... ,, 25 ,,
Thomas Chippindale and Alice Dixon... Lycence 3 Febry

1687.

Henry Chatburn and Elizabeth Readman ...Bans 1 May
Robert Burrow and Elizabeth Hutton... ... ,, 18 June
Tristram Ray and Jane Armistead ... Lycence 26 ,,
John Jackson and Isabel Groser... ... ,, 14 July
William Laurence and Ann Johnson ... ...Bans 13 August

1688.

William Robinson and Margret Taylor ...Bans 15 April
Thomas Robinson and Jennett Addison ... ,, 24 May
Tho Greenwood and Ellin Dickouson ... ... ,, 30 Jany

1689.

Robert Warde and Isabel Cocking ... ...Bans 6 August
John Leafield and Agnes Robinson ... Lycence 24 July
Thomas Casson and Alice Slater... ... ,, 3 Mar

1690.

Johes Braithw^te and Isabella Robinson Lycence 17 May
Edmond Dodgson de Casterton and Margret Dick-
   son de Whittington ... ... Lycence 15 Junij
William Richinson de Dent and Alice Harries de
   Newton ... ... Banes 19 June
John Margison de Docker and Agnes Wither de
   Brownedge ... ... Banes 26 Novr

1691.

Obadiah Burrow and Isabell Harleing... Lycence 15 April

1692.

James Downham and Mary Hackworth Lycence 28 Sep

1693.

Richard Todd de Longsledall in pch de Kendall
and Margret Robinson de Whittington...Bans   18 May

1694.

William Martin and Isabel Taylor ...	Banns	12 April
Robert Atckinson and Mary England ...	,,	24 May
William Cockin and Elizabeth Margison	,,	17 Junij
William Styth and Esther Battersby ...	,,	26 Sep

1695.

Henry Robinson and Ellin Tunstill ...	Banns	28 Aprillis
Richard Heblethwaite and Cathrine Harris	,,	8 May
John Styth and Jane Taylor...	,,	2 Junij
John Preston and Jane Cockin	,,	10 Decr

1696.

John Heblethwaite and Margaret Ward both of Newt	Banns	5 May
Thomas Heaviside and Isabell Cort ...	,,	9 ,,
Luke Corner and Agnes Denison... ...	,,	7 Junij
Edward Taylor and Elizabeth Johnson...	Lycence	28 Novr

1697.

Mr. John Statter and Agnes Bateson ...	Lycence	18 April
Richard Skirrow and Margaret Wadeson	Banes	8 May
James Johnson and Isabel Lupton ...	,,	23 June
Thomas Peck and Elizabeth Johnson ...	,,	19 July

1698.

Emanuel Swainson and Eliz Barker ...	...Bans	25 May
Witt Willan and Ann Hall	,,	25 ,,
John Procter and Isabel Burrow	,,	25 June

1699.

William Ball and Katherine Adcock ...	Lycence	17 Octr
James Lucas and Alice North	Banns	8 April

1700.

John Johnson and Margret Dixson ...	Banns	11 July

1702.

Richard Dodgson and Jane Burrow   ...   Banns   7 November

1703.

William Tomlinson and Elizabeth North... Licence   11 November

1704.

Hue Mattyson and Agnes Willan ...   ...   Banns   19 June
John Croft and Margret Crosfield ...   ...   „   30 November

1706.

Will: Bush and Joan Bentham   ...   ...   Banns   31 March
Wiłłm Overen and Eliz: North   ...   ...   „   5 April
Tho: Foster and Jenet Miller ...   .   „   27 July
Myles Willan and Isabal Batty   ...   ...   „   9 September
John Cocking and Isaball Tompson...   ...   „   2 Novembr.
Richard Hall and Margret Greenhow   ...   „   16   „

1707.

Thomas Willson and Agnes Tompson   ...   Banns   8 May
Henry Meals and Ruth Relton   ...   ...   „   1 September

1709.

Richard Tatham and Martha Williamson...   Banns   18 July
Will: Boardley and Ann Herdson ...   ...   „   12 Novembr
Mr. William Dawson and Mrs. Eliza: Boach Licence   3 January
John Willson and Mary Kue ...   .   Banns   2 February

1711.

Christoph Lawrence and Dorothy Thompson Banns   27 Novem

1713.

Thomas Hodgson and Eliz: Howson   ...   Banns   9 May
Edward Houghton and Margret Crawdson   „   25 Octobr
Robert Smallwood and Elizabeth Simonson Licence   17 Novembr
Martin Hutton and Elizabeth Burrow   ...   Banns   24 January

1715.

Richard Robinson and Mary Barrow   ...   Banns   13 November

1716.

John Heaton	Ellen Robinson...	Banns	23 June
John Borrow	Alice Jamsone ...	,,	1 Decr
John Stithe	Jane Dickson ...	,,	7 Janr

1718.

Tho: Atkinson	Ellin Jackson ...	Banns	17 Apr
Anthony Bird	Mary Marsdon ...	,,	15 ,,
John Couert	Agnes Wilson		
both of this Parish..Licence by William Withers			20 January

1719.

Joseph Robinson and Ann Balderston   ... Banns   26 Apr
John Warriner of Kerby Lonsdale Parish and Agnes
    Tod of this Parish   ... ... Banns   5 November
Thomas Baines of Bentom Parish and Isabel Sclater
    of this Parish   ... ... Banns   9   ,,
Wm. Jackson of Casterton and Margaret Daubikin
    of Wh. Parish   ... ... Banns   16 January
John Rentlay of Casterton and Agnes Sclater of
    Wh. Parish   ... ... Banns   24   ,,
Joseph Hodgson of Kerby and Margaret Batty of
    Wh. Parish   ... ... Banns   13 Feb:

1720.

William Womsley of Bradford in ye Parish of
    Mitton in Yorkshire and Sarah Towerson of
    Wh. Parish   ... ... Banns   24 April
Richard Skirrow of Dalton and Elizabeth Johnson
    of Wh. Parish   ... ...Licence frō Mr. Bryer   18 May
William Chatbourn and Alice Rowlinson both of
    Wh. Parish   ...   Licence frō Mr. Withers   27 November
John Atkinson and Margaret Scamler both of Wh.
    Parish ...   .Banns   19 January

1721.

Thomas Robinson and Jane Dixon both of this
    Parish... ... ...Licence frō Mr. Bryer   22 June
Wm. Martin and Sarah Needham both of this
    Parish ... ...Banns   13 January

P

1722.

Stephen Breaks of Kirby Lonsdale Margaret
    Burrough of ye Parish Licence frō Mr. Briggs 16 Feb:

1723.

John Barrow and Margaret Chester both of ye
    Parish ... ... Banns   4 May
William Durham of Kirby Lonsdale Parish and
    Jane Lawrence of ye Parish ... ... Banns 29 June

1724.

Timothy Wardley and Jane Peck both of this
    Parish ... ... Banns 31 May

1725.

James Tatham and Ann Dawson both of this
    Parish ... ... Banns 26 June
Edward Barton and Elizabeth Robinson both of
    this Parish... ... ... Banns 27 ,,
Mr. Giles Ridman, mayor of Kendal and Mrs.
    Elizabeth Lucas, of ye Parish ... Licence frō
                     Mr. Withers 20 Oct.

1726.

George Facet of Huton roof and Elizabeth Smith
    of Newton... ... ... Licence 2 June

1727.

John Hogart and Margaret Attkinson both of this
    Parish ... ... Banns 8 April

1728.

Charles Simpkin of Quarmore Park in ye Pish of
    Laucr and Mary Schamler of Newton in this
    Parish ... ... Banns 8 Febry

1729.

William Adcock and Dorathy Cornthwait both of
    Whittington ... ... Banns 12 May

1731.

James Tompson of Burrow and Ann Ridin of Whittington ... ... Licence   17 Janry

1732.

Robert Gibson and Dorathy Robinson both of
    Whittington   ... ... Banns   16 Octobr
Roger Boothman of Kirby Lonsdale and Mary
    Ballderstone of Whittington   ... ... Banns   30 Decembr

1733.

Robert Willson and Ellin Rennison both of Newton
    in ye Psh of Whittington ... ... Banns   11 August
Thos Smith of Elsewick and Ann Pearson of Whit-
    tington   ... ... Licence   1 Octobr

1734.

James Taylor of Kirby Lonsdale and DorathyWood-
    house of Whittington ... ... Licence   3 Septembr
John Lonsdale of Newbigin in ye Psh of Kirby Lons-
    dale and Ellin Huck of Docker in ye Pish of
    Whittington ... ... Licence   8 Febry
Oliver North of Newton and Alice Bordrigge of
    Whittington ... ... Licence   16   ,,

1737.

Robert Robinson and Ann Lawrence both in the
    Parish of Whittington   ... ... Banns   4 June
William Harrison of Casterton in ye Parish of
    Kirby Lonsdale and Agnes Carter of Whit-
    tington   ... ... Banns   18 September

1739.

John Altham of Feizer in the Parish of Clapham
    and Margaret Slater of Newton in ye Parish
    of Whittington... ... ... Licence   3 June
Robert Leigh of Natland in the Parish of Kendale
    and Ann Burrow of Selet Hall in the Parish
    of Whittington ... ... Banns   29 July

1740.

John Smith of Arckholme in the Parish of Melling
and Ellin Bordrigge of Whittington... Banns   5 June
John Burnet of Woodhouse in the Parish of Leeds
and Jane Burrow of Sellet Hall in ye Parish
of Whittington ...   . Banns   15 July
James Parker of Casterton in the Parish of Kirby
Lonsdale and Margaret Holme of Whitting-
ton   ...   . Banns   4 November
John Preston of Kirby Lonsdale and Ann Robinson
of Whittington ...   . Banns   27 December

1741.

William Lawrence and Mary Baynes both of Whittington   ...   . Banns   6 May

1742.

Richard Proctar of Kirby Lonsdall and Ann Thompson of Whittington   ...   . "Bands"   7 February

1743.

John Parkar Wenington in ye Parish of Melling
and Eling Lonsdell widow of this Parish Liceus   9 Aprill
Richard Thompson and Alieis Willon both in this
Town ...   . "Bands"   11   „
Edward Thornbergs and Jane Howton both of this
Parresh...   ...   . Bands   29 November
John Hodgshon and Elizabeth Turner both in this
Parish ...   . Bands   12 January

1744.

William Brown of Burton and Dorothy Kerby of
Whitington...   ...   . "Bands"   16 Aprill
John Johnson of Hutan Rouf in ye Parish Kerby
Lonsdell and Ann Hodgson of this Parish "Bands"   5 August

1745.

John Lund of Kirkby Lonsdale and Ellin Tomlins-
son of this Parish ...   . Banns   11 Novr
John Low of Sedbridge and Ann Barker of ye
same...   ...   . Licence   9 Jan

John Glover of Mansergh and Anne Dixon of this
Parish   ...   . Licence   11 Feb

1746.

Thomas Yeadan of Astwick and Mary Overende of
Whittington   ...   . Licence   8 December

1747.

Robert Howlm and Dorothy Johnson both of Whit-
tington   ...   . Bands   18 June
Joseph Johnson and Grace Walen both of Whit-
tington   ...   . Bands   29 July
Will Whited and Cateron Gray [?] both of this
Parish   ...   . Bands   28 December
William Dickson of Arkhowlm and Ledea Willkeson
of Whittington   ...   . Bands   10 Febury

1748.

Thomas Brenan and Mary Knowles both Whit-
tington   ...   . Banns   23 September
George Atkinson and Ann Adcock both Whitting-
ton ...   ."Bands"   14 Novembr
John Taylor and Margt. Heblethwaite both Whit-
ton ...   ."Bands,'   30 Jan
John Court and Ellin Robinson both of Whittington ...   . Licence   8 Febry

1749.

Robert Wildman of Tunstall and Agnes Leyton of
Whittington   ...   . Banns   25 November

1750.

Robert Heblethwaite and Ellinor Johnson both of
this Parish   ...   . Licence   21 April

1751.

Fardy Kitchin and Mary Wilson both of this
Parish   ..   .. Banns   14 April
Michael Hodgson and Isabel Johnson both of this
Parish   ...   . Banns   26 August

1752.

Thomas Heblethwaite and Ann Robinson both of
this Parish... ... ... Licence by Mr. Croft   6 February
John Lawrence and Elizabeth Ashton [? Ashson]
of this Parish... ...Licence by Mr. Letousey   9 August

1753.

William Lawrence and Allice Garnet both of this
Parish   ...   .   Banns   25 January
William Birket and Jane Hodgson both of this
Parish   ...   .   Banns   25 August
William Richardson and Bridget Dawson both of
this Parish...   ...   .   Banns   20 October

1755.

Christopher Williamson   Elizabeth Batty   30 March
        Tunstall Parish   Whittington
Witnesses: John Johnson, Richard Batty
                        Thomas Nicholson, Minister

John Wedderburn   Ann Hodgson   27 April
    Dalton in Furness Parish   Whittington
Witnesses: Christopher Hodgeshon, John Johnson
                        Robert Ravald, Minister

John Heblthwaite   Ellin X Bland   14 June
    Whittington   Whittington
Witnesses: John Johnson, John × Atkinson
                        Robert Ravald, Minister

James Willan   Isabel Johnson   30 August
    Kirkby Lonsdale Parish   Whittington spinster
Witnesses: Christr· Carus, John Johnson
                        Robert Ravald, Minister

George Willcock   Jane Wilkinson   2 September
    Whittington   Whittington
Witnesses: Thomas × Huck, John Johnson
                        Robert Ravald, Minister

Thomas Torver   Agnes Heblethwaite   18 October
    Tunstal Parish   Whittington
Witnesses: Thomas Nicholson, Robt. Coates
                        Robert Ravald, Minister

1756.

Myles × Ackrigg   Sarah × Lambert 12 May
 Whittington widower   Whittington
Witnesses: James Thompson, Edward Barton
          Robert Ravald, Minister

James Speight   Agnes × Dickonson 13 May
 Whittington   Whittington
Witnesses: John Tatham, Jas. Tomlinson
          Robert Ravald, Minister

1757.

William × Fryer   Anne × Noble 4 February
 Grassingham Parish   Whittington
Witnesses: John Johnson, Nicholas Croft
          Robert Ravald, Minister

Stephen × Emiley   Isabel × Knowls 30 October
 Whittington   Whittington
Witnesses: John Towers, John Johnson
          Robert Ravald, Minister

1758.

Richard Procter   Anne × Meales 8 January
 Whittington   Whittington
Witnesses: Francis Chippendale, John Johnson
          Robert Ravald, Minister

James × Brennan   Mary × Foxcroft 16 May
 Whittington   Whittington
Witnesses: Thomas North, John Johnson
          Robt. Ravald, Minister

1759.

Jonathan Robinson Anne × Proctar 22 December
 Kendal Parish   Whittington
Witnesses: John × Carter, John Johnson
          Robert Ravald, Minister

1760.

William × Willan   Ellin × Hodgson 23 April
 Kendal Parish   Whittington
Witnesses: Francis Chippindale, John Johnson
          Robert Ravald, Minister

Robert Williamson   Agnes × Harling   24 May
    Whittington   Whittington
Witnesses: George × Harling, John Johnson

               W. Wray, Vicar of Tonstal

William Shawe   Susanna Ravald   26 August
    Preston Parish   Whittington spinster
Witnesses: Jane Wilson, Eliz Walmsley

               Robert Ravald, Minister

1761.

John × Nutter   Alice Cockin   10 January
    Whittington   Whittington
Witnesses: Richd. Mason, Thos. Abbotson

               W. Wray, Curate

Richard Danson   Mary Hodgson   23 March
    Whittington   Whittington
Witnesses: Henry Gibson, James Johnson

               Robert Ravald, Minister

1762.

James Robb   Dorothy Lawrence   31 May
    Whittington   Whittington spinster
Witnesses: John Lawrence, John Johnson

               Robt. Ravald, Minister

1764.

Robert Mawdesley   Elizabeth Willis   8 Sep
    Clapham Par   Whittington
Witnesses: John Halsoo [?], Joseph Willis

               Robt. Ravald, Minister

Thomas Thebay   Susanna Adcock   20 Dec
    of Whittington   of Whittington
Witnesses: Richard Fell, John Adcock

               W. Wray, Curate

The following Miscellaneous Entries appear in various parts of Volume I. of the Register.

THE twentieth day of December Anno Dñj 1650 being the third publicue day appoynted for the pishoners and Churchwardenes of Whittington for Meeting at the Church concerning the Disposseing and selling for the benefitt of the Church now in great decaye the formes and seats therin that was new sett upp by way of adition to the former Ansent seats without piudic to the owners of the said Ancient seats which seats are now sould by the order of the Rector Churchwardens and all the Pishoners was then and there p'sent unto these psones and for these herafter mentioned that is to say unto John Carter for his house in the upper end of the towne the whole form in the middle ile upon the north syd abuting to the hyest pue in consideracion he forgoeth two seats in the next forme between paid in hand to the Churchwardens three shillings by ye year And the next whole forme before it unto these three, viz.:— Richard North Jun'. of Docker as an addition to his house puchased of John Whitthead one third pte and also to Thomas Johnson the elder as an adition to his mansion house in Whittington another third pte and unto John Bland Jun'. of Newton an adition to his mansion house there the other third pte in consideracion of fifteen shillings by them then paid in hand to the Churchwardenes. And also the one half of the form next above the pue towards the midle ile unto Thomas Johnson Jun'. of Whittington for his mansion house there in consideracion that hee did forgoe the third pte of the form on the syd of the belfrce and paid to the Churchwardnes five shillings. And also the other half of the form next above the pulpitt unto Thomas Hutton for his mansion house in Whittington in consideracion that hce did forgoe another third pte of the forme on the south syd of the belfree and paid in hand to the Church wardens five shillings and also unto Bryan Dicconson of Newton for his mansion housc there the third seat in that form next beyond John Cort as an adition to his mansion house and paid to the Churchwardens three shillings fower pence. This above is allowed and consented unto by us the Chū wardens and pishioners whose names are here [edge of leaf torn off.]

Richarde Jackson Rector   John * * *
Richard North   Tho: * * *
Willm ʌ Godsalf
      mark

And it is also wittnessed the day and yeare aforsaid being the twentieth day of December 1650 by the Rector and Churchwardens of Whittington that there was sould unto Thomas Dowthwayt of Newton for his house there the . . . seate in the

second forme next above the second piller on the north syde of
the midle ile which Mr. North did forgoe in consideracion that
hee paid then in hand to the Church wardens the somme of
three shillings and fouer pens.

[*At the top of a page which someone has numbered 21, is written
the following:*]

"Whittington Rigester in ye hand of J. S. [? John Statter]
Clerk."

[*Immediately after the Baptisms of 1648 are written the
following:*]

"Whereas the Church of Whittington in the County of Lancaster is out of repayres as allso ye bells and clocke therein
so as ye quindames for yt purpose will not extend to pay for
ye same therefore know yee yt wee Richard Jackson Rector,
Richard North ye younger of Docker John Bland ye younger of
Newton William Bordrigge ye elder and Bryan Dawny of Whittington Churchwardens within ye said pish upon consideration
thereof and for satisfaction of ye workmen for repaireinge of
ye said Church have severall lords dayes published ye sale of
severall vacant places within ye said Church and whosoever
would give ye most mony should have them and whereas
Lenard Jackson sonn of ye said Richard Jackson did after the
first meeting after publication offer thirteene shillings fourepence
for all ye place and portion of ground lying and being in ye
east end of ye south ile of ye said Church from ye east windowe
of ye said east end of ye aforesd south ile to extend into ye
new erected pew or inclosed seat of Mr. Brabin of Whittington
Hall afforesaid upon ye west to extend unto ye chancell of ye
sd church upon ye north, And afterwards ye last of December
being ye Lords day wee did againe publish ye same yt if any
would give any more mony for ye said place then ye said
thirteene shillings foure pence yt then they should have ye
same but none offering any more thirefore know ye to whome
these psents shall come yt wee ye said Rector & Churchwardens
with ye consent of ye parishoners within ye said pish for and
in consideration of ye said some of thirteene shillings foure
pence to us allreadie payed for ye use of ye said church have
by this our psent writing conveyed and sould ye aforesd pcell
of ground to ye only use and behoofe of ye said Leonard Jackson
his heires & assignes for ever with liberty for him and them
to erect a pew or seats therein & to enjoy ye same in pprijetie
for ye better accomodation of their soules in hearing ye word of
god receiueing ye sacrament and all other divine and religeous
duties of devotion in testimony whereof we have hereunto put
our hands the nynteenth day of Jan. 1654.

Richard Jackson Rector	Richard North
Willyam Bordrigg M marke	John Bland
Bryan Dawnie	

[*The succeeding Grants, all of same date, 19th Jan., 1654, are precisely similar in form, and so only the name and description of the Grantee, the description of the Pew and the price are given here.*]

[*Grantee.*]—"John Foxcroft of the Holme house."

[*Price.*]—"Twenty five shillings."

[*Pew.*]—"The vacant place or parcell of ground situate within ye said Church ajoyning to ye new erected Pewe of Mr. Brabins of Whittington Hall on ye east side & to ye little door on ye south side of ye said Church."

[*Grantees.*]—"Thomas Johnson ye younger and Simon Dawny son of ye said Bryan Dawny and Bryan Bland son of ye said John Bland ye younger of Newton."

[*Price.*]—"Tenn shillings."

[*Pew.*]—"All the space of & portion of ground from ye south end of the Pewe instiled John Newton Rector and to extend eastward to ye outside to ye south outside of ye Piler which joyenes to ye side and west end corner of ye Chauchel in a direct line westwards opposite to ye south west corner of ye said Pew and in yt corner to joyne to ye Pewe."

[*Grantee.*]—"John Foxcroft of ye Holme House."

[*Price.*]—"Twenty six shillings eight pence."

[*Pew.*]—"Foure of ye five single seats in ye North Isle of ye said Church from ye corner of ye North side wall over against ye cross Isle coming from ye little door of ye South side of ye said Church and in length extend five Inches beyond ye East of corner window with two lights in ye north side of ye said Church and one yeard from ye side wall unto ye said North Isle southwards."

[*Grantee.*]—"Willm Borrow."

[*Price.*]—"Six shillings and eight pence."

[*Pew.*]—"For ¹ of ye five single seats in ye North Isle in ye Corner over against ye cross Isle coming from ye little dore on ye south side and in lenght to extend two foote and one yard into ye North Isle Southward from ye said Wall."

Left blank in original.

[Next after the Baptisms of 1665 entered in Volume I. is written at the top of a page, the remainder of which is blank, the following words—the complete sense cannot be gathered as the top and corner of the leaf are much torn.]

" . . . . incumbent or pson & the . . . . clerke who enioyes & houses gleabs rents and tythes the . . . . wherof is about £120 the now patron is Thomas Carus Esquier November 28 Anno Dñj 1665."

[On the following pages, being the last of Volume I., are written the following:]

"[Collected in our] church at Whittington the . day of May 1664 the sum of 4s. 6d. towards the losses of the inhabitants of Houghington in the pish of Washingbrough in the parts of Kest-even in the county of Lincolne."

"Collected in our Church of Whittington 15th day of May the sume of 3s 9d. towards the repair of the church and steeple of Sandwich in the towne and port in county of Kent."

"Collected in our Church of Whittington the third day of July the year above said the sume of three shillings three pence towards the losses by the inundations of waters the inhabitants of the pish of Weedon in the county of Northampton."

"Collected in our church of Whittington the fower & twenteth day of July in the year above said the sume of five shillings nynepence towards losses of the towne of Grantham in the county of Lincoln."

"Collected in our church of Whittington the 18th . . . September Anno 1664 the summe of thre [shillings] five pence towards the losses of the town of Aughton and county of [Lancas] ter."

"Collected in our Church of Whittington towards the losses of Flookburgh the [sum] . . . . . [shill]ings sixpence."

1665.

"Collected in our church of Whittington the seventh day of . . in the yeare above sd towards the losses of Stiling . . . east riding of Yorke the sum of three shillings & , . ."

"Collected towards the poor distressed people in the south parts touched with the infection the first Wednesday £0 8 2
the second Wednesday 0 1 2
the third Wednesday 0 2 1

"Collect in our church of Whittington in the couuty of Lanc. the 18th of Feb. towards the losses in the towne of Sherifhales in the County of Staford two shillings."

"Collect in our church of Whittington for the repaire of the breaches of the fo[rt] or wall of Hartlepoole in the county of Durram, the 28th day of March the [sume] of nynteene pence."

"Collected in our church of Whittington towards the rebuilding of the Antient pish church of Clun [in the county] of Salopp, the sume of thre shillings eight pence . . . of Aprill Anno 1666."

[   ] 13th Anno Dei 1668.

"Collected in our Church of Whittington in the County of Lancaster for the Captives in Algers & Sally within the Turcks Dominions the sume of 6d."

"Collected at our Pish Church the sume of 3s. 8d. towards the losses of Haverhill in the County of Suffolk. Collected the 7th of February Anno Dnj 1668.

Daniell Garnett
Henry Collison
Miles Eykridge
Thomas Douthaite }Churchwar:"

December the 16th Anno Domj 1678.

"Collected w^thin ye Parish of Whittington and County of Lanc^r for & towards ye Rebuilding of ye Cathedrall Church of St. Paul's London ye sume of One Pound fourteen shill & four pence whereof Mr. Richd Jackson then Rector of Whittington gave ye sume of Twenty shillings.

James Whitehead
Andrew Cue
Bryan Manserge
. . . Harris }Churchwardens."

"Collected w^thin ye pish of Whittington in ye County of Lanc^r for & towards ye Relief of ye Irish Ptestants the summe of Sixteen Shillings & Eight pence."

[*The names of the Churchwardens are torn off.*]

March 17th Anno Dnj 1689.

"Collected w^thin ye pish of Whittington & County of Lanc the Summe of Eight shillings Six pence for & towards ye Second brief of ye poor exild & distressed Irish Ptestants.

Edw. Taylor
Rich. North."

April 7 A° Dnj 1690.

"Collected then within ye pish of Whittington in County of Lanc^r the Summe of Three shillings for & towards ye brief of St. Ives."

"Collected for Bungay Brief in County of Suffolk the sume of Four shillings & Eight pence."

[*The particulars of one Collection are entirely torn away.*]

"Collected within ye pish of [Whittington in the] County of Lancaster ye 12 day of . . . ye sume of 2s. 0d. for & towards . . . . of ye Town of Borough in ye County . . . . by fire &c.

George . . .

Churchwarden.

[*In margin can be read*] $-$ Cockin } Churchwardens."
$-$ Cockin

"Collected within ye pish of Whittington [in ye County] of Lancaster ye 9th day of December 169–, 2s. 3½d. for & towards ye losses . . . . of Bishop Lavington and County . . . . by fire."

"Collected within ye Pch of Whittingt[on in the County] of Lancaster ye 28 of March 1691 ye sume of 1s. 11d. for & towards ye losses of M . . . . in Leubestershire by fire &c."

"Collected within ye Pch of Whitt[ington in the County] of Lancaster ye 19th of Aprill 1691 ye [sume of] . . . . for & towards ye losses of two merchant . . . ."

"Collected within ye Pch Church of [Whittington in the] County of Lanc⁻· ye fifth day of July . . 2s. 1d. for & towards ye losses of . . . ."

"Collected within ye Pch Church [of Whittington] & County of Lanc⁻· ye 4 of October [ye sume of] 3s. 4d. for & towards ye losses . . . . the County of Brecon

James Bordridge
Will Slater
Thomas Dawney
John Margison
} Churchwardens."

"Collected within ye Pch [Church of Whittington] & County of Lancr ye 18 . . . . . the sume of 1s. 10d. for & towards . . . of Thomas Holme of K . . . by the River Lune."

"Collected the 3 of January 1691 [ye sume] of 2s. 3½d. for & towards the . . . of Thirske in the County of . . . ."

[*On the last page of Volume I. are written*]

"John Statter Clerk & Schoolemast⁻· of Whittington 1690."

" . . . Bond came to be Clarke & [Schoolmaster] of Whittington ye 14 day of [Jan]uary 1694."

[*On the fly-leaf of Volume II. are written:*]

"Georgius Hornby eccleciae Rectoris Whittington."

"Henry Foster, Clerk and Schoolmaster anno domi 1750-1751."

"Thomas Thistlethwaite Esquire and an Attorney at Law haveing [?] orders under ye hand of Lord Mawrley Mount Eagle Barran a Roy."

Indexes.

I.

Of Christian Names and Surnames.

Where a name has variants the Head-name has been selected which now exists or which most closely resembles the modern equivalent. All variants are separately Indexed with cross-references to the Head-name.

Where a name has an *alias* each form of the name is Indexed under its initial letter. The Christian names are with some exceptions Indexed under their modern form. Illegitimate children are Indexed under the Surnames of both Mother and putative Father.

"N.X.N." signifies "No Christian name." An asterisk following a page number signifies that that combination of Christian and Surname occurs more than once on the page number asterisked.

C. pp. 1—74; B. 75—133; W. 134—160.

Anderson, William, 16*
Aplegarthe, William, 134
Apley, Elisabeth, 78
Armistead [Armestead, Armystead],
 ,, Abraham, 68
 ,, Isaac, 68
 ,, Jane, 150
 ,, John, 66
 ,, Magaret, 67, 127
 ,, Nathan, 69
 ,, Richard, 69
 ,, Thomas, 66
 ,, William, 66,* 67,* 68,* 69,* 129
Ashburn [Ashburne],
 ,, Agnes, 2, 4, 6, 7, 90
 ,, Alice, 7, 79
 ,, Ann, 6
 ,, Edward, 1, 2, 4,'5, 6, 7, 78, 90
 ,, Elizabeth, 1, 5
 ,, Jenet, 4
 ,, John, 79
 ,, Lawrence, 5
 ,, Robert, 79
 ,, William, 2
Ashburner, Ellen, 140
Asheton *alias* Poulton, John, 101
Ashson [see Ashton]
Ashton [? Ashson], Elizabeth, 158
Astwicke, James, 18
 ,, Myles, 18
Atkinson [Adkinson, Atckinson,
  Atkison, Attkinson],
 ,, Agnes, 119
 ,, Alexander, 5, 6, 12, 75, 76, 83,
  85, 92
 ,, Alice, 115
 ,, Ann, 6,* 76, 129, 137
 ,, Edward, 23, 91, 95, 96, 138
 ,, Elizabeth, 85
 ,, Ellen, 126
 ,, George, 157
 ,, Gilbert, 5, 12, 15, 83, 85,* d. of
  85, 100, 135
 ,, Grace, 141
 ,, James, 141
 ,, Jane, 15, 85
 ,, Jenet, 75, 100
 ,, John, 23, 25, 55, 91, 153, 158
 ,, Mabell, 5, 6
 ,, Margaret, 43, 46, 57, 96, 154
 ,, Mary, 58, 59, 128
 ,, Matthew, 57, 119
 ,, Nicholas, 43, 46
 ,, Richard, 6, 56, 65, 66, 136
 ,, Robert, 55, 56, 57,* 58, 59,* 65,
  119, 124, 151
 ,, Stephen, 25, 139
 ,, Thomas, 66, 115, 118, 126, 145,*
  153

Atkinson, William, 145
Awrey [Aaura, Awray]
 [see also "Alrey"],
 ,, Alice, 7, 140
 ,, Dorothy, 13
 ,, Elizabeth, 88, 93
 ,, James, 5, 6, 7, 13, 37, w. of 82,
  90, 93
 ,, Jenet, 5, 6, 7
 ,, John, 5
 ,, Mabell, 6
 ,, Margaret, 139
 ,, N.X,N., 37
Aykrigg [Ackrigg, Ayckrigge,
  Aykridge, Aykrigge]
 [see also Eckrigg and Eskrigg],
 ,, Alice, 51
 ,, Ann, 33
 ,, Henry, 32, 33, 97, 101, 102
 ,, Myles, 32, 51, 97, 159
 ,, William, 101

B

BACKHOUSE [Bacchus, Bachouse,
  Backehouse, Backhousse,
  Backus],
 ,, Agnes, 20, 88
 ,, Alice, 90
 ,, Dorothy, 90, 100
 ,, Elinor, 71
 ,, Elizabeth, 88, 114
 ,, George, 18, 20, 21, 40, 41, 88,
  90, 94, 99, 115, 121
 ,, Isabel, 40, 108, 125, 142
 ,, James, 8, 90, 115
 ,, John, 70, 71*
 ,, Margaret, 78, 94, 139
 ,, N.X.N., 98
 ,, Richard, 8, 18, 21, 37,* 41, 70,
  98, 100, 104, 108, 125
 ,, Thomas, 79
 ,, William, s. of 80, 85, 88
Bailey [Balye, Bayley, Bayly,
  Baylye]
 [see also Bayliffe],
 ,, Alice, 147
 ,. Elizabeth, 20
 ,, Jane, 22
 ,, John, 18, 20, 22, 94
 ,, Margaret, 75
 ,, Miles, 11, 75
 ,, Richard, 18, 80
 ,, Thomas, 11, 94
Bainbridge, Edward, 139
Baines [see Baynes]
Baitson [see Bateson]

C. pp. 1—74; B. 75—133; W. 134—160.

C. pp. 1—74; B. 75—133; W. 134—160.

Borthrigg, Rowland, 32,* 105
,, Thomas, 2, 93
,, William, 13, 14, 23, 31, 32,* 33,*
    34,* 40, 41,* 56, 82, 86, 97,
    100,* 104, 105, 106,* 108,*
    132, 162*
Bouch [see also Boach],
,, Anthony, 53, 114
,, Elizabeth, 53
,, Jane, 54
,, Mary, 54, 57, 115, 118
,, Mr., 56
,, Mrs., 127
,, Thomas, 53,* 54,* 56,* 57, 115,
    118,* 122
,, Vigessima, 127
Bow, Agnes, 145
Bower, Mary, 97
Bowerdale [Bourdall, Bourdell,
    Bowerdall, Bowerdell]
    [see also Boardley],
,, Agnes, 22
,, Alice, 21
,, Christopher, 21, 141
,, Edward, 138
,, Elizabeth, 25, 26, 144
,, Margaret, 23
,, Tristram, 21, 22, 23, 25, 26, 93,
    138
Boyes, Ellen, 13
,, William, 13
Brabin [Brabing, Brabyn, Brabbyn,
    Bribin],
,, Alice, 11, 13, 14, 19, 87, 95
,, Ann, 23, 53, 93, 115
,, Elizabeth, 49
,, George, 95
,, Henry, 11,* 13, 14, 27, 30, 31,*
    33, 39, 87, 95, 101, 103
,, Jane, 13, 21, 30, 98, 138
,, John, 18
,, Katherine, 22, 52
,, Mary, 51, 53, 111
,, Michael, 51
,, Mr., 11,* 38,* 39, 49,* 51, 52,
    53, 95,* 100, infant of 101,
    101, 103,* 111, 162, 163
,, N.X.N., 134
,, Robert, 34, 101
,, Thomas, 11, 25, 31, 38,* 39, 49,*
    51,* 52, 53,* 92, 98, 101,
    103,* 111, 115
,, Ursula, 24
,, William, 11, 18, 19, 21, 22, 23,
    24, 25, 26,* 27, 33, 34, 92,
    93, 95, d. of 99, 100, 101
Bradley [Bradeley], Ann, 147
,, Francis, 71
,, Isabell, 112

Bradley, Margaret, 72
,, Thomas, 71, 72, 74*
Braithwaite [Braithait, Braithaite.
    Braythait],
,, Agnes, 47
,, John, 48, 110, 150
,, Rowland, 47, 48, 110
Bramell [see also Brumell];
,, James, 36
,, Nicholas, 36
Breaks, Elizabeth, 73
,. Ruth, 73
,, Stephen, 134
Brennan [Brenan], Francis, 73
,, James, 70, 73,* 74,* 159
,, John, 74
,, Mary, 132
,, Thomas, 70, 73, 74, 157
Briggs, Mr., 154
,, Rowland, 114
Brize, John, 140
Brockbancke, Isabel, 137
Brockherst [Brockherste],
,, Francis, 32, 98
,, Margaret, 32, 98
Brockhols [see next name],
,, Isabel, 20
,, Wilfride, 20
Brockhouse [see previous name],
,, Wilfred, 139
Brogten, Henry, 146
Bromley [see Brumley],
,, Dorothy, 112
Brough, John, 52*
Browen, Ann, 28
,, John, 28
Brown [Browne], Agnes, 70, 72, 131.
,, Edward, 69
,, Henry, 65*
,, Margaret, 71
,, Mary, 72
,, Thomas, 70
,, William, 69, 70,* 71, 72,* 73,*
    131, 156
Brumell [see also Bramell],
., Nicholas, 143
Brumley [see Bromley],
,, Margaret, 122
,, William, 122, 124, 149
Bryer, Mr., 153*
Buckley, Charles, 50
,, George, 50
,, John, 50*
,, Mr., 50*
Bunnell [? Brumell],
,, Nicholas, 103
Burnet, John, 156
Burroughs [see Barrow]
Burton, Ellen, 80

Chester, Margaret, 154
Chippendale [Cheppendell,
    Chipindale, Chipingdale,
    Chippendell, Chippindal,
    Chippindale],
,, Ann, 68
,, Elizabeth, 62, 72
,, Ellen, 61
,, Francis, 58, 59, 60, 61,* 62, 63,
    122, 123, 128, 159*
,, Isabell, 59, 122
,, John, 58
,, Margaret, 60, 72, 139, 131
,, Robert, 68, 69,* 131
,, Thomas, 63, 123, 150
Chorley [Chorlee], Ann, 74
,, Margaret, 73
,, Richard, 72
,, Thomas, 72,* 73, 74, 147
Cirkbryd [see Kyrkbride]
Claghton [see Claughton]
Clark, Henry, 61
,, Mary, 61
Clarkson, Elizabeth, 96, 140
,, Thomas, 82
Claughton [Claghton, Clagton],
,, Ann, 8, 78
,, Ellen, 8, 9
,, John, 8, 9, 76
,, Richard, 146
,, William, 9, 78
Coates, Robert, 158
Cockeram [Cokeram],
,, Ann, 138
,, Ellen, 97
,, John, 148
Cockin [Cocking, Cokin, Cokinge,
    Cokynge],
,, Agnes, 23, 41, 49, 51
,, Alice, 59, 61, 68, 114,* 129, 160
,, Ann, 33, 58, 59,* 60, 98, 110,
    120, 121, 122, 128, 142
,, Edward, 26, 27, 29,* 37,* 47,
    52,* 53, 54, 55, 58, 59,* 60,*
    61, 63, 98, 102, 104, 109, 113,
    121,* 122, 124, 127, 149
,, Elizabeth, 21, 92, 106, 108, 117,
    122, 130
,, Ellen, 26, 34, 59, 102, 121
,, George, 63
,, Hanna, 70
,, Isabell, 39, 49, 51, 58, 59, 65,
    104, 112, 125, 150
,, James, 55
,, Jane, 26, 32, 37,* 38, 42, 45, 51,
    52, 64, 95, 100, 113, 146, 151
,, Jenet, 56, 148
,, John, 11, 22, 32, 33, 34, 35, 53,
    59,* 60, 61,* 62,* 63,* 64, 65,

Cockin, John, *continued*—
    86, 92, 102,* 110,* 120, 121,
    122,* 125, 129, 130, 133, 152
,, Margret, 29, 103, 147
,, Marmaduke, 11, 21, 22, 23, 25,
    25, 27, 29, 34, 39, 41, 42, 45,
    47, 49,* 51,* 57, 95, 103, 109,
    112, 114, 116, 118, 138
,, Mary, 59, 127
,, N.X.N., 102, 106*
,, Paul, 59
,, Richard, 25, 34, 35, 36, 37, 38,
    40, 41,* 54, 56, 57, 58,* 59,
    68, 70, 100, 118, 121, 131
,, Robert, 51
,, Sarah, 58
,, Thomas, 36, 121
,, William, 40, 52, 151
Cokeram [see Cockeram]
Coles, Marie, 144
,, Mrs., 144
Collin [Colin], Abraham, 71, 72, 73,
    74, 133
,, Christopher, 72
,, Dorothy, 71, 133
,, Margaret, 74, 133
,, Mary, 73
Collison, Agnes, 112
,, Henry, 165
,, Nicholas, 147
Conder, Alice, 25
,, Elizabeth, 141
,, Jenet, 140
,, Mary, 68
,, N.X.N., 25
,, Sara, 68
Corner [Cornew, Corney, Cornuer],
,, Agnes, 56, 118
,, Ann, 70
,, Henry, 70, 71
,, James, 50, 51, 52, 114
,, Job, 51
,, John, 52,* 114, 115, 148
,, Luke, 56, 118, 151
,, Margaret, 52
,, Mary, 71
,, Richard, 50, 52,* 104, 113, 114,
    116
Cornthwaite [Cornthait, Cornthaite,
    Cornthwait, Cornthwayte],
,, Agnes, 127
,, Alice, 66
,, Ann, 67, 126
,, Benjamin, 125
,, Dorothy, 154
,, Henry, 50
,, Isabel, 61, 126
,, John, 61, 66, 67, 115, 122, 126,
    127

C. pp. 1—74; B. 75—133; W. 134—160.

C. pp. 1—74; B. 75—133; W. 134—160.

C. pp. 1—74; B. 75—133; W. 134—160.

C. pp. 1—74; B. 75—133; W. 134—160.

Lonsdale, Ann, 20, 105
,, Elizabeth, 18, 32, 101
,, Ellen, 33, 49, 109, 156
,, Joane, 148
,, John, 23, 33, 67,* 99, 109, 111,
127, 142, 155
,, Richard, 99
,, William, 16, 18, 20, 23, 32, 33,
49, 88, 95,* 110, 111, 148
Lorimer, Agnes, 30
,, Roger, 30
Low, John, 156
Loudg, Loydge [see Lodge]
Lucas, Agnes, 4, 10
,, Alice, 8
,, Edward, 10
,, Elizabeth, 57, 154
,, James, 57, 58,* 151
,, John, 3, 58
,, Leonard, 137
,, Margaret, 3, 4
,, Marmaduke, 8
,, Mrs., 154
,, Oliver, 58
,, Richard, 10
,, William, 3, 4
Lund, John, 156
Lupton, Agnes, 12, 76
,, Alice, 11, 98
,, Ann, 90
,, George, 76, 77, 136
,, Isabel, 151
,, Jane, 12
,, Margaret, 87, 137
,, William, 12, 84, 90

M

MADDISON [Maddyson, Madison],
,, Agnes, 113
,, Francis, 23
,, Jane, 107
,, Marie, 98
,, Rebecka, 142
,, William, 23, 98, 99, w. of 106,
107, 138
Mahan, Jenet, 144
Maiers [see Myres]
Maison [see Mason]
Makarell, Isabell, 3
,, Richard, 3
,, Thomas, 3
Man, Etheldrede, 5
,, Myles, 7
,, Tristriam, 5, 7
Mansergh [Manser, Manserge,
Manzer],
,, Agnes, 108, 117
,, Briggit, 148

Mansergh, Bryan, 40, 43, 45, 106, 107,
116, 118, 144, 165
,, Christopher, 137
,, Elizabeth, 52, 109
,, Ellen, 125
,, Ester, 116
,, Francis, 30, 108
,, John, 32, 43, 45, 53, 106, 107,
121, 149
,, N.X.N., 30
,, Richard, 30,* 32, 52, 53, 98, 109,
131, 140
,, Robert, 98
,, Thomas, 40, 112
,, William, 108
Margerison [Margeson, Margieson,
Marginson, Margison,
Margisson, Mergerison],
,, Agnes, 128
,, Ann, 141
,, Duke (Marmaduke), 31
,, Elizabeth, 43, 45, 105, 151
,, Ellen, 44, 46
,, Isabell, 19, 42, 141
,, John, 39, 54, 56,* 105, 119, 130,
150, 166
,, Margaret, 29, 48, 93, 98
,, Marmaduke, 12, 29, 30, 31, 93,
98, 101
,, Maud, 117
,, N.X.N., 31, 102
,, Sarah, 40, 148
,, Stephen, 117
,, Thomas, 30
,, William, 12, 19, 39, 40, 42,* 43,
44, 45,* 46, 47,* 48, 54, 90,
103, 105,* 107,* 110,* 116,
132
Marsdon, Mary, 153
,, William, 124
Marshall, John, 125
Martin [Marting, Marton],
,, Agnes, 56, 58, 117
,, Isabell, 117
,, John, 66
,, Leonard, 64, 70
,, Margaret, 67, 70, 125, 129
,, Robert, 65, 128
,, William, 55,* 56,57,* 58,64,65,*
66, 67, 117, 118,* 125, 126,*
130, 151, 153
Marton [see Martin]
Mason [Maison], Jonathan, 65
,, Margaret, 65
,, Richard, 160
,, Thomas, 105, 107
Mattyson, Hugh, 152
Mawdesley, Ann, 74
,, Elizabeth, 74

C. pp. 1—74; B. 75—133; W. 134—160.

N

NARDSDALLE, Thomas, 8
,, William, 8
Nealson [see Nelson]
Needham, Sarah, 153
Neilson [see Nelson]
Nelson [Nealson, Neilson, Nellson, Neylson],
,, Abraham, 142
,, Agnes, 8, 10, 136
,, Alexander, 24, 91
,, Alice, 27, 142
,, Bryan, 12, 21, 22, 23, 24, 25, 26,* 27, 41, 43, 46, 47,* 89, 90, 91, 92, 99, 101, 105, 107, 108,* 138, 142
,, Christopher, 18, 20, 22, 88, 90
,, Dorothy, 10
,, Edmund, 3, 26, relict of 96
,, Elizabeth, 43, 46, 121
,, Gilbert, 5
,, J, 2
,, James, 76
,, Jane, 8, 138
,, Jenet, 2, 3, 5, 20, 26
,, John, 78, 80 [?]
,, Jon [? Joan], 80
,, Mabell, 99
,, Margaret, 41, 105, 107, 111
,, Mary, 127
,, Mathew, 47, 108
,, N.X.N., 12
,, Richard, 23
,, Thomas, 18, 21, 25, d. of 86, 89, w. of 91, 91, 92, w. of 102, 105
,, William, 2, 3, 5, 8, 10, 12, 76, 82, relict of 84
Newby [Neuby, Nuby],
,, Agnes, 119
,, Ann, 108, 119, 133
,, Edward, 51
,, Elizabeth, 68, 113
,, George, 67, 68, 69, 70,* 71, 132
,, Isabel, 70, 133
,, James, 35, 104
,, Jane, 67
,, Jenet, 117
,, John, 69, 148
,, Mary, 71
,, Stephen, 70
,, Thomas, 35, 51, 104, 108, 113, 119,* 146, 149*
Newton, Agnes, 78
,, Ann, 12, 14, 119, 141
,, Bryan, 7
,, Christopher, 20
,, Dorothy, 14, 15, 29, 103
,, Edmund, 6, 7, 9

Newton, Elizabeth, 79, 137
,, Ellen, 81
,, Frances, 71
,, Francis, 71
,, Isabell, 6, 7, 9
,, James, 96, 140
,, Jane, 6, 15, 106, 107, 138
,, Jenet, 7,* 9, 18, 79, 105, 142
,, John, 7,* 14, 15, 16,* 17, 18, 19,* 20, 22, 89,* 97, 103, 105, 106, 107, 150, 163
,, Leonard [Lenard], 140
,, Margaret, 12, 86, 96
,, Marmaduke, 17, 90
,, Matthew, 10
,, Mr., 12, 78, 81, 86, 89, 112
,, "Rector," 135
,, Richard, 7, 16, 29, 78, 99
,, Robert, 9
,, Thomas, 7, 9, 12, 16, 76, 78, 79, 81, 86, 88, 89
,, William, 9, 22, 88, 112, 145*
Neylson [see Nelson]
Nicholson [Nichollson, Nickolson],
,, Christopher, 73, 134
,, Elizabeth, 120, 132
,, Ellen, 74
,, Jane, 73
,, John, 58, 71, 73, 120, 121, 130
,, Margaret, 25, 149
,, Mary, 71
,, Mr., 71,* 130
,, Richard, 25
,, Susanna, 71, 131
,, Thomas, 71, 72,* 73, 74, 131,* 132, 158*
,, William, 58, 124
Noble [Nowball], Andrew, 150
,, Ann, 63, 159
,, Edmund, 64
,, Elizabeth, 126
,, Jane, 130
,, John, 70
,, Katherine, 86
,, Mary, 66, 70
,, Thomas, 63,* 64, 65,* 66, 130
,, William, 63, 129
North [Northe], Agnes, 105, 141, 145*
,, Alice, 8, 30, 33, 50, 51, 108, 115, 124, 127, 136, 143, 151
,, Ann, 6, 20, 53, 62, 89, 91, 96, 118, 132
,, Benjamin, 61
,, Christopher, 20
,, Edward, 9, 10,* 11, 20, 41, w. of 84, 88, 91, 105, 107
,, Elizabeth, 4, 5, 6,* 8, 9, 10, 11, 15, 36, 52,* 59, 63, 78, 87, 93, 102, 110, 123, 137, 139, 148, 152*

C. pp. 1—74; B. 75—133; W. 134—160.

Parkinson, Elizabeth, 65
  ,, Mr., 111
  ,, William, 65
Parrate, Ellen, 138
Patchett [Pachet, Pachett,
    Padget, Pagett, Patchat,
    Patchet],
  ,, Alice, 92
  ,, Ann, 13, 83
  ,, Elizabeth, 3, 34, 86
  ,, Henry, 11, 81, w. of 84, 92, 93
  ,, Isabell, 33, 100, 137, 139
  ,, J: 100
  ,, Jane, 22, 33, 143
  ,, Jenet, 1, 3, 86
  ,, Joan, 81
  ,, John, 1, 3, 21, 33, 34, 75, 86, 100
  ,, Mabell, 11, 20, 110
  ,, Margaret, 24, 32,* 98,* 137
  ,, Richard, 1
  ,, Robert, 13, 83, 86
  ,, William, 11, 20, 21, 22, 24, 91
Pattison [Patison, Patteson],
  ,, Alice, 123
  ,, Ann, 45, 106, 108
  ,, Elizabeth, 110
  ,, Ellen, 103
  ,, Henry, 43, 45, 103, 106, 108, 110,
    111
  ,, N.X.N., 43
  ,, William, 113, 148
Patton, Alice, 34
  ,, Isabell. 32, 35, 101
  ,, Jenet, 33, 102
  ,, John, 11*
  ,, Richard, 32, 33, 34, 35, 101,*
    102, 142
Peandreth, Sibilla, 48
  ,, Thomas, 48
Pearson, Ann, 58, 155
  ,, Daniel, 58, 59, 60, 120, 122, 125,
    129
  ,, Ellen, 120
  ,, Frances, 125
  ,, Jane, 59, 149
  ,, John, 60
  ,, Mr., 59, 60, 120, 122, 125
  ,, Thomas, 122, 138
Peck, Annas, 104
  ,, Christopher, 121
  ,, Dorothy, 57, 120
  ,, Elizabeth, 123
  ,, Jane, 56, 154
  ,, Thomas, 56, 57, 120, 123, 124,
    151
Penny, Mary, 131
  ,, William, 131
Perkin [see also Parkin],
  ,, Edmund, 64

Perkin, Ellen, 64, 124
  ,, Ellenor, 66
  ,, Margaret, 63
  ,, William, 63, 64, 65,* 66, 124
Persevell [Parcevell, Parcible,
    Parcivle, Parsiball],
  ,, Elizabeth, 57, 119
  ,, Margaret, 57, 58, 119
  ,, N.X.N., w. of 83
  ,, Robert, 77
Petty, Isabell, 119
  ,, John, 111
Phillipson, Jenet, 102
Place, Elizabeth, 63, 64, 123*
  ,, James, 63, 123
  ,, Joseph, 63, 64,* 123*
Plummer, Margaret, 88
  ,, N.X.N., 88
Postlethwaite [Postlthaite],
  ,, Henry, 115*
  ,, Jenet, 145
Poulton *alias* Asheton, John, 101
Powe [Pow], Ann, 136, 143
  ,, Isabell, 144
Pratt, Margaret, 100
Preston, Francis, 117
  ,, George, 39
  ,, John, 117,* 135, 151, 156
  ,, Mary, 39
Proctor [Proctar, Procter,
    Prockter],
  ,, Alice, 141
  ,, Ann, 48, 111, 131, 159
  ,, John, 151
  ,, Magdalen, 148
  ,, Richard, 48, 111, 131,* 156, 159
Pauper [Paupercula],
  ,, Ann, 85
  ,, Anthony, 81
  ,, Ellen, 78
  ,, Margaret, 77
  ,, N.X.N., 89,* w. of 95

R

RACKSTRAW, Robert, 60*
Rallison [see Rawlinson]
Ratson, Thomas, 72
  ,, William, 72
Ravald, Robert, 158,* 159,* 160*
  ,, Susannah, 160
Rawlinson [Rallison, Rawlisson]
    [see also Rowlinson],
  ,, Elizabeth, 132
  ,, John, 145, 146
  ,, Mary, 63
  ,, Mr., 63
  ,, Mrs., 132
  ,, Thomas, 63

C. pp. 1—74; B. 75—133; W. 134—160.

C. pp. 1—74; B. 75—133; W. 134—160.

Stackhouse, John, 127
„ Joseph, 69
„ Margaret, 128
Stamper, John, 143
Staruthait, Ann, 63
„ Margaret, 63
Statter, John, 151, 162 [?], 166
„ Mr., 151
Stephenson, Elizabeth, 92
„ Robert, 89, 92
Stewardson, James, 57
„ Sarah, 57
Stith [see Styth]
Stones [Stons], Elizabeth, 83, 135
Stoory, Isaac, 109
„ John, 109*
„ Rebecca, 109
Stors, Addam, 138
„ Christopher, 88
„ Ellen, 141
„ Richard, 148
„ Thomas, 88
Styth [Stith, Stithe, Stythe],
„ Easter, 125
„ Elizabeth, 44, 46, 60, 100, 121
„ Ellen, 36
„ Francis, 34, 40, 103, 104
„ Isabell, 39, 116
„ James, 37, 57, 120, 121
„ Jane, 48, 116, 119, 132
„ John, 39, 56,* 119, 126, 129, 151, 153
„ Mary, 59
„ N.X.N., 41
„ Thomas, 35, 42, 43,* 44, 45,* 46, 48, 56, 110,* 114
„ William, 34, 35, 36, 37, 38,* 39,* 40, 41, 42, 56,* 57, 59, 60, 61,* 100, 104, 105, 121,* 124, 143, 144, 151
Sunderland, John, 69*
„ Judith, 69
„ Mr., 69*
„ Thomas, 69
Swainson [Svenson, Swenson],
„ Ellen, 40
„ Emanuel, 151
Syll, Sylle, Syls [see Sill]

T

TALLAN [Talens], Ann, 68
„ Edward, 66,* 67, 68*
„ Elizabeth, 145
„ James, 67
„ Ralph, 68
„ Thomas, 66
Tasker, Ann, 136

Tatham [Tathem, Tathum, Thatham],
„ Agnes, 126, 136
„ Alice, 54,* 57, 61, 115, 116, 117, 118
„ Ann, 22, 93, 125
„ Dorothy, 33, 47, 105, 110
„ Edmund, 12, 22, 23, 24, 42, 45, 79, relict of 81, 93, 110
„ Gilbert, 78
„ Isabell, 63, 123
„ James, 33, 53,* 54, 55, 56,* 57,* 116, 118, 120, 125, 150, 154
„ Jane, 23, 53, 105
„ Joan, 55
„ Joana, 120
„ John, 44, 46, 60, 67, 127, 159
„ Jonathan, 60
„ Margaret, 82
„ Martha, 126
„ Mary, 60, 120, 122
„ Reynold, 136
„ Richard, 12, 24, 33, 42, 43, 44, 45, 46,* 47, 53, 60,* 61, 63, 82, w. of 84, 85, 105, 110,* 111, 114, 120, 126, 127, 133, 149, 152
„ Thomas, 43, 46, 54, 57, 67, 117, 123, 126
Taylor [Tailer, Tayler, Tayller, Telar, Teyler],
„ Agnes, 42, 50, 101, 106, 108, 148
„ Alice, 91
„ Ann, 117
„ Catherine, 48, 114, 147
„ Christopher, 28, 34, 35,* 39, 49, 50, 51, 100, 112, 120, 148
„ Dorothy, 9, 33, 37, 99, 100, 104
„ Edward, 30, 35, 56, 84, 101, 117, 122, 149, 151, 165
„ Elizabeth, 7, 8, 9, 10, 36, 114, 119, 127
„ Francis, 19
„ Isabell, 8, 55, 151
„ James, 25, 92, 155
„ Jane, 36, 56, 70, 108, 109, 145, 151
„ Jenet, 120
„ John, 6, 7, 8, 9, 10, 24, 26, 37,* 41, 49, 70,* 104, 109, 140, 157
„ Margaret, 146, 150
„ Mary, 70
„ N.X.N., 26, 102
„ Richard, 7, 25, 33, 34, 38, 46, 47, 52,* 70,* 71, 86, 99, 100, two infants of 101, 101, 102, 106, 108, 109, 112, 132, 142, 143
„ Robert, 145

C. pp. 1—74; B. 75—133; W. 134—160.

Topping, Robert, 47, 48,* 49,* 50, 51,
 52, 58, 109,* 110, 111, 114, 146
,, Thomas, 15, 51, 58, 121, 139
,, William, 49, 110
Torver, Thomas, 158
Towers, Elizabeth, 53
,, Ellen, 35
,, Henry, 54
,, John, 35, 131, 159
,, Robert, 53, 54, 55*
,, William, 104, 141
Towerson, Elizabeth, 47, 48, 109, 112
,, James, 48
,, John, 48, 55,* 147
,, Margaret, 123
,, Sarah, 55, 153
,, Thomas, 47, 48, 109, 146
Towne, Gyles, 134, 137
,, Margaret, 136
Townson [Tounson, Towneson],
,, Agnes, 121
,, Alice, 149
,, Anne, 98
,, Edward, 149
,, John, 96, 125
,, Margaret, 40
,, Maude, 141
,, William, 40, 98, 144
Trotter, Mary, 65
,, Richard, 65
Troughton, Hanna, 46
,, Jane, 149
,, John, 43, 44, 46,* 106, 107
,, Joseph, 73
,, Leonard, 46, 106, 107
,, N.X.N., 43, 44
,, Peter, 73
Tunstill, Ellen, 151
Turner, Anna, 40
,, Elizabeth, 156
,, Francis, 142
,, Jane, 28, 149
,, John, 28, 140
,, Mary, 149
,, Thomas, 145,* 149
,, William, 40, 145
Tydeman, Robert, 2
,, Thomas, 2
Tyeson [Tison], Agnes, 57, 118
,, George, 57, 118

U

Ubank [see Eubank]
Ullacke, Agnes, 149
,, Jane, 149
Ustenson [Ustonson, Vstenson,
 Vstinson, Vstison, Vstonson],
,, Ann, 22

Ustenson, Christopher, 9, 89*
,, Edward, 76
,, Ellen, 135
,, Isabell, 52, 142
,, Jane, 6, 90, 144
,, Janet, 9,* 20, 89, 111
,, John, 26, 52, 98, 104
,, Margaret, 9, 76
,, N.X.N., 104
,. Richard, 6, 20, 22, 24, 96
,, Thomas, 9, 79
,, William, 6, 9, 22,* 24, 26, 27,*
 83, 90, 96, 106, 108

V

Vapor, James, 39
,, Thomas, 39
Vin [see Ewan]
Vstenson [see Ustenson]

W

Wadeson [Waydson],
,, Margaret, 151
,, Mary, 140
Waithman [Wethman, Wetheman],
,, Alice, 78
,, Bryan, 7
,, John, 7
,, Mabel, 136
,, Margaret, 4
,, Richard, 4, w. of 81
Walen, Grace, 157
Walker, Ann, 104
,, Christopher, 19, 20,* 137
,, Elizabeth, 48
,, Isabell, 26
,, James, 4*
,, Jane, 28
,, Jenet, 4
,, John, 104, 118
,, Leonard, 140
,, Mr., 48
,, Richard, 19, 147
,, Stephen, 139
,, Thomas, 26, 28, 48
Wallen, Jane, 143
Waller, Ann, 4
,, Brian, 148
,, James, 4
,, "Vidua," 81
,, Thomas, 139
Walmsley [Wallmsley],
,, Elizabeth, 160
,, John, 140
 [see also Womsley]
Ward [Warde], Ann, 63

C. pp. 1—74; B. 75—133; W. 134—160.

II.

Index of Places.

[All places left without the addition of a County may be presumed to be in Lancashire. Great care has been taken, but the Indexer was unable to trace all the names.]

C. pp. 1—74; B. 75—133; W. 134—160.

C. pp. 1—74; B. 75—133; W. 134—160.

C. pp. 1—74; B. 75—133; W. 134—160.

III.

Index of Trades, Descriptions, and Various Matters.

C. pp. 1—74; B. 75—133; W. 134—160.

C. pp. 1—74; B. 75—133; W. 134—160.

JAMES CLEGG, THE ALDINE PRESS, ROCHDALE.